# *America's First* Highways

## Auto Trails and the Quest for Good Roads

Stephen H. Provost

**DRAGON CROWN**

All material © 2020 Stephen H. Provost
Cover concept and design: Stephen H. Provost
Cover photograph: Lee Highway c. 1920, Library of Congress
Back cover: Lee Highway, U.S. 11-70, Lincoln Highway, 2020, Stephen H. Provost
All contemporary photographs © 2020 Stephen H. Provost
Historical images are in the public domain, except where noted

No part of this book may be reproduced, or stored in a retrieval system, or transmitted in any form or by any means, electronic, mechanical, photocopying, recording, or otherwise, without the express written permission of the publisher.

Dragon Crown Books 2020

All rights reserved.

ISBN-13: 978-1-949971-11-8

# Dedication

To the pathfinders, trailblazers and the memories of those who have gone before.

*A car on a cross-country auto tour encounters a covered wagon near Big Springs, Neb., in 1911.*
*A.L. Westgard, National Archives*

# Acknowledgments

Thanks to the many researchers, journalists, historians and photographers whose primary work has been invaluable in compiling this volume. Thanks also to Dan R. Young for suggesting the topic of this book, and to the University of Michigan Library (Special Collections Research Center, Transportation History Collection) and Boca Raton Historical Society & Museum for their gracious permission to reproduce their archived photos in this volume.

# Contents

*Introduction*     7

**Part I: Trail Blazers**
Breaking the Cycle     13
Cars and Drivers     35
Road Tests     57
Great Races to Strange Places     81

**Part II: Trail Builders**
Carl's Creation     99
Great Lakes to the Gulf     135
Eisenhower's Eye-Opener     157
Land of Confusion     169
Primitive Cool     215
End of the Trails     233
The End is the Beginning     255

*Timeline*     275
*Index of Trails*     279

# Volume II
# America's Historic Highways

Man pushing a stalled car that truly resembles a "horseless carriage," c. 1900. Note the bicycle-style wheels. *City of Toronto Archives, Creative Commons CCBY2.0*

STEPHEN H. PROVOST

# More Reading

Check out these other great highway-themed books by the author.

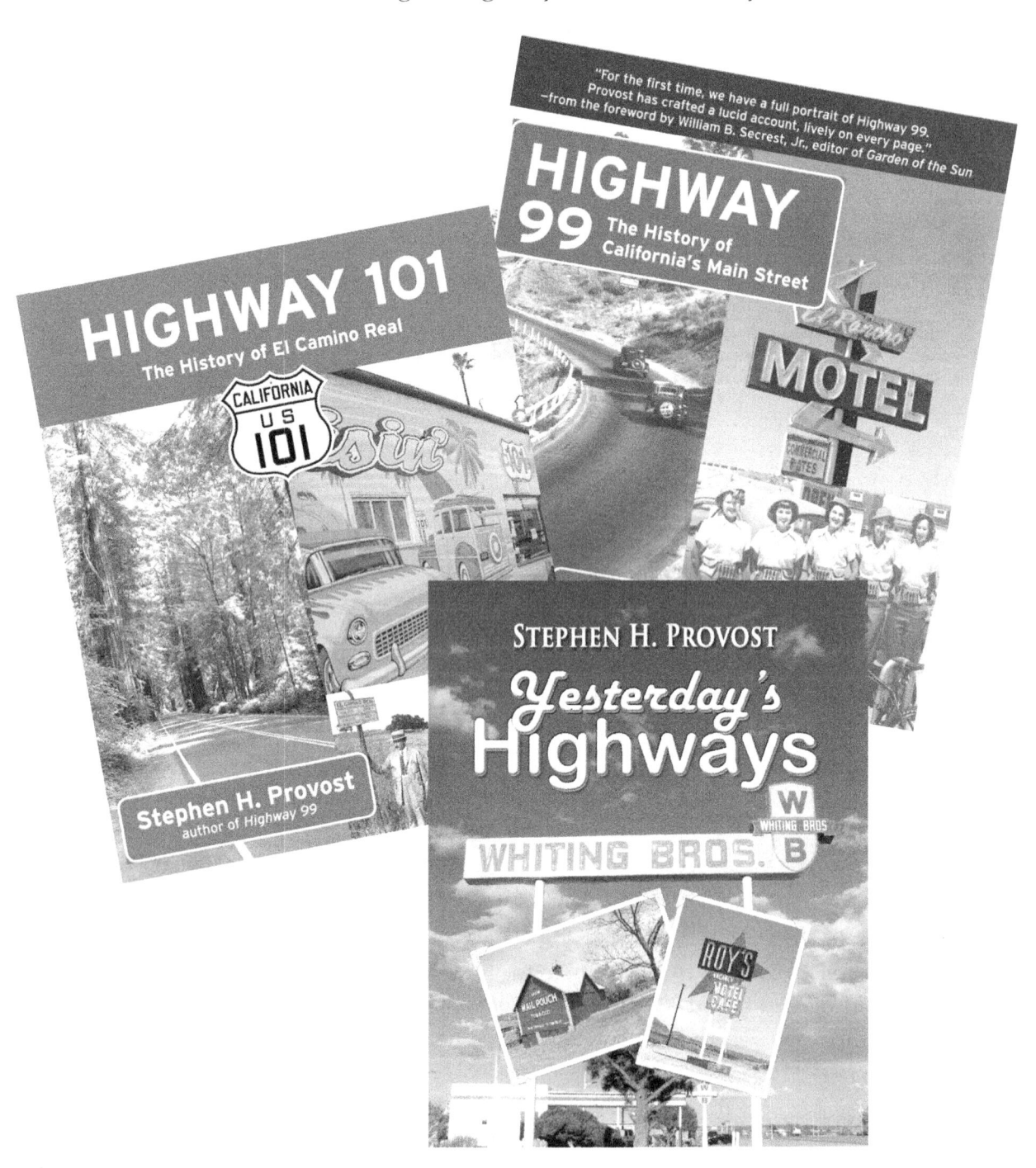

Abandoned Grapevine section of the Ridge Route south of Bakersfield, once part of the Pacific Highway auto trail that ran through Washington, Oregon and California. *Author photo*

# Introduction

One of the most fascinating aspects of traveling the country investigating the history of our highways is finding bits and pieces of pavement that belong to now abandoned sections of road. Sometimes, they're off in the middle of nowhere, slabs of concrete or short stretches of brick that had been chipped and overgrown by weeds. Other times, they've been repurposed as driveways, frontage roads or parking areas you'd never even know were once part of our highway system.

My first three highway books focused largely on the history of our nation's roads since 1926, when the U.S. government created the first federal highway system. That was natural for me. I grew up in the 1960s and 1970s, when interstates were just starting to replace some of those roads (although many remain in use today). I grew up traveling up and down Highway 99 in California, the subject of my first book in this subject, one of the original federal roads from '26, but one that had been handed over to the state for safekeeping when Interstate 5 replaced it.

Later, I moved to the coast and commuted for several years along Highway 101, which remains a federal road even now, more than a half-century into the interstate era. That became the subject of my second highway book. A third book, *Yesterday's Highways*, was the product of my travels along those highways, the legendary Route 66 and U.S. 30, among other roads. I looked at motels, gas stations, diners, roadside attractions and, of course, the highways themselves.

But this last project led me to start researching an earlier era — a time before the federal highway system, when privately funded roads called auto trails crisscrossed the country. The brief but colorful history of these roads, which consisted of about 15 years (from around 1911 to 1926), produced a wealth of stories and information that provided a vivid backdrop to the studies I'd already done. Highway 101, I already knew, had been based on El Camino Real, the trail that linked the 21 missions in what used to be called Alta California. Highway 99 was a newer name for the Pacific Highway, which itself began as a privately funded auto trail, as did U.S. 30, much of which was once called the Lincoln Highway.

But that was just the tip of the iceberg. It turned out that, in that brief span of about 15 years, more than 250 auto trails had sprung up across the country, some of them part of grand visions for linking the Atlantic and Pacific, the Great Lakes and the Gulf. The Lincoln Highway might have been the most famous transcontinental trail, but it wasn't the only one. Others bore names like the National Old Trails Road, the Yellowstone Trail and Pike's Peak Ocean to Ocean Highway. Then there were the north-south trails, like the Jefferson, Dixie and Meridian Highways. All were famous in their day, drawing on history and geography to create a sense of belonging for those who traveled their strips of concrete, sections of gravel and stretches of unimproved dirt road.

Other auto trails were regional in character or confined to a single state. There were the Ozark Trails, a network of roads in the Southwest, and the Great White Way in Iowa, which was marked by a series of white poles. Though we've mostly forgotten them today, we still often travel their remnants without realizing it. Some were abandoned, but most were broken up into fragments, then pieced back together in different combinations by the highway system of 1926.

The creation, in that year, of the federal highway system marked a major change in the character of our roads. They went from private operations to public thoroughfares. They shed the romance of their historical connections and replaced it with the efficiency of Arabic numerals, much to the chagrin of some. The name "Lincoln Highway" had been chosen after the federal government had, in an earlier time, declined to fund its own road honoring "The Great Emancipator" and had opted instead to build the Lincoln Memorial in Washington, D.C. How would it have been, some wondered, if they had torn down that memorial instead for the sake of greater efficiency?

But with so many competing trail markers creating confusion on the roadway, and more than a few smooth-talking grifters collecting "assessment fees" for highways they never built, the government felt it had little choice. For years it had stayed out of the business of funding roads, and now that it had committed to doing so, it wanted to be sure motorists were getting their money's worth.

As time has passed, most of the old names have faded — some justifiably so. Highways that pay tribute to Confederate champions of slavery and division have a place in history, and so are chronicled here, but not in any moral society. The actions of men who fought and killed because they wished to enslave and abuse others should be remembered — but only as reminders of the evils we humans are capable of inflicting. Such men and their actions should never, in any sense, be celebrated.

Unlike many books on old highways, this is not a travel guide; it's a glimpse back into an era of history that seeks to preserve some bit of the past so we can better understand the present. The pages ahead contain the story of how and why the auto trails came to be, how they struggled and left their mark on the American landscape, and how they ultimately faded into the shadows of a near-forgotten past.

I hope you enjoy the ride.

## Part One
# Blazing Trails

The Veterans Memorial Bridge, which opened in 1930, carries the Lincoln Highway across the Susquehanna River between Columbia and Wrightsville, Pa. *Author photo*

## The Good Roads Movement

A horse and buggy on a macadam road in the 1850s.

# Breaking the Cycle

It all started with bicycles.

There weren't any cars on America's roads in 1880, when a group of cycling enthusiasts met in Newport, R.I. The fact is, there weren't many roads, either. Most of them were barely beaten paths or trails. In fact, it was common to actually *call* them trails.

The cyclists at that meeting formed the League of American Wheelmen. The gathering (which included a parade) attracted more than 100 cycling aficionados from 29 clubs in New England, on the Eastern Seaboard and from as far west as Chicago.

The object of their fascination, the bicycle, was still a new phenomenon: The first one had been built in 1817 by a German baron named Karl von Drais and dubbed a "velocipede" or "hobby-horse." You didn't pedal it; you had to kick and push off against the roadway.

Pedals weren't attached to the front wheel until the 1860s, when the French produced several different prototypes. One popular version, known as a "penny-farthing," had a huge front wheel and a smaller rear wheel (a British penny being about twice the size of a farthing).

There was a method to this odd design: The large front wheel covered more ground with every pump of the pedal, pulling the rider along at a faster clip.

The penny-farthings weren't cheap, which meant that cycling was, at least initially, a pastime for the well-to-do. And if you could afford to buy one, you could also afford to make a fuss in defense of their rights. At the top of their agenda was their insistence on a share of the road. In the days before bike lanes, there were those who had little tolerance for this new form of transportation. In 1881, for instance, three cyclists were jailed for violating a ban on riding in New York's Central Park.

Laurie A. Perkins stands next to a tall penny-farthing bicycle, around 1900. *State Library and Archives of Florida*

But in 1890, a Kansas court found that bicycles were vehicles with the same rights as wagons, horses or any other means of transport. That freed up the Wheelmen to focus on another priority: the state of the roads they traveled — which was, everyone agreed, abysmal.

Meanwhile, cycling was going mainstream.

In 1884, Thomas Stevens of England had pedaled a bike around the world, shining a spotlight on the pastime. Still, penny-farthings like the one he rode scared a lot of would-be cyclists away. It was hard enough to get up on the big wheel, which was a good 4 feet high, but if you fell... ouch!

# AMERICA'S FIRST HIGHWAYS

The following year, another Englishman created a less-daunting alternative. John Kemp Starley designed what was known as a "safety bicycle" (it was safer because, if you fell off, it wouldn't hurt as badly!). With wheels of equal size and a chain drive that connected the pedals to the back wheel, it was very much like the modern machine, and it made cycling accessible to thousands of Americans who had hesitated to give it a try.

The number of cycling clubs, and their membership rolls, exploded, as did the number of bikes on the road. In 1890, a mere 27 manufacturers made 40,000 bikes. By the end of the decade, 321 bicycle companies were churning out an astonishing 1.2 million a year.

Cycling, however, remained a largely urban pursuit.

There were more Wheelmen in Massachusetts alone than in 26 states in the South, Great Plains, Southwest and Rocky Mountain regions combined. But that was slowly changing, as riders began to explore beyond the city limits.

Beyond simple recreation, the attractions of cycling were obvious. In a word, it was all about freedom. Riders didn't have to rely on trains, avoiding the "rush to the railway station and "wading through timetables." They could ride with whomever they chose — or alone, if they preferred. There was no need to be boxed in on a rail car and feel "oppressed" by "unseasonable companions."

Cycling created a world of new opportunities. Newspapers and touring magazines published articles, along with maps and descriptions of various routes. The League of American Wheelmen, meanwhile, posted signs showing the best ways of getting from one place to another, steering riders away from hazards and indicating how far ahead their destination lay.

The League even helped its members pick the best hotels, evaluating potential overnight stops and granting its seal of approval to 7,000 of them. Each recommended inn had to provide good food, ensure its accommodations were clean and comfortable, and offer "a discount or rebate" to members of the League who showed a membership card.

Sound familiar?

It's basically the same template used by the American Automobile Association, which would — a few years later — create a similar network of member inns and lodges. It would also, like the Wheelmen, take up the task of posting informational signs by the side of the road.

Car stuck on a rutted, muddy road. *Malmazan, Creative Commons CCBY4.0*

## Railroaded and Sidetracked

Even with all that, though, the roads themselves remained a problem. It was hard enough to ford a stream or navigate a muddy road in a heavy wagon, with its sturdy wheels. Ever try riding a two-wheeler through the mud? You might as well turn around and go home.

So, many riders still had to take the train — at least if they wanted to get from one town to the next. In 1894, no fewer than 430,000 cyclists rode the rails, "going to or coming from some point from which a cyclist was about to start on a tour, or to which he had returned, having completed it."

The railroad was, indeed, a big part of the problem. At the country's founding, Congress had been far more interested in roads than it was by the end of the 19th century. It had supplied funding for a National Road stretching westward from Cumberland, Md., and had established 37,000 miles of "post roads" for mail delivery. But fiscal conservatives chafed at the cost of these programs, even as the need for them grew with the nation's expansion thanks to the Louisiana Purchase. (President Thomas Jefferson, who engineered the Purchase, ironically opposed large-scale spending on post roads, fearing it would "open a bottomless abyss for public money.")

As the century wore on, however, the government pulled back from its commitment to good roads. It stopped building post roads and stopped doing maintenance on the National Road, leaving it up to the states.

It wasn't as though the federal government stopped supporting transportation — it merely shifted its focus, and its *means* of support. The government was stingy about doling out cash, but the Louisiana Purchase and other acquisitions in the mid-19th century meant it had plenty of land. In the 1840s, the U.S. added territory that would become the states of Texas, New Mexico, Utah, Arizona, California, Nevada, Oregon, Washington and Idaho. Land was so plentiful it could be given away, and it effectively was with the Homestead Act of 1862.

But homesteaders weren't the only beneficiaries of the new land-rich government. The biggest windfall went to an emerging form of transportation: the railroad. The feds might not want to spend money on good roads, but they had land, which they gave to railroad companies in the form of grants to encourage their expansion. It was a win-win situation. The government, for its part, could invest in transportation without actually spending a dime. The railroads, however, were the real winners. Before the middle of the century, railroads were small potatoes, with fewer than 10,000 miles of track laid nationwide. They couldn't get banks to loan them money, because lenders worried they'd take too long to pay it back. But the land grants changed everything: The railroads took the government's free land, sold what they didn't need, and used the profit to build more rail lines.

With this kind of windfall, the railroads became rich — filthy rich. Tycoons like Cornelius Vanderbilt and Leland Stanford made their fortunes thanks to the railroad.

The secret to the railroads' success was simple. Each rail line had a virtual monopoly within its geographic area: All roads led to the train depot, which became the hub of society and commerce.

Until the railroads came along, manufacturers, farmers and merchants had relied on roads to carry their goods. Gravel toll roads like the Louisville and Nashville Turnpike did a booming business. In fact, there 175 companies ran about 3,000 miles of pikes in the first part of the 19th century. The Great Valley Road in northern Virginia was another mainstay. But Civil War troop movements tore it up around the same time the railroads were coming into their own. You could ship a lot more goods a lot faster by rail than you could by loading up a horse-drawn wagon, so it was only natural that commerce migrated to the tracks.

The railroads thrived, while the old toll roads, no longer making enough money to pay for their upkeep, fell into disrepair. The roads that remained viable were, by and large, those that led to the train station. They didn't connect communities at all. They were basically on-ramps to the depot.

The Arcade Depot in Los Angeles, 1891.

New towns popped up like weeds along rail lines, some given names by the railroads themselves. Hotels were built near the depot for easy access; so were restaurants like the Harvey House, where Fred Harvey created his famous blue-plate specials to serve train travelers quickly during stopovers at the station. Factories were built near the depot, too, so goods could be easily loaded onto boxcars for shipment far and wide. In Martinsville, Va., the B.F. Gravely & Co. tobacco plant set up shop right across from the train station, and it was far from the only business to do so.

Atlanta began its history as the terminus of a state-sponsored railroad. Other towns boomed with the railroad's arrival: Barely 5,000 people lived in Los Angeles in 1870 before the arrival of the Southern Pacific (1876) and Santa Fe (1885). When the turn of the century arrived, it was 20 times larger. By that time, those 10,000 miles of rail line had mushroomed to more than 193,000 nationwide.

While new towns with train terminals prospered, established towns bypassed by the railroad, withered up and faded away. Millerton, the first seat of government in Fresno County in California, wasn't chosen as a railroad stop; it was too far out of the way, up in the foothills. The city of Fresno was founded as a depot on the Central Pacific line in 1872. Two years later, the county government was transferred there, and today, Fresno is the fifth-largest city in the state. What happened to Millerton? The town was abandoned, and the site became submerged beneath a manmade lake when a dam was built there in 1944. Millerton had been built along a Gold Rush route, the Stockton-Los Angeles Road, but it didn't matter because *roads* didn't matter.

Railroads did.

## Rough Road Ahead

Isaac Potter, an early president of the League of American Wheelmen, wanted to change all that. He wanted to make roads relevant again. And he knew it was possible, because some places were already doing it. American roads, he noted, were a far cry from those in France — even its rural byways. Never mind that there were more people in places like Massachusetts and New Jersey than in 70 of the 87 French administrative districts.

Roads in Italy, Belgium and elsewhere in Europe were similarly well maintained.

Why couldn't the same be done in America?

Potter made his case in 1891, when he penned a lengthy "Letter to the American Farmer," the subtitle of his pamphlet, *The Gospel of Good Roads*. He even included a photo of a tree-lined French country road, taken after a heavy rain, to hammer home his point.

"The road surface is smooth and dry," he noted. "The tall poplars on either side have been trimmed to the upper branches so as to let the sun and air hasten the drying of the road after a storm. Then notice the heaps of broken stone on each side of the road. These are used by the workmen in making constant repairs from day to day whenever the least imperfection occurs."

It might seem odd that Potter should have directed his appeal to farmers. Most cyclists were, at least in the early days, city folk who took up the pastime as a social outlet. They weren't too keen on venturing into the mud and muck of rural roads; they were the kind of dandies who preferred more genteel surroundings. What did such folks have in common with rural farmers?

One thing: the road.

Potter and his fellow cyclists recognized that, despite their growing numbers, they would need allies in their cause — preferably, allies with a financial stake in the game. And no group had a bigger stake than farmers, as Potter was quick to point out.

"A little while ago," he said, "a very clever and intelligent citizen of Indiana estimated that bad roads coast the farmer $15 per year for each horse and mule in his service." This added up, he said, to a "loss in the aggregate" of $250 million a year. That wasn't even taking into account wear and tear on wagons and harnesses, which Potter said amounted to $100 million, and depreciation in farmland values, which he pegged at $2 *billion*. In case you're wondering, that would be $56 billion in 2020.

It was a powerful argument, and one that got a boost from the U.S. Postal Service in 1896, when it passed a bill recommitting the country to the idea of post roads and establishing a new program called Rural Free Delivery. (If you're old enough to remember a sixties television show called *Mayberry R.F.D.*, you may already know that's what the initials in the title stood for.)

Before the era of Rural Free Delivery, the Postal Service didn't deliver to addresses out in the country. Roads beyond the city limits were simply too poorly maintained — if they were at all. The stalwart postal courier might let "neither snow nor rain nor heat nor gloom of night" keep him from completing his appointed rounds. But washed-out roads and axel-busting potholes were another matter.

If farmers wanted to collect their mail, they had to drive all the way into town to get it. This wasn't just an inconvenience for them, it was a problem for another group with a financial stake in good roads: catalog houses. By the 1890s, catalog businesses like Sears, Montgomery Ward and Butler Brothers were growing by leaps and bounds, shipping goods out across America from their Chicago warehouses. But they couldn't get their merchandise to a good chunk of the country, because the Post Office didn't deliver to rural routes.

This old post road in Fishkill, N.Y., was photographed in 1907. Post roads were established to deliver mail to rural areas, an effort that accelerated with the adoption of Rural Free Delivery in 1896. *Library of Congress*

They lobbied to change this, and farmers were happy at the added convenience of having goods brought right to their doorstep.

But the RFD service came with a price: Farmers had to make sure the roads to be used for delivery were passable. In doing so, they helped the Wheelmen take a step toward their goal of improving roads across the country. That didn't mean, however, that the battle had been won. In fact, it was just beginning. The farmers, not the government, were still responsible for keeping the roads up, and private roads would remain the rule for more than a quarter-century.

## On the Surface

The government's involvement in road building was intermittent, at best. One 1911 article pointed out that the feds had spent $3 million each on roads in two far-flung territories that weren't even states: Alaska and the Philippines. In the continental U.S., meanwhile, most of the burden fell on states, counties and private landowners.

New Jersey passed a bill in 1891 that put the state in the road-building business, if only indirectly.

The counties actually had to get the ball rolling.

They'd identify projects, to be overseen by the Board of Agriculture and, later, by a commissioner of public roads and funded by a combination of sources:

- The state would pay 33%.
- Adjacent property owners would kick in 10%
- The county would pay the remaining 57%.

The process hit several potholes, though. The public roads commissioner declared the law "simple and easy" to implement. But he had limited power. He had no way of making sure state roads were linked to significant highways (if there were any), and he lacked the power to maintain them once they were built.

A Massachusetts law passed in 1892 set up the first state highway panel, which had more power than the New Jersey commissioner. Project requests still came from the counties, but the Massachusetts commission could accept or reject them. A couple of years later, the state put the panel in charge of funding the roads in their entirety — after which it could bill the counties for 25% of the costs. The state also gave the commission $300,000 to carry out its plans.

California set up a Bureau of Highways in 1895.

But private parties continued to take the lead.

In 1899, a wealthy railroad man named Sam Hill had founded the Washington (state) Good Roads Association, noting that the U.S. "ranks with Turkey as one of the worst roaded countries in the civilized world."

Hill made it his mission to change that.

The next year, the Wheelmen abolished their racing division to focus even more attention on what had come to be known as the Good Roads movement. They were already holding conventions in various states and pushing state legislators to support their cause.

Yet, despite the best efforts of the Wheelmen and the advent of rural free delivery, roads across the country remained primitive at best. There were some cobblestone streets through town, but most roads were little more than dirt tracks, with a few surfaced with what was called macadam — what we'd call gravel roads today.

It was the invention of John Loudon McAdam, a Scotsman who improved upon the work of pioneering English road-builder Thomas Telford. Over the first two decades of the 19th century, Telford supervised the construction of 920 miles of road (not to mention 1,200 bridges). His technique: Use dirt to fill in the spaces between large foundation stones, then cover the surface with smaller stones. Drains were placed across the 18-foot-wide road every 100 yards to siphon off water.

One improvement McAdam made was dispense with the foundation stones, trusting the soil itself to support the surface of densely packed small stones set with water. Then, instead of using drains, he built his roads with a gentle slope so they were a few inches higher at the center. This allowed water to flow off naturally to one side or the other.

The first "macadamized" project in the United States was a 10-mile stretch of road between the Maryland towns of Boonsboro and Hagerstown. It was completed in 1823. A more ambitious project followed: McAdam's technique was used on a 73-mile segment of the Cumberland Road, the first federally funded road in U.S. history. The road itself was commissioned by Congress in 1806, and construction began five years later. Work started on the macadamized portion in 1825 and wasn't completed until five years later.

The road — which eventually ran all the way from Cumberland, Md., to Vandalia, then the capital of Illinois — was called "The Main Street of America" a century before that title was conferred on Route 66. Sometimes called the National Road or National Pike, it became the major wagon road for shipping goods between the Atlantic and the inland frontier.

Other roads were soon macadamized, as well. In the 1830s, the Valley Turnpike Company used the technique to improve 68 miles of the Great Wagon Road in the Shenandoah Valley. Merchants paid tolls at regular intervals to maintain the road so they could ship goods from Atlantic ports south, into the heart of Virginia and beyond.

But macadam wasn't the only option available to road-builders.

A variation on McAdam's technique used tar as a binding agent instead of water. This cut down on the amount of dust and dirt kicked up by wagons (and later, cars) once the water dried. The material was first used in Nottingham, England, in 1848, and was applied stateside to roads in Knoxville, Tenn., 18 years later. "Tar macadam," as it was called, came to be known as "tarmac" for short, a term still used for airport runways.

Other materials soon surfaced, too.

A section of the Cumberland Road, also known as the National Pike, is seen west of Brownsville, Pa. (south of Pittsburgh) in this 1910 photo by John Kennedy Lacock. *Library of Congress*

James Elbert Feltner photographed this railroad crossing on the National Pike in 1922. *Library of Congress*

# AMERICA'S FIRST HIGHWAYS

**Left:** This tollhouse on Cumberland Road, seen in a 1933 photo by A.S. Burns, was built c. 1812-1814, before the road was macadamized. *Library of Congress*

Concrete pavement was used for many early federal highways, such as Route 66 and U.S. 99 in California. You can still see old concrete alignments along sections of both roads. Brick was used on some sections of the Lincoln Highway, the Dixie Highway and other auto trails.

A 1906 headline dubbed Cleveland "the City of Brick Streets": Of its 280 miles of paved roadways, 165 were made from brick. And they weren't "confined to the down-town section" but were "all over the city." With pavement planned on portions of 100 streets that year, 90% were set to be covered in brick.

A stretch of brick pavement survives today on the Lincoln Highway at Elkhorn, Neb., west of Omaha. *Author photo*

In Seattle and Spokane, too, brick was the material of choice in the early 20th century. In 1905, Denny Clay Brickworks of Seattle came up with a brick hard enough to stand up to the pounding of horses' hooves. The red brick produced by Denny Clay bears the company imprint: D.C. Co.

T.J. Cannon improved on the concept two years later and started producing sandstone blocks.

Seattle also experimented with creosoted wood-block paving on 4th Avenue. As of 2019, the city still had 100 sandstone streets, half of which were set aside for historic preservation in the 1990s. (An example is seen below on 3rd Avenue South in 1922.) The sandstone was mined in quarries at Wilkeson, a town about 45 miles south of Seattle, then cut into brick shapes and laid down on the city streets.

In Spokane, meanwhile, 40 blocks of brick streets remain exposed, most of them laid down in 1910 and 1911, with many more miles hidden beneath less-expensive modern asphalt.

*Wikimedia Commons*

# AMERICA'S FIRST HIGHWAYS

Auto enthusiasts prepare for a trip from Tampa to Jacksonville, Fla., on a brick road c. 1910. *Florida State Archives*

Asphalt, also known as bitumen, occurs naturally in just a few places. Three of them are in California, including the famous La Brea Tar Pits in Los Angeles, and two others in South America. The fourth is in Venezuela, and the fifth can be found near the town of La Brea on the island nation of Trinidad and Tobago. No, that's not a misprint: Both the town and the California tar pits really are called "La Brea," which translates into English as "The Pitch."

It was Trinidad's Pitch Lake — the world's largest asphalt deposit, containing some 10 million tons of the stuff — that served as the source of material used to pave the some of the earliest asphalt roads in the United States.

A chemist named Edmund De Smedt had tried to use bitumen from West Virginia to pave a street in Newark, N.J., as early as 1870.

The trial was a failure.

But De Smedt didn't give up. Between 1876 and 1878, he used asphalt from Pitch Lake to pave Pennsylvania Avenue in Washington, D.C., the road that runs past the White House. This time, it worked. Cyclists loved it and came from all over to try out the new surface. Soon, other manufacturers got into the act, too, and by 1907, asphalt from refined petroleum was being used more often than natural asphalt in paving projects.

Which of these surfaces was the best? That's what Washington state Good Roads pioneer Sam Hill set out to discover. In 1911, he set up a $100,000 project at his planned town of Maryhill (named for his wife, Mary Hill) to test several different surfaces over the course of a 10-mile road:

- Concrete
- Macadam
- Oil-treated crushed rock macadam
- Sand and gravel macadam
- Decomposed rock macadam
- Asphalt macadam

Hill was so eager to tout the future of paved roads that he invited the governor and state legislature to visit the site, at his own expense, to see the results firsthand. (This wasn't Hill's only grand gesture: He later built a replica of Stonehenge to honor the dead from World War I and a Peace Arch where the road now called Interstate 5 crosses the U.S.-Canada border.)

Hill's friendship with one Canadian in particular was significant. A.E. Todd of Victoria, B.C., had spent the summer of 1910 driving the length of the Pacific coast with his wife, from Vancouver to Tijuana. The purpose of his trip was to draw attention to the need for better roads and publicize plans to create a Pacific Highway along the coast.

It was an ambitious project, which would take time and money. But there was no question it was needed.

After Todd drove through Oregon on the fledgling highway in 1912, he found "only a few miles of good macadam or gravel roads." Barely one-third of the total distance was properly graded, he said. "All the rest is mud and boulders, impassible in winter and difficult in summer." The state was the site of the Pacific Highway's only toll gate, "and that is on a very bad section of road, too!" Todd declared.

# AMERICA'S FIRST HIGHWAYS

A car passes over a section of concrete on the Old Ridge Route, a section of the Pacific Highway (later U.S. Highway 99) crossing the Tehachapi Mountains, c. 1925. *University of Southern California Libraries and California Historical Society*

Large sections of the Pacific Highway — such as the Ridge Route across the Tehachapi range, linking Northern and Southern California — wound up being paved in concrete. So did other highways built in the 1910s and '20s. But as time went on, asphalt roads become more common. The reason was simple: Although asphalt wasn't as durable (think about those potholes that appear out of nowhere after a heavy rain), it was a whole lot cheaper.

In the long run, even some sections of concrete were paved over with asphalt. If you visit the Old Ridge Route today, you can see sections of asphalt that have been poured over the original concrete roadway. But the asphalt hasn't lasted. It's been worn away in sections, revealing the concrete underneath, and with it, buried history from a time when the road was new.

(For more on the fascinating history of the Old Ridge Route, see my book *Highway 99: The History of California's Main Street*.)

Old concrete is visible beneath a layer of asphalt on the abandoned Grapevine section of the Old Ridge Route, north of Lebec, Calif. *Author photo*

Changes were taking place out in Michigan, too. There, a Good Roads pioneer named Edward Hines had worked to improve road surfaces since 1888. He was taking his girlfriend out for a bicycle ride when he became frustrated at the quality of the roads in the Detroit area. The couple would marry later that year.

Two years after that, Hines formed the Good Roads organization of Michigan.

He and Henry Ford were both founding members of the Wayne County Road

Commission in 1906, where Hines would serve continuously as president for 15 years. In 1909, he oversaw a project that made a stretch of Woodward Avenue in Detroit (between Six and Seven Mile roads) the world's first full mile of paved concrete road.

On Hines' watch, the commission would also become the first to resurface an old concrete road with a thin, concrete-wearing surface, and the first to implement a snow-removal program.

Perhaps his most famous contribution, though, was the invention of the highway center line in 1911. The idea came to him by chance: He had an epiphany when he saw liquid pouring from the back of a milk truck, leaving a white trail behind it. He asked himself: Why not do the same thing on purpose, to divide the road into lanes and clearly separate oncoming traffic?

*Michigan Roads & Construction* magazine would later describe it as "the most important single traffic safety device in the history of auto transportation." And Hines' 1938 obituary in the *Detroit Free Press* declared, "No other man in the country did more for the promotion of good roads than Mr. Hines."

The first center line made its appearance on River road in Trenton, Mich. Still, it took a while for the concept to catch on.

Even in Michigan, it wasn't until 1917 that the first line was painted on a rural highway: an area known as Dead Man's Curve in Michigan's Upper Peninsula. Kenneth Sawyer, a county roads superintendent, had noticed that traffic from Marquette on Lake Superior to the town of Negaunee ten miles inland had "become heavy enough to make travel dangerous unless some means of control" were adopted.

He wrote: "The handling of motor traffic upon our main trunk highways through the country is rapidly becoming as serious a problem as traffic control has ever been in our cities."

Sawyer's solution?

"White 8-inch center lines upon a black surface of the road upon dangerous curves, with an arrow pointing down the right-hand side of the road at either end."

At first, center lines were only painted (by hand, using a paintbrush) on hazardous sections of road such as curves, narrow bridges and hills. There were limitations: As Sawyer pointed out, you needed a black surface to make the lines stand out, and you

Kenneth Sawyer's centerline, with white directional arrow, at Dead Man's Curve on what was then Michigan State Highway 15 between Marquette and Negaunee. *Wikimedia Commons*

couldn't very well paint one on a gravel or dirt road — which constituted by far the majority of roadways in that era.

So, it's probably not surprising that the idea didn't spread quickly from Michigan.

But it did, eventually, take root.

Also in 1917, quite independently, Dr. June McCarroll was driving on a concrete road between Indio and Palm Springs, Calif., near dusk, when a truck came along going the opposite direction. Its driver, who was apparently having trouble seeing where his side of the road ended, allowed it to drift far enough toward McCarroll that he forced her off the road.

"My Model T Ford and I found ourselves face to face with a truck on the paved highway," she later recalled. "It did not take me long to choose between a sandy berth to the right and a ten-ton truck to the left!"

Later, while driving on a newer road, she noticed it had been widened from 8 to 16 feet, creating a visible center ridge between the older and newer lines of concrete.

# AMERICA'S FIRST HIGHWAYS

Road crews found a way to add dark center lines to lighter concrete, as seen here in this 1924 photo of the Yakima River Canyon in Washington state. *Wikimedia Commons*

This gave her an idea: She went home, got a can of paint, then went back out and hand-painted a 4-inch-wide stripe down the center of the road in front of her home on Indio Boulevard (which would later become U.S. Highway 99). It wasn't until 1924, however, after seven years of lobbying, that McCarroll and her allies were able to persuade the state legislature to authorize center lines on California's highways.

Meanwhile, up in Oregon — also in 1917 — Deputy Peter Rexford painted a yellow center line below Crown Point on the Columbia River highway. He came up with the idea while riding on a bus from Salem, Ore., on a rainy night that year.

"I'm a farmer, just a kid raised on a farm," he later recalled, "and I remembered the guide line my dad once had." It led across a ravine to a bunkhouse on that farm in Hubbard, Ore., helping Rexford find his way.

He went to county officials with the idea, but they declined to fund it, so he paid for it out of his own pocket, painting the Columbia River highway line in April.

The roads were getting better, but they still had a long way to go.

**Top:** A pile of discarded Warrenite sits beside a road in the Seattle suburb of Bothell, Wash., in 1912, beneath a sign advertising the paving material — a bitulithic asphalt invented by the Frederick J. Warren. *Webster and Stevens*

**Above:** Modern traffic arrows and center line in a Martinsville, Va., shopping center parking lot. *Author photo*

## Automotive Pioneers

Henry Ford with the first and 10 millionth Ford in 1924. *Library of Congress*

# Cars and Drivers

Four years before Henry Ford produced his first Model T, he built a car that wouldn't run.

So, he sold it to his partner and a bicyclist who'd never even driven a car before he got behind the wheel of Ford's 999. That cyclist became the Babe Ruth of auto racing and found so much success with the car that Ford bought it back — and set the land speed record in it. But we're getting ahead of ourselves.

The 999 wasn't Ford's first entry into the racing game. By 1901, his first car company — the Detroit Automobile Co. — had already debuted ... and failed. Eager to restore his

Henry Ford

reputation, he decided to design a race car: a two-cylinder model with a primitive form of fuel injection and possibly the first spark plugs ever to feature porcelain insulators. Those insulators were made by a Detroit dentist.

The 26-horsepower car topped out at 72 mph in speed tests, which doesn't sound too fast. But you have to remember that, at the time, the official land speed record was just short of 66 mph, so those horses had a pretty impressive kick.

All Ford needed was a way to prove his car's mettle. The idea he settled on was as audacious as the assembly line that would make him wealthy and famous less than a decade later: He would take on the country's most successful driver in a race.

Alexander Winton was a car manufacturer in his own right and, at the time, and his reputation as a driver was second to none.

Everyone thought Ford was nuts. Surely, he and his two-cylinder creation didn't have a chance.

It didn't even have a name yet.

The two met in October of 1901 on a horse racing track in Grosse Point, Mich., for a 10-mile sweepstakes race that highlighted a full day of racing and motorcar exhibitions. (An inspired Ford decided to christen his own car "Sweepstakes" in honor of the occasion.) An overflow crowd of 8,000 people turned out to view the spectacle.

The big headline, according to the *Detroit Free Press*, came when Winton broke the world's track record by covering a mile in 1 minute, 12 seconds, and Edgar Apperson of Buffalo captured the Detroit Free Press Cup in another 10-mile race.

The sweepstakes race between Ford and Winton was actually supposed to feature six other drivers, but only three showed up — the third being Pittsburgh millionaire William Murray.

Murray predicted he would improve upon Winton's just-

Alexander Winton

established speed record, but he never got the chance. Before he could even get started, Murray's mechanic found a cylinder leak in his entry, and he was forced to withdraw. The *Free Press* described it as "a great disappointment," because Murray had "given up a hunting trip in the Adirondacks in order to race."

That left Ford and Winton to go ahead as planned. (According to one account, Winton — who would register more than 100 automobile patents in his career — gave Ford one of his own complete steering mechanisms because he was worried Ford's design might get him killed.)

The race started predictably enough, with Winton dashing out to a lead of 300 yards over Ford. The newbie didn't quit, but Winton was clearly the more accomplished driver, and he managed to extend his lead to a half-mile nearly two-thirds of the way through the race. Because of his inexperience, the *Free Press* observed, Ford "did not dare keep (his car) on the pole."

In those days, mechanics rode along with drivers to fix the cars if they broke down. The *Free Press* reported that Ford's mechanic and his mechanic "hung far out in his effort to ballast the car, but she swung wide at every turn, and Mr. Ford had to shut off the power."

By the seventh mile, however, Winton's car was in trouble. The vehicle was starting to overheat: "A thin wreath of blue smoke appeared at the rear of the machine, and it gradually increased to a cloud." Winton's mechanic poured oil on it, but to no avail. And Ford, seizing the initiative roared past them on the main straightaway "as though they were standing still."

"Down the stretch he came like a demon, and the crowd yelled itself hoarse," the *Free Press* declared.

Ford's wife Clara later described the bedlam in a letter to her brother. "The people went wild," she recalled. "One man threw up his hat, and when it came down, he stamped on it. Another man had to hit his wife on the head to keep her from going off the handle. She stood up in her seat (and) screamed, 'I'd bet $50 on Ford if I had it!'"

Ford wound up winning the by three-quarters of a mile. Before he even left the racetrack, he received a pair of offers from businessmen wishing to purchase the car, which he eventually sold in May but repurchased years later in 1930. His success had the desired effect: It drew the attention of investors, whose backing enabled him to start the

Henry Ford Company later that year.

This wasn't the Ford Motor Co. that would bring him lasting fame. In fact, he was only a minority shareholder, and the investors he'd recruited weren't happy about his priorities: He was spending more time working on a race car prototype than he was on the company's stated goal of producing a lightweight roadster it could sell for $1,000.

Ford, meanwhile, was unhappy with being told what to do at a company that bore his name. He wanted a bigger stake in the ownership and, ironically enough, he'd decided that he wanted to pursue racing rather than manufacturing.

"There is a barrel of money to be made in this business," he wrote to his brother-in-law in 1902. "My company will kick about me following racing, but they will get the advertising, and I expect to make $ where I can't make ¢'s at Manufacturing."

So, Ford left.

Not to be deterred, the owners he left behind forged ahead without him, finding a new name for the company he'd founded: Cadillac.

Ford's focus on racing set the stage for an unlikely chain of events that brought together perhaps the two biggest names in motorcars during the first half two decades of the 20th century, Ford and a champion cyclist named Berna "Barney" Oldfield.

A year after he made headlines with his "Sweepstakes" win, Ford teamed up with a bicycle racer named Tom Cooper to build a pair of four-cylinder race cars: the red 999 (named for the first locomotive to go faster than 100 mph) and the yellow Arrow. It wasn't cheap: The 999 alone cost $5,000 to build — more than $150,000 in 2020 dollars.

Oldfield was a friend of Cooper's, so the pair invited him up to Michigan to test the 999. It wasn't unusual for bicycle racers to make the transition to motorcars, and Oldfield had already driven a gasoline-powered bicycle at a race in Salt Lake City. In fact, his ability to slide into turns like a motorbike racer was one of the keys to his success behind the wheel.

Ford had assembled his team, but at some point around this time, problems arose. The cars, it seemed, refused to start. Chagrined, Ford sold his stake in them for $800 to Cooper and Oldfield, who eventually resolved the issue and got the cars up and running. A rematch of sorts with Winton in Grosse Pointe a year after Ford's victory ended the same way the second time out. With Oldfield at the wheel this time, the 999 won going away in a 20-mile race, a mile ahead of second-place Charles Shanks. Winton's car once again broke down.

The Ford 999 on display at the Henry Ford Museum in Dearborn, Mich. *John Ross, Creative Commons CCBY2.0*

Oldfield and Cooper then toured the country with the two cars, and Oldfield set a record by covering a mile in 55.54 seconds at the Empire City race track in Yonkers, N.Y. After that, though, Oldfield jumped ship and joined Winton's racing team, leaving Cooper to take the wheel of the Arrow himself.

At an event in Milwaukee, however, he turned the car over to a driver named Frank Day, who decided to push the car in his quest for a new record. The track was wet, but Day was undeterred: Instead of slowing down as he leaned into a turn, he accelerated ... and skidded. The tires flew off the machine, which flipped, tearing a hole in the track before slamming into a fence and stopping.

Day was crushed beneath the wrecked vehicle and died eight days later.

That might have been the end of the Arrow if it hadn't been for Ford, who bought the wreckage and rebuilt it, calling it the "Red Devil 999."

The year was 1904, and despite his intent to return to racing, Ford himself hadn't gotten behind the wheel the previous year.

When he finally did so, he made quite a splash — metaphorically speaking, that is, because the surface on which he made his return was, in fact, water. Frozen water.

In January, Ford hauled his reborn 999 out onto Lake St. Clair, northeast of Detroit, which was frozen solid in the depths of winter. He then proceeded to shave a full 10 seconds off the world land (ice?) speed record, hitting 91.37 mph in what the *Detroit Tribune* called "the wildest ride in the history of automobiling."

The newspaper related the scene: "Humped over his steering wheel, the tremendous speed throwing the machine in zigzag fashion across the fifteen-foot roadway, Ford was taking chances that no man, not even that specialist in averted suicide, Barney Oldfield, had dared to tempt."

But Ford had committed to the attempt, and he knew that calling off the ice sprint wasn't an option.

He later wrote that "the ice seemed smooth enough, so smooth that if I had called off the trial, we would have secured an immense amount of the wrong kind of advertising. But (actually), instead of being smooth, that ice was seamed with fissures which I knew were going to mean trouble the moment I got up to speed."

However, "there was nothing to do but go through with the trial, so I let the old Arrow out. At every fissure, the car leaped into the air. I never knew how it was coming down. When I wasn't in the air, I was skidding, but somehow I stayed top-side-up and on course, making a record that went all over the world."

The record didn't last long, though. William Vanderbilt bested it by going 92.29 mph in a Mercedes at Daytona Beach less than a month later. Before the year was out, it had been broken four more times, topping 100 mph in July, when Louis Rigolly of France drove a car made by Gobron-Brillié 103 mph.

Two years later came another milestone, when the steam-powered Stanley Rocket obliterated the previous record by nearly 18 mph, becoming the first car to go faster than the contemporary *rail* speed record. Its 127.66 mph run made it the second and last steam car ever to claim the record, which endured as the standard for steam-powered vehicles all the way until 2009.

Ford tried and failed to reclaim the speed record in 1905 with another car, dubbed the Model K, and eventually returned his focus to manufacturing: His Ford Motor Co. produced the first Model T in 1908.

Barney Oldfield, left in 1915 with his trademark cigar, wrote a column in which he dispensed advice on automotive matters. *Library of Congress*

Oldfield, meanwhile, became all but synonymous with the race game. The image of him behind the wheel with the fat stub of a cigar in his mouth became iconic. But the cigar, it turns out, wasn't just for show. He explained: "I used that cigar for a purpose, and a mighty good one, too. I keep the cigar in my mouth to protect my teeth in case of an accident, and it has served me many a good turn. Of all the accidents that I have had, I have never lost a tooth, and it has been due to the fact that I always had a cigar between my teeth…"

Oldfield's career was a mix of official races and colorful exhibitions. He drove a Mercedes to victory at the Indianapolis Motor Speedway in August of the track's inaugural 1909 season. Meanwhile he staged best-of-three match races in which he would purposely lose the second leg in order to set up a dramatic win in the final run.

In 1914, he took part in barnstorming tour in which he raced his Fiat against Lincoln Beachey's biplane in a series of 35 races across the country. Two years later, he became the first person to record a 100 mph lap at the Indianapolis Motor Speedway. He even wrote a "Dear Abby"-style advice column for auto enthusiasts, long before Dear Abby was doing her thing. He finally retired at the age of 40 in 1918, although he raced a couple of times after that.

Later in life, the story goes, he was stopped for speeding after leading three motorcycle cops on a chase. When they finally caught up to him, one of them walked up to him and asked, "Who do you think you are? Barney Oldfield?"

Before he died, Ford and Oldfield met up again, by which time they were both legends, linked forever by their exploits in the 999.

Ford reportedly said to Oldfield, "You made me and I made you."

But Oldfield just shook his head and declared, "Old 999 made both of us."

Actress Fannie Brice with an Oldsmobile in 1922. *Library of Congress*

## Early Carmakers

It's easy to look back and imagine Henry Ford dominating the car industry in the first two decades of the 20th century — and in a sense, he did. But he started out as just one among a slew of ambitious automakers seeking to make their mark in a fast-growing industry.

Henry Leland was nearly 60 years old and sported a bushy Van Dyke that would have put Colonel Sanders to shame when he got into the fledgling auto industry. He'd made his name and his money as Detroit's leading manufacturer, making everything from stoves to Pullman railroad cars. By 1902, he was supplying auto parts, too.

That year, Leland became involved in the first Henry Ford Company, which at the time was on the verge of producing an economically priced roadster. Ford, however, had become fed up and departed to design the race car that would become the 999 — leaving lead investor William Murphy and his partners high and dry.

Murphy wanted to fold up his tent and liquidate the year-old company's assets. It was natural that he should turn to Leland, the city's leading parts man, to find out what they were worth. But, to Murphy's surprise, Leland told him *not* to close up shop. The roadster was already designed, and the factory was ready to go. Why not get things started and see if he could sell some cars? Leland even had the perfect engine for the new car: a single-cylinder gas motor he'd built for another automaker.

Murphy was so impressed he not only kept the company open, he hired Leland and to run it.

With Ford gone, it needed a new name, and the backers settled on "Cadillac" — for Antoine de la Mothe Cadillac, the French nobleman who had founded the city of Detroit. Leland put his own engine in Ford's roadster, which hit the market in 1903. It carried the Cadillac nameplate but bore an uncanny resemblance to the Model A produced by Ford Motor Company that same year.

Go figure.

The next six years, however, were kind to Leland. He built Cadillac into one of the nation's premier automakers, eventually selling the business to William Durant of General Motors in 1909 for a cool $4.5 million. He joined GM as an executive but left in a dispute with his new boss: Leland wanted the company to build engines for U.S. airplanes fighting in World War I, but Durant, a pacifist, shot him down.

Leland took the government contract himself, decided to pocket the $10 million that went with it and started another luxury car company, named for Abraham Lincoln. The Lincoln Motor Company started producing V-8 engines based on the airplane's designs, and Leland appeared to be off and running with another successful venture. There was just one problem: The government never paid Leland the full $10 million he was due, and when a recession hit in the early 1920s, he wasn't equipped to weather it.

The company, valued at $16 million, went into receivership and was put up for auction.

Who should put in the winning bid but the man whose design Leland had used for the very first Cadillac? That's right, Henry Ford. Adding insult to injury, Ford offered a paltry $5 million for the company, which was raised to $8 million only on the insistence of the bankruptcy judge. Not long after the deal was finalized, Ford fired Leland's son, and the 79-year-old Leland himself resigned in protest. Ford had his security officers march in and escort both men personally off the premises.

What ever happened to the other automaker who used engine Leland put in his first Cadillac — the man for whom it was originally designed?

Ransom Eli Olds found a good deal of success in his own right.

One might say that Olds was not only ahead of his time, he was ahead of Henry Ford's time, too. He got started in the business before Ford did, building the first car with a steam engine in 1894 and producing a gas-powered model two years later. By 1901 he had a factory staffed by 300 workers and a full line of cars ready for production. But one of the fastest-spreading fires the city had ever seen broke out at the plant in early March, and there was no time to save the building's contents. Ten men even jumped out of windows to escape the flames. (Although four were injured, they all survived.)

The loss was estimated at nearly $73,000 — the equivalent of roughly $2.2 million in 2020. All but one of Olds' 11 prototypes went up in flames, too: Workers managed to wheel the Curved Dash model out of the plant before it was fully consumed.

But if the fire was fast, Olds was faster.

He had a trick up his sleeve, a little something he invented called the assembly line. Yes, it was Olds who invented it, not (as you might think) Mr. Ford, who only improved upon Olds' concept. It was, indeed, Ford who created the *moving* assembly line. But it was Olds who had the idea of handing workers interchangeable parts and having them walk up and down an assembly line as they built the Curved Dash.

The car was named for its curved dashboard, which made it look like a sleigh from the front. It sold for $650 and was the nation's first reasonably priced, mass-produced car. Olds believed so strongly in it that, when one dealer offered to purchase 500, Olds suggested he buy 1,000. He did. It was the top-selling automobile in 1903 and again the following year, and Olds built more than 19,000 by the time production ended in 2006.

Olds left the company that bore his name, Olds Motor Works, in 1904, to form a new business called the R.E.O. Motor Works.

The original company, which produced Oldsmobiles, eventually became part of General Motors. Olds, meanwhile, quickly built the new company that bore his initials into a major player. It was one of the four largest car manufacturers by 1907. Sales declined gradually after that, but the company stayed in business until 1975, producing cars with names like the Flying Cloud and Reo Royale 8.

Apart from his contributions to the auto industry, Olds is known for a quirky link to musical pop culture. In 1905, a song called *In My Merry Oldsmobile* became a smash hit for vaudeville recording star Billy Murray. It told the story of one "Young Johnny Steele" and his Oldsmobile, in which he courted his true love, Lucille ("the queen of his gas machine").

The lyrics were somewhat suggestive, especially for the day, relating that the smitten pair "love to spark in the dark old park."

It goes from there:

> Each day they spoon to the engine's tune
> Their honeymoon will happen soon
> He'll win Lucille with his Oldsmobile
> And then he'll fondly croon:

"Come away with me, Lucille
In my merry Oldsmobile
Down the road of life we'll fly
Automobubbling, you and I

To the church we'll swiftly steal
Then our wedding bells will peal
You can go as far as you like with me
In my merry Oldsmobile

But that wasn't Mr. Olds' only musical connection. In 1967, a rock band that formed in Champaign, Ill., took its name from one of Olds' models, the 1915 R.E.O. Speed Wagon truck (the band styled "Speedwagon" as one word).

One of the founding members saw the name on the blackboard in his History of Transportation class at the University of Illinois.

The reason for the choice was simple. As explained on the band's website, the Speed Wagon "was very high-speed and heavy-duty for its day, and was considered a milestone of early transportation. It was sometimes outfitted as a fire engine."

That last bit makes sense: a precautionary measure, perhaps, for a man whose factory was once burned to the ground.

As of 2020, the band was still together, having lasted far longer than the model of truck that inspired its name.

## The Need for Speed

Henry Ford might have made a temporary miscalculation in 1902 when he said there was more money in racing than making cars. But he was right about one thing: If your company had a winner at the races, it gave you loads of free publicity.

In the early 1900s, carmakers didn't just enter races for the fun of it. It was free advertising. Even today, race fans keep track of which car companies excel on the banked oval or at the 24 Hours of Le Mans. (For the record, Chevrolet had racked up the most NASCAR cup titles as of 2019 with 39 , including runs of nine and 13 straight; Chevy was followed by Ford with 16, with Toyota and the now-defunct Hudson — winner first three cups, starting in 1952 — having collected three apiece.)

It's fitting that Chevrolet should have built such a stellar record on the track, because founder Louis Chevrolet started out as a driver, earning a reputation to rival Barney Oldfield's. Sometimes, he even eclipsed Oldfield's records on the track.

The Swiss-born Chevrolet arrived on U.S. soil in 1900, becoming the first of three brothers to immigrate. At 210 pounds, he stood out immediately with his thick moustache and barrel chest. Like Oldfield, he was a former bicycle racer making the transition to the new world of motorcar racing. In 1905, he used his Fiat to best both Oldfield and another driver, Walter Christie, in a three-mile sprint. That same year, he beat Oldfield's record for the fastest mile by two-tenths of a second, covering the distance in 52.8 seconds.

By 1911, Chevrolet was designing a prototype for a four-door touring sedan he dubbed the Classic Six: Its six-cylinder engine could do 65 mph "without taxing itself" and go from 0 to 50 in an "astounding" 15 seconds. He had the backing of none other than William F. Durant, who had founded General Motors in 1908 and engineered its rapid rise through the acquisition of Cadillac, Oldsmobile and Oakland Motor Car.

Chevrolet had been working for Durant at GM, racing Buicks and making a car that, according to General Motors' history "would bring race-type handling to the public."

Louis Chevrolet, the founder of the company that bears his name, behind the wheel for the 1916 Astor Cup race at Sheepshead Bay Speedway on Long Island. *Library of Congress*

But Durant had overextended himself with the purchases of other companies, and a group of bankers forced him to give up control of GM. Chevrolet was Durant's ticket back into the game. The Chevrolet Motor Car Company sold nearly 3,000 Classic Six cars in 1912, its first year of production, at $2,150 a pop, and its output doubled the following year. But Chevrolet left the company that bore his name, selling his stock for far less than what it was worth, over a dispute with Durant about whether to focus on a luxury car (Chevrolet's preference) or more affordable models.

Durant maintained control, and his investment ultimately proved so lucrative that, in 1916, he was able to regain control of GM by trading in his Chevrolet stock for shares of General Motors. The coup was such that writers said it was like "Jonah swallowing the whale," hailing it as one of the greatest feats in the history of American business. Chevrolet, the company, subsequently became GM's nameplate for — as Durant had envisioned — its most affordable models.

Chevrolet, meanwhile, returned to the race track, creating the Frontenac racing engine and also serving as vice president of a short-lived company called American

Motors (*not* the AMC of the much later Hornet, Pacer and Gremlin).

The Frontenac engine powered back-to-back winning Indy 500 entries in 1920 and 1921, with Louis' younger brother Gaston taking the checkered flag in the first of those two races. Gaston Chevrolet was the first driver to make it through the entire race without a tire change. Unfortunately, he never got the chance to defend his title. Less than six months later, during the final race of the season, his car flew up over the embankment at Beverly Hills Speedway in California. He died instantly. Even so, he was declared the national points champion for the 1920 season.

A year later, with Tommy Milton behind the wheel, Louis Chevrolet's Fontenac team won at Indy again.

Other cars and manufacturers, now largely forgotten, created milestones in the early years of the automotive era. The Mors automobile factory in France produced one of the first V-shaped engines and installed shock absorbers on its cars in 1902. That same year, its cars set three consecutive land-speed records in rapid succession, pushing the limit to 77.13 mph in November.

Another French company, Darracq, set back-to-back records in 1904 and 1905 before the Stanley Rocket shattered them with its 127.66 mph showing at Daytona Beach the following year. It was only the second time the record had been set on U.S. soil, following Henry Ford's successful "ice run" two years earlier.

The record might have gotten even more impressive the next year, when driver Fred Marriott tried to better it in an improved version of the '06 model. He had it running at close to 150 mph when it hit a rut and flew into the air, smashing in two when it landed and injured Marriott, who had no interest in making a repeat try after that.

The Stanley Motor Carriage Company took a different approach than most of its rivals, employing a steam engine rather than an internal-combustion motor that ran on gasoline. Often referred to as the Stanley Steamer or "Flying Teapot," the car was the nation's most popular automobile in the industry's formative years from 1900 to 1904. It was quiet, fast and environmentally friendly.

But there were disadvantages, too. The Stanley company never mass-produced the cars, which were overwhelmed on the market by Ford's Model T. By 1914, Ford was producing twice as many cars in a day as Stanley Motors was in a full year. They were a lot cheaper, too: You could buy a Model T for one-quarter of what you'd pay for a

Steamer. Add to that the convenience factor — you had to stop every ten miles in a Steamer to refill the boiler — and the Steamers were at a big disadvantage, especially when the electric starter replaced the hand crank on gas-powered vehicles.

The founding Stanley brothers sold the company in 1918 after making more than 10,000 cars, and it went out of business six years later.

Fred Marriott in his record-setting Stanley Steamer Rocket, which obliterated the land speed record with a 127.66-mph showing in 1906. *Wikimedia Commons*

Steamers were expensive, and so was another fast car of the early 20th century, the Stutz Bearcat, created by Harry Stutz. With a price tag of $2,000, the Bearcats were luxury cars, but they were also built to win on the track. The Bearcat debuted at the 1911 Indy 500, finishing an impressive (for a newcomer) 11th place and leading the company to call it "the car that made good in a day." In 1912, the Bearcats did even better, winning 25 of 30 races they entered.

The winner of that 1911 Indianapolis race, the first "500" at the Brickyard, was Ray Harroun in a car called the Marmon Wasp. Harroun came out of retirement for one race to run at Indy, and his car featured an innovation that helped him take the checkered flag: the first rear-view mirror ever used on a moving vehicle. Harroun later said the mirror bounced around so much it was hard to use, but even so, it helped eliminate the need for a mechanic to ride alongside the driver.

The Bearcats stopped rolling onto the streets in 1923, and Marmon ceased production of its cars a decade later.

# AMERICA'S FIRST HIGHWAYS

**Top:** A couple with a Marmon automobile in Jacksonville, Fla., 1927.

**Left:** Hudson dealer in Florida, 1926.

*Florida State Archives photos*

## Gone but Not Forgotten

Just in the past couple of decades, four long-established car brands have ceased production — two of them at General Motors. Pontiac, founded by GM in 1926 as a cheaper alternative to its Oakland line, was so successful it rendered Oakland obsolete seven years later. But in 2010, it became the second GM division to bite the dust in six years, following the demise of Oldsmobile in 2004.

Over at Chrysler, that company's entry-level alternative to Ford and Chevy — Plymouth, which debuted in 1928 — halted production in 2001. A year earlier, Ford's mid-priced Mercury brand reached the end of the (assembly) line. Mercury had been introduced in 1938 by Henry Ford's son, Edsel, whose name became attached to an ill-fated line of automobiles introduced by Ford in 1958.

It was gone two years later, having cost the company more than $200 million.

Fewer people probably remember other early automakers that found initial success but eventually fell by the wayside: companies with names like and Packard, Hudson and Nash.

Packard began producing its luxury car in 1899, three years before Studebaker brothers got into the automotive business, having started out during the mid-1800s producing carriages and wagons. The two companies merged in 1954, but even combined they couldn't halt the brands' decline. The Packard name was gone by 1962, and the entire business closed up shop four years later.

Hudson and Nash were both founded by corporate giants. Hudson was backed by retail mogul Joseph Hudson, whose department store in Detroit was once the tallest in the world. Charles Nash, meanwhile, succeeded founder William Durant — who had hired him 20 years earlier as an upholstery stuffer at his carriage company — as president of GM when Durant was forced out in 1912.

Durant regained control of the company four years later and offered Nash $1 million a year to stay on, but Nash resigned instead and bought the Wisconsin-based maker of the Rambler motorcar, which had been around since 1897. Nash put his own name on the company, which merged with Kelvinator appliance (the company that would later create the first side-by-side refrigerator) in 1937 and bought out Hudson in 1954 to create American Motors.

In that merger, both firms brought something to the table. Nash had reintroduced the Rambler name in 1950 and slapped it on the first successful American compact car, while Hudson's six-cylinder Hornet won the first three NASCAR points titles.

Unfortunately for the new company, American tastes soon began trending toward larger cars, spelling the end of the Nash Rambler in 1955. The Rambler name, however, continued as a full-fledged division within AMC.

The 1921 Hupmobile. *Library of Congress*

Production of the Hornet was discontinued in 1957.

AMC's most enduring success was the Jeep, a brand created by Willys-Overland Motors during World War II. Jeep later became part of Kaiser Motors, and when AMC purchased Kaiser in 1970, the vehicle became that company's most recognized model. The company brought back the Hornet name that same year, when it also introduced the first U.S. subcompact, the Gremlin. It came out with a wide-bodied small car called the Pacer that had a funky bubble-car look in 1975 (*Car and Driver Magazine* dubbed it "The Flying Fishbowl"), but that model only lasted five years.

AMC struggled in the 1980s and finally gave up the ghost in 1987, when Chrysler bought the company. Jeep, however, survived as a Chrysler nameplate.

One of the less-remembered early automakers was Hupp Motors, which produced a car called the Hupmobile.

Bobby Hupp founded the company that bore his name in 1909 and made an immediate impression on none other than Henry Ford, who enthused, "I recall looking at Bobby Hupp's roadster at the first show where it was exhibited and wondering whether we could ever build as good a small car for as little money."

Of course, he could. And did.

Even so, the Hupmobile was an early success, churning out 5,000 cars in its second year of production. Sales had reached 65,000 by 1928, but the Depression and an ill-advised change in focus from smaller, four-cylinder cars to more expensive eight-cylinder models doomed Hupp Motors. It closed up shop for good in 1938.

Nonetheless, Hupp left two lasting marks on the American landscape — if only indirectly. In 1914, Carl Wickman established a Hupp dealership in the mining town of Hibbing, Minn. But the miners couldn't afford the Hupmobile, and the dealership went belly-up. Hoping to salvage something from the experience, Wickman started offering the miners rides from Hibbing to their homes a couple of miles away in Alice. He charged them a one-way fee of 15 cents and a round-trip fare of a quarter for a ride in the only car he had: a seven-seat touring Hupmobile.

The shuttle service was such a success that Wickman eventually expanded it into a bus service that would become known as Greyhound.

Ralph Hay

An even more successful business was born in the showroom of a Canton, Ohio, Hupmobile dealership owned by Ralph Hay in 1920. It was there that 15 men gathered in a room equipped with just ten seats to launch an endeavor they called the American Professional Football Conference. The five people who didn't have chairs had to sit on a Hupmobile's running boards.

Each of the men represented a team in the proposed new league, with Hay owning the Canton Bulldogs. His team had won three consecutive titles in its last three years competing in a loosely organized "Ohio League," but it had lost money, and Hay was looking for a way to control salaries. Jim Thorpe, an Olympic hero who coached and played halfback for the Bulldogs, came up with the idea of forming a more formal league across the Upper Midwest and Northeast.

That led to the meeting in Hay's Hupmobile dealership, where the men in attendance paid $100 apiece for the right to join the new league.

Hay was asked to become the league's commissioner, but he deferred to Thorpe, whose name recognition would raise the new circuit's profile. Shortly after that meeting, the league changed its name to the American Professional Football Association and competed for two years under that banner before adopting yet another new name: the

National Football League.

Hay's team went unbeaten and won the league championship in 1922, but the Bulldogs continued to lose money and he sold them before the next season began. Under new ownership, they posted another unbeaten record the following year and won a second consecutive title.

After 1926, the Canton Bulldogs were no more. But in 1961, the NFL chose Canton as the site for the Pro Football Hall of Fame. Despite being recommended for inclusion by no less a personage than Chicago Bears owner George Halas — one of the people in attendance that day at the Hupmobile dealership — Hay himself isn't in the Hall. But a plaque at the site where the dealership once stood pays tribute to him alongside Thorpe.

Hay died in 1944 at the age of 53.

## Auto Tours and Reliability Runs

AAA founder Augustus Post takes part in the New York-to-St. Louis run of 1904. *Estate of Augustus Post/Wikimedia Commons*

# Road Tests

Cycling enthusiasts had done their best to lobby for better roads, but they'd only managed to get so far. The railroads weren't eager to give up their monopoly on long-distance shipping and travel, so they had no interest in a network of interstate highways. Even an alliance of cyclists, farmers and catalog houses wasn't strong enough to stand against the almighty iron horse. A more powerful challenger was needed.

At the turn of the century, just such a challenger was starting to emerge. The cycling fad of the 1890s was waning, but many of the same people who'd been so taken by two-wheelers were turning their attention to the latest craze: the automobile. This love affair, while still in its infancy, would prove far more lasting than the nation's dalliance with cycling. And, even more important to the Good Roads movement, there would be a lot more money behind it.

Nineteenth century railroad moguls would give way, in due course, to automotive tycoons like Henry Ford, William Durant and Carl Fisher, who had both the visibility and the financial clout to make Congress sit up and take notice. Eventually.

Of course, it didn't happen overnight. In fact, some people thought the automobile would prove a fleeting fancy, simply because there were so few good roads. Buyers wouldn't flock to a new contraption that didn't have much use outside the few decent streets in major cities — at least, so the thinking went. But it didn't quite work out that way. Americans were so taken with the motorcar that, instead of being discouraged by the poor quality of roads, they started demanding improvements.

In 1900, there were just 8,000 motor vehicles in all the nation. But just five years later, there were ten times as many. In 1908, the year Durant founded GM and Ford introduced the Model T, the figure was just shy of 200,000, and five years after that, it was 1.25 million. This meant there was not only a growing number of drivers eager to expand their horizons, there was an increasingly wealthy group in the auto industry who wanted to accommodate them.

The mighty railroads, meanwhile, were beginning to feel the pinch of regulation — and competition.

In 1887, railroads became the first U.S. industry subject to federal regulation, under the newly created Interstate Commerce Commission. Then, in 1906, the Hepburn Act empowered the ICC to set maximum rail rates, and the Valuation Law of 1913 gave the commission authority to assess the value of railroad property — and set shipping rates accordingly. Regulation limited the railroads' profits, and their options.

It was about that time that the auto trails movement really got rolling. But even with the railroads weakened, there was still a major obstacle to highway improvement. A lot had changed in 100 years, but one thing remained the same: Fiscal conservatives in Congress were loath to spend tax dollars on better roads. It was one thing to give away surplus land to the railroads, but quite another to dig into the treasury and pay for a nationwide system of highways.

# AMERICA'S FIRST HIGHWAYS

**Top:** Along the Columbia River Highway in 2016. *NOAA Photo Library*

**Above:** Buggies and cars share Ocean Avenue in this 1914 photo taken in Garden Grove, Calif. Most "improved" roads were still dirt. *Orange County Archives, Creative Commons CCBY2.0*

During the first part of the 20th century, most of the nation's roads were unimproved. That is to say, no one did anything to maintain them. An "improved" road was still a dirt road, just one that had been consciously graded and topped with a mixture of sand and clay.

In other words, such roads were just a small step up from beaten paths: dirt trails, where the brush had been cleared away and wheels had worn visible paths in the earth. Sometimes, this actually made things worse. Early tires were thin, hard, solid rubber or wagon-wheel wood. They dug into the soil and created troublesome ruts — which motorists who came along afterward had to contend with.

The Goodyear Tire and Rubber Company improved the situation in 1905 when it began producing an inflatable tire that was easier on the road. And Henry Ford helped matters further when he ordered 1,200 sets of them for his first Model T. But dirt was still dirt, subject to wear not just from tires but from rainstorms, snow, flooding and other factors. Unimproved roads were endemic to rural areas, especially in the West and South. Only 16% of the roads in New York state were improved by 1909, but that was still more than Tennessee's 11.5% and Georgia's 7%.

With bad roads still the norm and the federal government still hesitant to invest in better ones, car lovers needed to make the case for improving them — and suggest how to make it happen. Like cyclists before them, they were more than ready to take up the challenge.

By the turn of the century, clubs for auto enthusiasts had started to form in much the same way cycling clubs had begun a few decades earlier. And just as those cycling clubs had gotten together to form the League of American Wheelmen, nine car clubs joined in common cause to create a similar group for car enthusiasts. In March of 1902, those clubs gathered in Chicago to form the American Automobile Association, which identified six specific goals a month later:

1. To secure rational legislation
2. To formulate proper rules governing the use of the automobile
3. To protect the interest of automobilists against unjust discrimination
4. To maintain their lawful rights and privileges
5. To encourage the use of the automobile and its development
6. To promote the "Good Roads" movement

# AMERICA'S FIRST HIGHWAYS

Where's the road? Often, there wasn't one. At left, a car crosses a dusty stretch of Nebraska in 1915, and below, vehicles struggle to deal with rocky terrain and sagebrush as they make their way through California's Death Valley in 1926.
*NOAA Photo Library*

Water could be a formidable obstacle, as these photos show. Sometimes, you needed a ferry to get across, as seen at left in this 1915 photo taken at the Snake River in Idaho. Other times, you might need help from some four-legged friends, as seen above in this 1921 photo taken on the Red River near Granite, Okla. *NOAA Photo Library*

It paid to take along plenty of spare tires and be ready for some steep hills, as illustrated by these photos. **Top:** Dragging a pine tree down a place labeled in the photo as Pine Mountain, 1926. **Above:** Somewhere in the Pacific Northwest, 1915. *NOAA Photo Library*

Charles and Lucy Glidden in London during their 1902 trip around the world in their Napier. *Wikimedia Commons*

## The Glidden Tours

If there was any doubt about AAA's interest in promoting interstate roads, a brief November report in the *Minneapolis Journal* laid it to rest with the opening sentence: "A national highway from the Atlantic to the Pacific coast is to be the leading issue henceforth for the American Automobile Association."

Not long afterward, the AAA decided to stage a gala event to highlight its mission: an automobile "run" from a variety of different starting points to the 1904 World's Fair in St. Louis. AAA Secretary C.H. Gillette of New York announced that "in connection with our work, we expect to bring at least 150 automobiles with us on this run, and are planning to get into an encampment for a week."

The event would be a tour, not a race. Participants would be able to go at their own pace, stopping along the way to tout AAA and the Good Roads movement at hotels and city centers. Most of the participants would start out from three locations on the East Coast: New York, Philadelphia and Baltimore. Other vehicles would head to St. Louis along secondary routes from Minneapolis, Kansas City (the shortest run at roughly 250 miles) and Birmingham, with additional cars joining in along the way.

The field of official participants didn't quite live up to the 150 originally advertised, with 77 cars starting from the various locations, although 200 local cars did join the finishers in a parade at the end of the run. The largest contingent also went the farthest: 18 cars traveling 1,350 miles from New York, with five others from Boston meeting up with that group at Albany and going the rest of the way.

Two in the group from Boston were notable: Percy Pierce drove his father George Pierce's car, the Great Arrow, and Charles Glidden was behind the wheel of a 24-horsepower Napier.

Glidden had already made a name for himself as an automobile pioneer. In 1901, he and his wife had taken his Napier to a place where no roads even existed: the Arctic Circle. They'd made it back safely, and immediately set their sights on an even more daunting goal, a trip around the world. They'd completed this journey, too, becoming the first people to circumnavigate the globe in a motorcar… and then, they'd done it again, logging more than 46,000 miles on a journey through 39 countries.

Charles Glidden's participation in the AAA run was a harbinger of things to come.

President William Howard Taft's Pierce-Arrow, 1909. *Library of Congress*

The same could be said for Pierce, the son of luxury automaker George Pierce, whose Pierce-Arrows were some of the most efficient — and expensive — cars on the road. In 1905, he would produce a model that was priced as high as $5,000: nearly $150,000 in today's (2020) currency, or comparable to the price tag for a modern Porsche 911.

The Arrow stood Percy Pierce in good stead during the run to St. Louis. He was the first driver to arrive in Buffalo from Rochester en route to the World's Fair, getting there more than an hour ahead of the other cars on the New York leg. During his Buffalo stopover, he made sure everyone knew that the motorists took their role as goodwill ambassadors seriously.

"The greatest care is being exercised by all in the party" that no accidents should occur, he said. "And if any of the party finds his car is likely to frighten a horse, it is slowed up and, if necessary, a man gets out and keeps the animal quiet. Especially is this the case where women are driving or in the carriages."

Local pace cars rode out ahead of the main pack, dropping rubber-weighted confetti in the road to make sure drivers knew the proper route to take. Local residents gathered as the main drivers drew closer, eager for a look at these adventurers braving the open road in their newfangled contraptions.

When the drivers rounded the bend and came into view, the spectators who had gathered beside the road were more than welcoming, greeting them enthusiastically. Pierce was duly impressed by their hospitality: "In scores of places we found the people looking out for us, and literally loaded with bouquets for us," he said. "I received enough bouquets along the run to completely cover my dash."

Despite Pierce's early arrival in Buffalo, he insisted it wasn't a race. "The drivers are all gentlemen out for a pleasant run, and most of the time the speed is held so low that they do not wear their goggles," he said, adding that "everyone is trying to do all possible to further the interests of good roads and of the automobile."

Despite encountering some rough roads, the cars to that point had come upon few difficulties beyond the occasional tire problem. That wasn't, however, the case on all the chosen routes to St. Louis. On the National Highway, for instance, only two of the ten cars that set out from Baltimore managed to make it through the Cumberland Mountains.

Still, the run to the World's Fair was an unqualified success. In all, 66 of the 77 cars that had embarked upon the journey made it through. Glidden for one was so impressed by the results that he became determined to repeat the experience the following year. As an incentive, he offered a $2,000 prize to the most successful driver in a sequel, to be run in 1905.

Suddenly, it was a race, after all. Or, rather, a "reliability run." Time limits were established between checkpoints, and a scoring system was set up, which called for points to be deducted for mechanical mishaps.

The change to a competitive format had two immediate results. First of all, as speed became more of a factor, some locals found themselves less enamored of the visiting drivers.

Pace cars left trails of confetti in the road, as they had the previous year, to mark the route. But local residents annoyed by the cars that came whizzing past sometimes removed the confetti or pointed it in the wrong direction, sending Glidden drivers off into the hinterlands.

Elsewhere, police set speed traps for the passing cars.

The *Manchester Union* in New Hampshire complained that motorists "seem to think they have the right to use the road to the exclusion or discomfort of other people, to say the least."

"Take for instance the record of the run from Concord to Nashua — 18 miles in 40 minutes! Have they the right to do such a thing? Take the list of accidents they caused: an old man thrown out of his wagon and his arm injured, while his horse ran away and smashed the wagon and harness to bits; a collision with a lumber wagon and the driver of the automobile hurt; a horse and a mowing machine badly frightened and cut up. All these things without redress offered or obtained from the man who owns the machine."

As a second consequence of the new "reliability run" format, carmakers became eager to prove their products were the best on the market. They entered the Glidden in the hope of racking up perfect scores, so they could tout their achievements to potential buyers in newspaper ads and other promotions.

Percy Pierce was more than prepared for the new focus. His father's Arrows became the standard-bearers for the Glidden Tour over the next several years, with Percy at the wheel and additional Pierce entries also posting perfect marks. In fact, Percy won the 1905 Glidden Tour (as the run came to be called) by collecting 996 out of a possible 1,000 points in a run from New York to Breton Hills, N.H. He topped that performance by racking up perfect scores each of the next four years.

The Arrow continued its dominance through 1908, with the tour routes restricted to the Northeast.

Then, in 1909, the tour's organizers became a little more ambitious. The tour that year was the longest yet, and the first to take drivers west of the Mississippi River. The route was a 2,600-mile loop that began in Detroit and headed west to Chicago before veering north to Minneapolis and dipping south again through Iowa to Omaha. It then took drivers across Nebraska and all the way to Denver before circling back south and east again to the final destination: Kansas City.

The contest committee examines entries before the 1910 Glidden Tour in Cincinnati. *Library of Congress*

Poorer road conditions, made worse by rain, led to a number of point deductions between Fort Dodge, Iowa, and Kearney, in central Nebraska. Several cars got stuck in the mud and were penalized for making necessary repairs. One car, for example, lost 1.6 points for fixing a broken steering arm after it became stuck on a muddy road. Another entry lost 16 points for fixing a hub flange after an accident that sent the car into a ditch.

The difficulties were such that they gave rise to rumors the tour would be cut short.

Glidden put those rumors to rest, declaring, "This is only the beginning of these tours. This tour is the most wonderful in the history of automobiling. If plans now under consideration are carried out, next year's run will be from San Francisco to New York."

Despite the difficulties, five touring cars and three roadsters finished with spotless scores. Four of the eight perfect entries were Pierces.

The 1910 tour, it turned out, wasn't a transcontinental journey from San Francisco to New York, after all. Instead, the route began in Cincinnati and headed south into Tennessee and Arkansas, then all the way to Dallas, before turning north again and passing through Oklahoma, Kansas, Nebraska and Iowa en route to Chicago. The total mileage was even greater than the previous year's run: 2,851.

The 1911 tour took participants into the Deep South for the first time, beginning in New York City and concluding in Jacksonville, Fla.

The roads proved to be even more challenging than the western roads of the previous two years. The official press car was "completely demolished" in Charleston, W.Va., when the brakes went out and it hurtled into a ditch, then knocked down a telephone pole, ending up on its side.

Things only got worse when the tour hit Virginia, as the motorists, in the words of the *New York Times*, "gave good-bye to good roads when they left Staunton" in the northwestern part of the state, adding that "evidently, there is no such thing (as good roads) anymore, especially going in this direction, for reports from all sources say the worst is yet to come…"

The newspaper continued: "Old dyed-in-the-wool tourists say they never knew a run as hazardous as" the 38-mile stretch from Natural Bridge — a limestone rock arch on land once owned by Thomas Jefferson — to Roanoke. A downpour "like the cloudbursts they have in the tropics" left wild mountain roads a mucky quagmire of yellow mud two feet deep. Swollen streams had to be forded, delaying any progress by a day, and Glidden himself reportedly said he'd never seen a stretch of road so bad.

A car carrying the governor of Georgia skidded off the road and hit a telephone pole, and after the AAA president's car flew into a ditch, three women in the vehicle were forced to take shelter in a nearby farmhouse.

But the worst was yet to come. A car carrying Samuel Butler, chairman of the AAA contest board, crashed when its steering gear — which had been tightened to contend with sandy roads — jammed on a road in rural Georgia. The Cunningham pace car was going 33 mph when the gear locked up, sending it into a ditch. It overturned and came to rest on its side, pinning Butler beneath one of its wheels. He was killed instantly, and the car's other occupants were injured after being thrown clear.

The tour continued to Jacksonville, but it might well have been the beginning of the end for the annual event. Plans were laid for another Glidden run in 1912, this time a "Great Lakes to Gulf" tour to begin in Detroit on Oct. 7 and wind up 12 days later in New Orleans. But by late September, the starting date had been pushed back a week, "because of the slowness of prospective entrants to nominate cars for the run." A few days later, the run was called off entirely, reportedly because would-be participants didn't want to be so far away from home just before the presidential election.

The tour returned for a final run in 1913, but only three manufacturers (Metz, Krit and Hupmobile) took part in the run from Minneapolis to Glacier Park in Montana, and the scoring system was relaxed, with cars losing points only for lateness and not for mechanical failures. Metz won the Glidden Cup, which was never awarded again.

## Other Auto Tours

The Glidden Tour wasn't the only reliability run, nor was it even the first.

In 1902, the Brooklyn Daily Eagle announced the Automobile Club of America was sponsoring a 500-mile reliability run from New York to Boston and back again. The event was open to "all classes of self-propelled vehicles made in the United States and abroad," the article said.

Seventy-five cars entered the event, and contestants were limited to an average daily speed of no more than 14 mph. This was necessary, in part, because Connecticut had adopted the nation's first speed limit in 1901, restricting vehicles to 12 mph in the city and 15 in the country. Gasoline-powered cars dominated the field with 55 entries, although there were also 19 steam-engine vehicles and one electric car. Cups were offered in three weight classes, along with a President's Cup.

The cars were decidedly out of their element in what was still almost exclusively a horse-and-buggy world. Two horses attached to one such buggy got spooked by one of the motorized marvels and bolted, "doing no greater damage than injuring the vehicle," a press account related. Another car suffered a bent axle after colliding with a trolley in New Haven, and there were bovine obstacles, as well:

"A herd of cattle crossing the narrow roadway near Warren (Mass.) caused some delay, and some of the vehicles ran into a cow without seriously damaging either cow or machine." At 14 mph, there was only so much damage that could be done. The cow, presumably, was going slower still.

Sixty-eight of the cars that started the event made it to Boston and back again, with Frank Duryea winning top honors in a vehicle of his own design, a Stevens-Duryea. (He'd founded the company a year earlier, and it would stay in business until 1927.) Two cars had to be towed across the finish line after breaking down: a steam-powered Locomobile and a Fiat — the Italian automaker was in just its second year of business. Still, steam-car drivers had something to crow about: More than half of them wound up with perfect scores, while just 18% of the gas-powered vehicles could say the same.

England hosted its own reliability run the following year, and soon, they were all the rage, quickly spreading across the country to the West Coast.

Auto enthusiasts gather for a reliability run at the Palomares Hotel in Pomona in April of 1904. *Wikimedia Commons*

STEPHEN H. PROVOST

*"When we left New York for Chicago, we were tourists. When we left Chicago for California, we were pioneers."*

— Early auto tourist, 1924

**Above:** Heavyweight champion Jack Johnson at the wheel of a Thomas Flyer.

**Left:** Journalist and playwright Sophie Treadwell takes part in an auto tour.

## AMERICA'S FIRST HIGHWAYS

The tours and runs went all over the place. A 1911 ad for the Flanders Model 20 crowed that it had placed first in runs from Minneapolis to Montana and St. Louis to Kansas City, as well as "America's Greatest Annual Hill Climbing Contest" in Worcester, Mass. (The company, co-founded by former Ford employee Walter Flanders, went head-to-head with the economically priced Model T in 1910 but ultimately failed to keep pace and was absorbed by Studebaker in 1913.)

Another big event in 1909 was the New York to Atlanta Good Roads Tour, which featured 61 cars — including a Chalmers Detroit Model 30 piloted by Detroit Tigers baseball great Ty Cobb. Chalmers, which would claim top honors in the 1910 Glidden Tour, decided before that season started to give a free car to the player in each major league with the highest batting average. That sounded like a great deal for Cobb, who led the American League in that category every year from 1907 to 1915.

Cobb himself certainly liked the idea: "I am glad that something besides medals and trophies is offered for the championship in batting," he said before the season got underway. "I think the offer of a Chalmers '30' is simply great, and I hope to be lucky enough to own a new Chalmers next fall."

He almost wasn't. Napoleon Lajoie of Cleveland would have caught him in a season-ending doubleheader if his final at-bat hadn't been ruled an error instead of a hit (defensive errors are treated as outs by official scorers in determining a player's batting average). An attempt to bribe the official scorer into ruling Lajoie's final at-bat a hit deepened the scandal. In the end, Cobb was ruled the official batting champion with an average of .385 to Lajoie's .384, but Chalmers awarded a car to each man.

The following year, the company changed things up, giving the car to the league's MVP instead of the batting champ. Cobb won car again in 1911 anyway, after hitting for a lifetime-best .420 average. The award was discontinued after 1914, and Maxwell Motors bought Chalmers in 1922, but the combined company struggled and was forced into bankruptcy. Walter P. Chrysler bought its assets and formed the Chrysler Corporation from its ashes.

Perhaps the most famous road runs of the early automobile age owe their enduring fame to later motion pictures: a Blake Edwards comedy called *The Great Race* in 1965 and the *Cannonball Run* in 1984. There's more about the real Great Race in the chapter.

*Cannonball Run* (and its sequel) starring Burt Reynolds, Roger Moore and Farrah

Fawcett, took its name from the exploits of Erwin "Cannon Ball" Baker, who started out as a motorcycle racer and won the first event ever staged at the Indianapolis Motor Speedway, in 1909.

Five years later, he set the first of his 143 driving records when he rode an Indian motorcycle coast to coast in 11 days. A year after that, he drove a Stutz Bearcat from Los Angeles to New York in the same amount of time, and improved on that showing in 1916 when he covered the same distance in less than 7½ days driving a Cadillac 8 roadster.

Baker's most famous feat came later, in 1933, when he made it from New York to L.A. in 53½ hours, driving a Graham-Page 57 Blue Streak 8. The record stood for nearly 40 years and inspired the Cannonball Baker Sea-to-Shining-Sea Memorial Dash, an unsanctioned event held five times during the 1970s, which in turn served as the direct inspiration for the Reynolds films.

## Transcontinental

One of the first great auto excursions, however, took place as the result of a $50 bet following a chance bit of eavesdropping in San Francisco.

A group of men were saying it would be impossible to travel across the United States in an automobile.

The year was 1903, and so far, no one had done it.

But that didn't mean it couldn't be done — at least according to the man who overheard the conversation, a 31-year-old former physician from Vermont named Horatio Nelson Jackson. The good doctor had retired young in 1900 after marrying Bertha Wells, the daughter of a patent medicine tycoon. The couple just happened to be there on a brief stop during a trip to scout out mining investments in Alaska and Mexico.

"I heard some men at the University Club in San Francisco one day declare that such a feat as crossing the continent in an automobile was impossible," Jackson said. "That, as an enthusiast, I resented."

Jackson wasn't the only person who believed it could be done. In 1899, a driver who set out from New York City quit by the time he got to Syracuse, after a one-armed bicyclist passed him on the road.

The car had been given a 10-day head start.

# AMERICA'S FIRST HIGHWAYS

Horatio Nelson Jackson surveys the landscape, above, in a display at the Smithsonian National Museum, and crosses the desert in his Winton Touring Car, left, in 1903.

*Above: Kevin Burkett, Creative Commons CCBY2.0. Left: Wikimedia Commons*

Two years later, Alexander Winton had tried to go the opposite direction, from San Francisco to New York. He'd made it across the Sierra Nevada, only to be halted by the Nevada desert. This wasn't, of course, the only setback Winton suffered in 1901; it was in that same year that he lost a race to then-unknown automaker Henry Ford in Grosse Pointe, Mich. A year earlier, he'd raced to a tie with Ransom Eli Olds of Oldsmobile fame: Winton followed Olds onto the course, and both reached identical speeds of 57 mph on the sands of Daytona Beach — the first auto race ever held there.

Olds, like Winton, wanted one of his cars to be the first to cross the continent. In fact, by the time Horatio Jackson made his $50 bet, Oldsmobile and Packard had both been planning their own attempts to travel from sea to shining sea. They'd recruited top drivers, expert mechanics and were working on modified versions of their best cars at the time.

Jackson recruited a mechanic of his own: 22-year-old Sewell Crocker, a former bicycle racer who'd worked in a gasoline engine factory. Jackson asked both his wife and Crocker what they thought about his idea.

After hearing the men at the club dismiss the concept of a transcontinental trip, Jackson said, "I returned to the hotel and told my wife what I had heard. She thought the trip could be done. Crocker, with whom I talked it over later, thought so too, provided we took a northern route."

But Jackson needed a car. So, four days later, he purchased an automobile for $2,500 plus an undisclosed bonus — quite an investment to win a $50 bet. It was, ironically, a Winton, manufactured by the man who had failed in a similar endeavor two years earlier. The two-cylinder, two-seat touring car was just the beginning of Jackson's expenditures: Before the trip was done, he would end up sinking $8,000 into the enterprise.

"By paying a bonus, I secured a 20-horsepower Winton gasoline machine of this year's model, and in four days we were off on our journey."

By starting from San Francisco on May 23, he and Crocker would be tackling the hardest part of the journey first. Only 150 miles of road were even paved nationwide, and what few decent roads there were at the time were almost all on the East Coast, so they had to rely heavily on improvisation at the outset. They popped a rear tire just 15 miles outside San Francisco and had to replace it with the only spare they had.

Then the drove up through Northern California and into Oregon, crossing the Sierra and heading on to Idaho. It was a bit out of the way.

"Of course, the distance by rail is much shorter," Jackson said, "but we went in and out and sometimes even back. For instance, we rode 69 miles to avoid a ravine, strayed 64 miles to Swanton Falls in Wyoming, and were sent 54 miles out of the way in California by a red-headed woman with a white horse just so we should pass her house and let her folks see an automobile."

Cars were that rare in those days. (Most people viewed a motor vehicle, in Jackson's words, as "an unreliable novelty.")

In fact, he said, "along 3,000 miles of our journey, an automobile had never before been seen." It was almost like an alien landing. "The people would telephone and wire ahead that we were coming, and the inhabitants would gather to see us pass. Cowboys would ride 60 miles to see the 'go-like-hell machine' for the marvelous stories of its speed possibilities."

The roads were, as expected, rough going. It took them nearly a week just to get through California, usually going from 7 a.m. to 7 p.m. and, sometimes, from 5 in the morning until midnight. The car jostled the two intrepid explorers to such an extent that it sent Jackson's coats and spectacles overboard. Before they even reached Utah — the third of 11 states they had to cross — the Winton lost its cyclometer: a device that told them how fast and far they had gone.

"In California and Idaho there are no bridges," Jackson said, "so we had to ford the rivers." They were 10 to 30 feet wide, but shallow enough to cross. "We would rush these streams and push and pull ourselves through as best we could when we got stuck. When we encountered railroad bridges, we would hunt for a place where we could get on the track. Sometimes, we had to go five miles to find it."

Jackson and Crocker had to stop to remove boulders from the road, and once, a team of horses had to pull the car out of some quicksand. Over a particularly sandy stretch, they created a 100-foot path of sagebrush to drive across; then, when they reached the end of it, they walked back, picked it all up, and repeated the process by moving it in front of the Winton.

Crocker's experience as a cyclist came in handy when a leak in their gas tank had them running on empty. He had to ride 26 miles to the nearest town, but then his bike tire went flat, too, and he had to walk most of that distance back. Crocker paid $15 for a bulldog named Bud in Idaho, but he wasn't the good luck charm they might have hoped. They got lost in Wyoming, where the Medicine Bow Mountains posed the stiffest climbing challenge of their journey, but they made it across by staying in low gear. When they reached the crossing at Medicine Bow River northwest of Cheyenne, their gas tank was nearly empty. But the shopkeeper there was far from sympathetic, charging them an outrageous $1.05 a gallon for gas.

They then hit what Jackson called "our first good road since we left the Sacramento Valley."

"Just watch us now," he cabled his wife in Vermont.

But they weren't out of the woods yet. The Winton broke down east of Cheyenne, and they had to wait five days for parts to arrive from the manufacturer so they could make repairs. In Nebraska, they got bogged down the "buffalo wallows," where they needed a block and tackle — or, in more extreme cases, a team of horses — to get free. When they finally hit another patch of good road as they neared Omaha, their front axle broke and they had to do a makeshift repair until they could find a blacksmith.

Amid all these tribulations, there came news that the Packard entry in the cross-continent sweepstakes had left San Francisco on June 30, with the Oldsmobile just a week behind. When the two other hopefuls left the Bay Area, the Winton was still in eastern Wyoming. Would they, could they, catch up to the Winton?

Bud the Bulldog. *Wikimedia Commons*

Despite "severe and continuous" rain that made for more muddy roads through Illinois, Jackson and Crocker began to make better time. Now, they were traveling 150 miles a day, and they were met in Ohio by Winton advertising manager Charles Shanks. The company was based in Cleveland, and Shanks offered to have Winton's own mechanics give the car a thorough once-over. But Jackson declined: He wanted to do this on his own.

Still, the Winton company made sure to capitalize on Jackson and Crocker's exploits, trumpeting their car's feats in the press, calling them "without parallel in American automobile history." Of course, that was still less than 10 years.

By the time Jackson was done, he'd dropped 21 pounds from the 225 he weighed at the outset — all of it, he said, from girth. According to the *New York Sun*, "a thick coating of dirt, a broken mud guard and a bent front axle were the only outward visible signs of 5,600 miles of roundabout and tortuous journey from the Pacific to the Atlantic."

**Above:** A later model Winton, the 1910 Winton Six, outside a Hupmobile dealership in Salt Lake City. *Wikimedia Commons*

**Right:** A Seattle ad for the Winton Model K, touting that it "goes everywhere on high speed" and "is built for Washington roads."

# WINTON MODEL K

Goes Everywhere on High Speed

$2650 F. O. B. Seattle

## An American for American Roads

A car to be right must be able to take the poor roads as well as the good. In buying a car for this section of the country pay great attention to its road clearance. Nothing is more important in touring. If a car is built too low to clear rough spots in country roads what good is it?

The Winton Model K is built for Washington roads. We can show you.

## Broadway Automobile Co., Inc.

BROADWAY AND MADISON STREET.

SEATTLE, WASHINGTON

SUNSET PHONE: EAST 3125    INDEPENDENT PHONE: 1190

AGENTS

CADILLAC, WINTON, PIERCE GREAT ARROW, WOODS ELECTRICS
SUNDRIES AND SUPPLIES

The Winton arrived in New York 63 days after it left, and the Packard, although it shaved three days off that mark, couldn't catch it. The chagrined driver apparently started a rumor that Jackson had cheated by loading his Winton onto a freight train for the most arduous sections of the journey. But when Shanks and Jackson offered a $25,000 reward for anyone able to substantiate the claim, no one cam forward to claim it. (It took the Oldsmobile 74 days to complete the journey.)

Unfortunately for the Winton Motor Carriage Company, both Packard and Olds would outlive it: The last Winton touring car was assembled in February of 1924. The company, one of the first to manufacture diesel engines, continued producing engine parts independently until 1930 and after that as an arm of General Motors.

Jackson returned to Vermont with his bulldog Bud and became involved in a granite-manufacturing business with his brother Hollister, who served as the state's lieutenant governor. Horatio Jackson served as an active-duty captain in the Medical Corps during World War II, and was promoted to the rank of major. He was awarded the Purple Heart after being wounded in the Battle of Montfaucon.

After the war, he was a founding member of the American Legion.

He died in 1955 at the age of 82. And in all that time, he apparently never collected on that $50 bet.

## The Pathfinders

The New York-to-Paris race around the world drew crowds of interested onlookers in 1908. *Library of Congress.*

# Great Races to Strange Places

Blake Edwards' *The Great Race* was, at the time of its release in 1965, the most expensive comedy ever made. It featured an all-star cast headlined by Tony Curtis as the archetypal hero, Jack Lemmon as the melodrama "Snidely Whiplash"-type villain, and Natalie Wood as a photojournalist driving a Stanley Steamer. The three were competitors in an automobile race from New York to Paris that, it turns out, was loosely based on a *real* race from New York to Paris back in 1908.

Six cars signed up for that event — three from France and one each representing

Italy, Germany and the United States. One of the French teams was led by a Norwegian who claimed to have sailed a Viking ship to the North Pole all by himself. He would be driving a De Dion-Bouton, manufactured by the company that had been the world's largest carmaker at the turn of the century.

The American driver was Montague "Monty" Roberts, behind the wheel of a Thomas Flyer and accompanied by mechanic George Schuster, who had gotten his start a few years earlier building radiators for at the Thomas Motor Co. factory in Buffalo. According to legend, the Flyer was a last-minute addition, with the Thomas company answering a call from President Teddy Roosevelt, who was chagrined that no American had entered the race.

Natalie Wood in a 1966 publicity shot for *The Great Race*, which was loosely based on the 1908 New York-to-Paris race. *Wikimedia Commons*

Despite Pierce-Arrow's dominance of the Glidden Tours, the company reportedly turned down the opportunity, as did other domestic automakers. Thomas pulled a newly minted Flyer out of its Buffalo plant at the last minute and sent factory employee Schuster along to ensure everything was in working order.

It needed to be.

At the time, only eight cars had ever crossed the North American continent, and the proposal here was far bolder: The cars would make their way up to Alaska, cross the 80-mile Bering Strait (on the ice!) and drive from there through Siberia to Moscow, Berlin and, finally, Paris.

It didn't quite work out that way, though.

Still, spirits were high as some 230,000 people converged upon Times Square for the start of the race, which was scheduled for 11 o'clock on the morning of Feb. 12. But the mayor, who was supposed to fire the starting gun, was late, and when he hadn't arrived by 11:15, a railroad financier named Colgate Hoyt took the pistol from the table where it was lying and fired it into the air.

Cars line up for the start of the New York-to-Paris race in 1908. *Library of Congress*

One of the French cars broke down and dropped out after just 96 miles, and a team of six horses was needed to extricate the three leading cars from a swampy morass in upstate New York, west of Syracuse.

The U.S. entry set the early pace, arriving first in Chicago and departing for points west on Feb. 28. It got stuck in the snow west of Cheyenne, Wyo., but remained in the lead on March 10, when the Italian entry was still moving through Nebraska and the French car piloted by the Norwegian stuck for repairs in Iowa.

The American team got a further boost when the Union Pacific Railroad allowed the Thomas Flyer to use its tracks across the mountains of Wyoming — a common strategy for drivers in rugged terrain where there were no roads — but denied the Italians the same courtesy. The railroad insisted its decision was "not through any desire to discriminate against the Italian, nor in favor of the American car, but simply a plain business proposition." The Flyer had done more damage to the tracks than the railroad had anticipated, so the company decided not to let any other drivers go through.

The Italian team was livid. A journalist named Antonio Scarfoglio, who accompanied driver Emilio Sirtori, declared: "I do not like the Americans as a whole, just as I do not like the cheesemonger whom a prize in a lottery or a sudden rise in the price of potatoes has made wealthy."

The Viking quit the French team around the same time, after their car got stuck in a snowdrift and his French teammate berated him for failing to get it unstuck in a timely manner. They agreed to a duel with pistols, but cooler heads prevailed, with the Norwegian declaring he could beat the De Dion on foot across Siberia.

A short time later, Roberts left the American team with the intent of competing in the Grand Prix at Paris in May, calling in relief driver named Harold Brinker to join Schuster until he could take over again in Europe. The Thomas Flyer had built up a sizable lead by this time, and although the car got lost "in the swamps of Los Banos" east of San Francisco overnight, Brinker and Schuster managed to find the road again and arrived at the City by the Bay on March 24.

It was the first time anyone had ever made it all the way across the continent during winter.

At this point, Schuster unceremoniously kicked Brinker off the team.

The Italian car was still in Utah, undergoing repairs, with the De Dion and the German entry, a Protos, farther back in Wyoming. The other remaining French car had dropped out in Iowa after running into mechanical problems. The driver was all set to cheat by having it shipped ahead to San Francisco by rail, but abandoned the idea when a photographer saw what he was doing. He subsequently received a mandate from the vehicle's owner to just sell the car and quit the race.

The De Dion broke down in Delano, Calif., and had to be towed to Tulare, while the Flyer was about to be loaded onto a ship for a journey north to Seattle and, thence, to Valdez, Alaska. The cars were supposed to travel north from there to Fairbanks and then west toward the Bering Strait. Once the Flyer arrived, however, Schuster took one look at the snowfields and decided to turn back the way he had come. He and the other teams had already agreed that, if conditions were too poor to continue across Alaska, they would ship their cars from Seattle to Vladivostok in Siberia instead.

The Flyer was loaded back aboard a ship bound for Seattle.

Meanwhile, however, the French and Italian teams had already arrived in Seattle and, rather than going farther north to Valdez, simply had their cars shipped directly across the Pacific. As a result, the American entry, which had built a seemingly insurmountable lead by the time it hit the West Coast, was suddenly in last place.

Even the Germans were ahead of Schuster.

The De Dion dropped out soon after arriving in Siberia, leaving three teams in the race. The Italians quickly fell behind, but a wrong turn in Russia cost Schuster 15 hours, and the Flyer was down for repairs for a day after getting stuck in a mudhole.

While still nearly 900 miles from Moscow, Schuster got a cable from the Thomas factory asking whether they should send Roberts to drive the Flyer the rest of the way.

The Thomas Flyer rides across railroad tracks in the snow during the New York-to-Paris race. *Library of Congress*

He told them not to bother: He'd make it to Paris on his own, thank you, within 15 days.

By the time Schuster reached St. Petersburg, Russia, however, he was three days behind the Germans with little hope of catching up before Paris.

As it turned out, it didn't matter.

The German car did, in fact, reach Paris while the Flyer was still in Berlin. But the German team had been penalized 15 days for shipping their car by rail from Utah to San Francisco, and the American car had picked up a 15-day bonus to offset the time lost on its futile trek to Alaska. Instead of being three days behind the German car, Schuster was almost a month *ahead*. He arrived in Paris on July 30 as the winner.

**Top:** McKinley Avenue in Valdez, Alaska, in 1908, the year the Flyer arrived in the New York-to-Paris race. *John Nathan Cobb/Wikimedia Commons*

**Above:** Getting across Nebraska was still a challenge in 1913, five years after the Great Race. *NUAA Photo Library*

# AMERICA'S FIRST HIGHWAYS

The Italians finished, too, but they didn't arrive in the French capital until December.

Schuster returned to the States and got a hero's welcome from 10,000 people in Buffalo, home of the Thomas factory — where he soon returned to work doing what he'd done before his great adventure started.

Unfortunately, the carmaker failed to capitalize on its fame as winner of the Great Race: Within five years, it was out of business. Schuster, for his part, went to work for Pierce-Arrow after that, but he never drove in another race again. Still, he lived a long time to tell the story many times over of how he won what remains the longest automobile race ever staged: He died in 1972 at the age of 99.

There was no mistaking the American entry in the New York-to-Paris race, with the large U.S. flag draped over the back. Here, it follows a trolley through the snow. The Flyer crew went prepared with snow chains and plenty of spare tires. *Library of Congress*

A car crosses the desert on the National Old Trails Road near Holbrook, Ariz., c. 1915. *Wikimedia Commons*

## Blazing Trails

While car companies used auto tours to promote their products, the ultimate goal remained to promote good roads. And part of that mission was to identify the best routes for those roads. Cars leading the Glidden Tours were labeled "pathfinders," tasked with mapping out the best possible paths for the tours and, consequently, for future roads.

The Flanders 20, for example, was the pathfinder car for the 1911 Glidden Tour of what was being called the Dixie Trail from New York to Jacksonville. This was, however, not the same as the Dixie Highway, created farther inland a few years later (more on that ahead).

Some of the pathfinders' work had been done for them. Many old toll roads and wagon trails already existed, such as the Cumberland Road in Maryland and the Santa Fe Trail in the Southwest. Some, like the Great Wagon Road in Virginia, had been routed along older Native American trails; El Camino Real in California was a trail connecting 21 Catholic missions that dated back to a time when the area was Spanish territory.

Even so, there were plenty of gaps in those older trails — and a need to find suitable paths over open land to fill them. This was especially true in the land west of the Mississippi. In Southern California, for example, a stretch of land near the Arizona state line was covered in sand dunes worthy of the Sahara Desert. Even if you built a road there, it might disappear a few hours later beneath the shifting sands.

Los Angeles was a booming city in 1912. Its population had more than tripled in the previous decade, and this was before the arrival of the motion picture industry. It was already one of the 20 largest cities in the country (although it still ranked behind San Francisco in the Golden State), and had become a transportation hub with the coming of the railroad. Businesses there saw it as a natural endpoint for an interstate road, the proposed Ocean-to-Ocean Highway.

The *Los Angeles Examiner* newspaper led the charge in promoting that route.

San Diego to the south — then a sleepy town of fewer than 40,000 people barely one-tenth the size of L.A. — had other ideas. San Diego businessman Ed Fletcher wanted to see *his city* become the terminus of the transcontinental highway. The town was already preparing to host a major event in 1915, the Panama-California Expo, to celebrate the opening of the Panama Canal. A grand exposition complex (which is still there today) would be built at Balboa Park, and Fletcher envisioned the new road bringing travelers from all over the country to San Diego for the gala event.

Together, the expo and the road would put San Diego on the map.

In question: whether it was feasible to run a highway west across the Imperial Valley from Arizona to San Diego, because the Algodones Sand Dunes — a mini Sahara Desert — stood in the way. *The Examiner* argued a path to the north was a better alternative.

To settle the issue, a road race to Phoenix was planned, with some cars starting from Los Angeles and others from San Diego. The *Examiner* issued a personal challenge to Fletcher, who promptly accepted and dashed off a letter to Arizona's attorney general, offering to put up $3,000 if the Grand Canyon State (which had just been admitted to the Union earlier that year) would bring $1,000 to the table. Arizona agreed to the terms.

The idea of races across the desert wasn't new. The Automobile Club of Southern California had sponsored a series of such races starting in 1908 as a way of promoting improved roads. The races, known as "Cactus Derbies," started either from San Diego or Los Angeles, but in 1913, it was decided that cars would embark from both locations, with civic pride on the line.

The Auto Club agreed to sanction the race, which also included several cars in both locations. About a dozen participants signed up to start from Los Angeles, driving cars that included three Cadillacs, a Buick, a Mercedes and a Hupmobile. They would follow a route through San Bernardino, Indio and Blythe, bypassing Yuma. The path from San Diego was more direct by at least 100 miles, so Fletcher agreed to give the Los Angeles car a 24-hour head start. Still, one San Diego driver boasted: "We will beat the Los Angeles cars by a full twelve hours, at the very least."

Several thousand dollars in prize money was up for grabs, and 22 drivers committed to racing from San Diego. But the main attraction, when it came right down to it, was the pathfinder duel between the *Examiner* car and Fletcher's automobile, which preceded the actual race. Fletcher reduced his tire pressure to traverse the desert sands, but he still had to deal with twigs from desert scrub brush infiltrating his engine. When he stopped to check on a popping noise, he saw the motor was on fire and had to throw sand on it to extinguish the flames.

Fletcher, it must be admitted, had some help: He hired a team of six horses to pull his 20-horsepower Franklin across the Algodones Dunes.

When he got to the Colorado River, he missed the day's last ferry, so he improvised by crossing the Southern Pacific Railroad bridge, laying down blankets to keep his tires from popping. In the end, he made it to Phoenix at 6:05 p.m. on Oct. 27, having been delayed for two hours by a sandstorm and a cloudburst in the hills west of Phoenix. The storm knocked down eucalyptus trees, which blocked their path, and Fletcher's team had to saw through the trees to continue.

Even so, they managed to beat the L.A. pathfinder (which broke down near Blythe) easily, completing the course in 19½ hours and cementing San Diego's status as the destination city for the road.

Overall, only four drivers who had started from Los Angeles made it all the way to Phoenix, while seven San Diego entries completed the course. The best time was turned in by D.C. Campbell in a Stevens-Duryea, who arrived in just a minute under 17 hours. Ralph Hamlin took 18 hours and 45 minutes to make it from Los Angeles, the best time among L.A. starters.

A headline in the *San Diego Union* boasted: "San Diego car beats Los Angeles."

And Fletcher did some bragging of his own. "By making it in a touring car before the first racer arrived at Yuma from Los Angeles, we conclusively show which is the more feasible route" for the highway, he crowed. "Our eight hours to Yuma does not count some small delays, so I may claim that the time ... in good weather ... is much shorter."

Despite the race's success, the dunes remained an obstacle. It was hardly reasonable to expect that every driver traveling across the dunes would hire a team of horses to drag them through. So, Fletcher raised money from local interests to purchase 13,000 wooden planks for a slightly raised causeway across the desert. Imperial County kicked in $8,600 for labor on the 6½-mile-long wooden road, which consisted of two sets of 25-inch-wide, parallel planks that looked a little like a rail line.

The second version of the old plank road on the Imperial dunes was already badly damaged when this photo was taken, c. 1920. *University of Southern California Library and California Historical Society*

Unfortunately, the wear and tear of traffic splintered the planks, while the continual efforts to scrape away the shifting sands damaged the road further. As a result, it had to be rebuilt with a new design a year later. Since it was only wide enough for traffic going one way, pullouts — each marked by an old tire hanging from a post — were built every quarter-mile to allow passing.

Some motorists weren't patient enough to wait, though. In one case, a line of 20 cars heading one way came upon a single car heading the opposite direction. When that car refused to back up to use a turnout, the men on the other side got out of their vehicles, strode up to the car and lifted it onto the sand, leaving their wives to drive past and meet them on the other side.

The Automobile Club of Southern California was wary even of the "improved" plank road. It issued a warning on the front page of the El Centro newspaper in April of 1919 that "travel to Yuma via the plank road is dangerous."

It continued: "Several cars which recently attempted the trip were badly damaged and owners were put to heavy expense to get through. Cars are injured in the drive, engines are racked and shattered, and in many cases the machines have to be pulled miles by teams." Those attempting to cross were in danger of suffering from thirst and even death, the statement said.

Drivers learned to bring along shovels, jacks, extra planks and provisions such as blankets and water in case they became caught in a blinding sandstorm and unwittingly drove off the road. Many cars wound up mired in the sand and had to be left behind, with the stranded motorists forced to hitch a ride on other vehicles.

The Old Plank Road today shows what it used to look like, foreground, and the remnants of the road itself, rear. *Author photo*

An up-close look at a section of the Old Plank Road today. *Author photo*

But that didn't stop Fletcher from continuing to champion the route, especially since the rivalry between his beloved San Diego and Los Angeles remained heated.

Fletcher's victory in the 1912 Cactus Derby challenge had been only the beginning of a struggle that escalated the following year, following another race from El Paso to Phoenix. Upon arriving, some of the drivers got together and created what they called the Borderland Route Association, with the intent of promoting a highway along the southern border.

In 1915, the National Highways Association produced maps of the Borderland Route. The NHA president proposed making it a transcontinental highway by extending it eastward from El Paso, as well, through Houston, New Orleans, Mobile, Tallahassee and on to Jacksonville.

Meanwhile, something called the Dixie Overland Highway Association was forming in Georgia "to foster the construction and use of a highway from Savannah, Georgia, to Los Angeles." The new road would have an advantage on other cross-continent routes such as the Lincoln and Pike's Peak Ocean to Ocean highways, because it would traverse states with mild climates and therefore be passable all year round.

The new highway association — whose road was not to be confused with the north-south Dixie Highway — incorporated in 1917, declaring itself "the shortest and only year-round ocean-to-ocean highway." But the route wasn't as firmly set in stone as it might have appeared. A year later, the association was mulling the question of whether, in fact, the road's western endpoint should be Los Angeles, after all. Or, should it instead be San Diego?

The governor, it appeared was in San Diego's corner. He dispatched a representative — who also happened to represent the San Diego Chamber of Commerce — to the association's convention in Shreveport, La. There, he argued that the Dixie Overlanders should ditch L.A. and end their highway in San Diego. To bolster his case, he brought a letter from none other than the plank road pathfinder, Ed Fletcher himself.

In it, Fletcher extolled the virtues of San Diego as "a city of one hundred and fifteen thousand inhabitants, with a perfectly land-locked bay and twenty-two miles of ocean dockage in the most southwesterly harbor of the United States."

The argument must have impressed the folks attending the convention, because they not only voted in favor of San Diego, they decided to elect Fletcher as president of their organization. Even though we didn't personally attend. Fletcher said he was honored and happy to accept, but made a point of saying he wouldn't have even considered doing so unless his city had been made the road's Pacific terminus — via the plank road.

Even the improved version of that road, however, wasn't the ultimate solution to the problem of the dunes. An upgraded plank causeway was considered in 1924, with room for traffic to travel both ways, but the state Highway Commission ultimately decided on a concrete replacement built atop a manmade sand embankment. It opened in 1926, and the plank road was history.

On the plank road in Imperial County. *California Bureau of Land Management*

# AMERICA'S FIRST HIGHWAYS

**From top:** Residents of Ehrenburg, Ariz., greet a pathfinder in 1911; a AAA official drives near Glendive, Mont., in 1912; a car on a cross-country trip is pulled through a sandy wash by a team of horses northwest of Yuma, Ariz., in 1911.

*Photos by A.L. Westgard*

# Part Two
# Building Trails

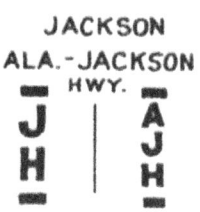

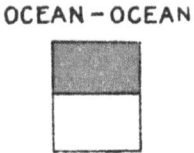

Just 30 of the more than 250 markers used in the late 1910s and early '20s on U.S. auto trails.

## The Lincoln Highway

The Lincoln Highway near the Pennsylvania Tunnel, 1922. *Wikimedia Commons*

# Carl's Creation

By 1911, the auto tours had led to "an agitation for a national highway, to connect the Atlantic and Pacific coasts," *The Grizzly Bear* reported on the Sporting Page of its September 1911 edition.

Illinois Sen. Shelby Moore Cullom introduced a bill to construct a system of seven national highways that would, based on the Roman model, come together at the hub of the nation's capital. Each of the highways would be named for a significant figure in American history.

| Proposed Highway | Washington D.C. to... |
|---|---|
| Washington National Highway | Portland, Maine |
| Roosevelt National Highway | Buffalo |
| Lincoln National Highway | Seattle |
| Jefferson National Highway | San Francisco |
| Grant National Highway | San Diego |
| Monroe National Highway | Austin, Texas |
| Lee National Highway | Miami |

The monikers had little or nothing to do with several auto trails that would ultimately bear those names. (The eventual Lincoln Highway, for example, would run from New York to San Francisco.)

Cullom's proposal would cost $48 million, to be paid using construction bonds, with tolls being used to fund maintenance. But it was just one of nearly 50 bills put forth over a two-year period. Some suggested specific highways, while others would have sent surplus money from the U.S. Treasury to the states for roads.

Shelby Moore Cullom

The bills were all sent to committee. None of them ever made it any further.

But that didn't discourage Good Roads activists, who just pushed all the harder for a transcontinental highway. One idea that gained traction was the concept of cobbling together several "old trails" into a single interstate highway to be called — naturally — the National Old Trails Road.

The proposal was set forth by Elizabeth Butler Gentry of the Daughters of the American Revolution in 1911. In a publication called *The Old Trails Road, the National Highway*, she set forth a route that would begin with the National (or Cumberland) Road in Baltimore, hooking up with Boone's Lick Road in eastern Missouri, then forking in two just west of the Kansas state line. The northern branch would follow the Oregon Trail, with the southern branch dipping south into New Mexico and Arizona along the Santa Fe Trail.

## AMERICA'S FIRST HIGHWAYS

Boone's Lick Road was the lynchpin in the proposal that connected east and west. The road took its name from a salt lick (where deer and other wild animals came to lick the salt) in western Missouri. At the beginning of the 1800s, two of Daniel Boone's sons began boiling down the water they found there and extracting salt, which they used for preserving meet. They used an old Native American trail to access it, but soon the path had blossomed into a full-fledged wagon road.

The town of Franklin, founded in 1816, grew up south of the lick, and stage routes were soon established. The road ultimately served as a gateway to the west, with travelers either going north along the Oregon Trail or south along the Santa Fe Trail.

Elizabeth Butler Gentry

The road, also called the Ocean-to-Ocean Highway, was officially dedicated the following year, but it didn't satisfy the growing desire for a transcontinental highway.

Far from it.

For one thing, much of the Santa Fe Trail section remained unpaved, and parts of it were less visible than the tumbleweeds that dotted the landscape in the desert Southwest. The portion of the route from Las Vegas, N.M., to Los Angeles would eventually become a section of Route 66 (a stretch of road that runs through the Mojave Desert in southeastern California is still signed as the National Old Trails Highway). But this was still nearly a decade and a half into the future, and even when the "Mother Road" was established in 1926, it still included many miles of unimproved trail.

Just because someone dedicated a highway, that didn't mean it existed. Usually, it was a work in progress, with the very real question looming as to whether it would ever be finished. Carl Fisher knew this all too well.

## 'Crazy Carl'

Fisher was a promoter: He knew how to sell things, and he was the driving force behind two of the most important, and highly touted highway projects of the 1910s — the Lincoln and Dixie highways. Modern journalists have compared him to P.T. Barnum and Elon Musk.

Like so many others in that era, Fisher got his start in cycling, opening a bike shop in his hometown of Indianapolis when he was just 17. One of his first publicity stunts was to ride a bike on a wire between two buildings.

It wouldn't be his last.

In 1900, he attended a car show in New York and became hooked on the automobile, getting behind the wheel to win a number of races. The Premier Car Company of Indianapolis built him a massive eight-cylinder racer called the Comet in 1904, and he used it to set world records for one and two miles, at 59.4 seconds and 2 minutes, 2 seconds, respectively. That same year, he drove a Mohawk Racer to victory in a match race against Earl Kiser of Dayton before more than 4,000 spectators at the Indianapolis Fair Grounds.

But Fisher wouldn't remain behind the wheel for long.

In 1904, he made an investment that would earn him a fortune while shedding new light on the road ahead for drivers. Literally.

At the time, motorists had to finish up their business during the daytime, especially if they lived in the country, away from city streetlamps. Cars didn't have headlights at the time, so motorists either had to get home before nightfall or engage in the risky proposition of hanging a kerosene lantern over their radiator. This didn't provide much light and could be an explosive proposition if the lantern fell and broke.

Carl Fisher

P.C. Avery believed he could light up the road by compressing acetylene gas into portable cylinders. It could then be burned inside transparent glass enclosures (the headlights) to provide illumination. Fisher took the idea and ran with it, buying the rights to the patent and forming a company called Concentrated Acetylene with Avery and James Allison. Avery left the business in 1906, and the two remaining partners changed the name to Prest-O-Lite. In 1911, they sold the company to Union Carbide for a cool $9 million.

Fisher was already wealthy by that time, having gotten into the business of selling cars — with his trademark flair for the dramatic. In a daring stunt, he attached a car to a hot-air balloon and set it aloft over a crowd in downtown Indianapolis. He prudently took the precaution of ordering it specially reinforced so it would survive the fall and letting most of the air out of the tires so it wouldn't bounce.

It so impressed one teenage girl in the crowd named Jane that she eventually became his wife. (In a scandal, Fisher broke off a six-year engagement to his fiancée, who responded by hitting him with a lawsuit for breach of promise. He eventually paid her $25,000.)

Fisher seems to have liked balloons a lot. So much so, that a balloon race was the first event he held at a new venue he opened in 1909. It had been in the planning stages for four years, perhaps inspired in part by the large crowed that had showed up to see Fisher's match race with Earl Kiser.

Whatever gave him the idea, Fisher was convinced that the city of Indianapolis needed a dedicated track for auto racing, so he set out to build one. Allison was one of the investors, as was Arthur Newby, a friend from his days as part of a local bike club (their names both appear with Fisher's on the poster above).

Fisher's $400,000 track was five miles long and surfaced with gravel, limestone and tar rather than the concrete being used elsewhere.

This proved a fateful — and fatal — miscalculation.

A steamroller works on the Indianapolis Motor Speedway during its initial construction. *Library of Congress*

After the opening balloon race, the first motorized event at the new Indianapolis Motor Speedway was a motorcycle race on Aug. 14. Thirty riders lined up including local racer Cannon Ball Baker and Walter Davidson, the Davidson in Harley-Davidson. But the riders had a hard time with the huge curves and the condition of the track, which kept spitting rocks and sand into their faces on a hot summer day. Only four of them managed to finish the 10-mile event, with Baker emerging as the winner.

Sixteen days later, the venue got its first test as an automobile racetrack, drawing the likes of Barney Oldfield and Louis Chevrolet for a series of 16 races over three days. The main event, which was set for Sunday, would be a 300-mile affair. (The first "500" wouldn't take place until two years later.)

But the track wasn't in any better shape for the cars than it had been for the motorcycle races. As drivers took to the track for a practice run, they were quickly caked in tar, oil and dirt as the track came apart on the turns and spat up gravel, shattering their goggles and blooding their faces.

## AMERICA'S FIRST HIGHWAYS

Despite being hailed by the *Indianapolis News* as "the first ideal racecourse ever built in America," it simply wasn't constructed to withstand the pounding of high-speed auto racing. One historian noted that "driving at Indy was like flying through a meteor shower."

On the very first day, William Bourque and his mechanic, Harry Holcomb, both died when their car — which was running second after 145 miles of the 250-mile race — careened into a fence before a crowd of 16,000 shocked spectators. "It was all over in an instant," the *Indianapolis Star* reported. "His machine skidded. Something broke. The maddened demon of speed rushed headlong into a ditch beside the track. The car was hurled and thrown over and over and to the ground against the fence. The two unfortunate men were tossed helplessly to either side."

Holcomb died instantly when his head hit a fencepost, and Bourque survived only about 15 minutes.

The accident cast a pall over what would have otherwise been a successful debut, with Barney Oldfield setting the world record for a mile at 48.1 seconds in his Benz and Chevrolet winning the second event, a 10-mile race, in a record time for that distance of 8 minutes, 56.4 seconds.

Saturday brought better results, as 22,000 people turned out to see Louis Strang shatter nine world records in his Buick, with two other records also falling. Oldfield was injured in an accident, but there were no serious crashes, giving rise to hopes that the track was safe, after all.

Those hopes were dashed on the third and final day of the meet, which drew the biggest crowd of the weekend: 37,000 fans. Two of them would not survive the day, and a third would suffer a broken nose and crushed arm.

Cars kicked up stones and debris from the start of the action, with two drivers and two mechanics blinded by dust. There were five accidents in all. Driver Johnny Aitken, who had set a record in winning a five-mile race the previous day, pulled out of the main event after 100 miles, declaring, "Someone would surely get killed before long because the track was being all torn to pieces."

His words, sadly, proved prophetic.

Three people were killed in the main event when a tire blew on Charles Merz's car in the southern turn, sending it flying into the fence. It took out five fenceposts, tore through a stone railing and wound up in the crowd, killing two spectators and Merz's mechanic. Merz, somehow, was uninjured, even though his car had flown 100 feet in the air.

After it all was over, he proclaimed himself the luckiest man on earth.

"I remember my car hitting the fence," he said. "There was a blurred vision of men falling beneath us as we swept through the air. Then the rest came in an instant: The car turned over, and I found myself under it on the other side of the creek." He thought his legs were broken at first, but to his surprise, he was able to crawl out through the mud and water to safety.

Somehow, the race continued. But just 30 minutes later, a Marmon driven by Bruce Keene struck a support pillar on a pedestrian bridge near the spot where Bourque and Holcomb had been killed two days earlier. Keene and mechanic James Schiller both survived — Schiller despite a fractured skull — but the referee had seen enough: He called off the rest of the race after 94 laps.

Original brick from Indianapolis Motor Speedway, dated 1909. *Native History & Heritage Command, Creative Commons CCBY2.0*

Indiana's lieutenant governor, Frank Hall, said the state legislature should consider banning the sport. "They talk about bullfights in Mexico, but did you ever hear of several people getting killed in a bullfight? Yet right here in Indiana, great crowds go out to witness an event in which it may be expected that human life may be sacrificed."

Hall was in the minority when it came to banning auto races, but it was clear that something had to be done. AAA was threatening a boycott, and the condition of the track was such that it simply couldn't withstand the pounding it had taken. If changes weren't made, more tragedy was bound to follow.

Fisher, seeing what was at stake, acted quickly. In September, he brought in 3.2 million bricks and used them to completely resurface the track, eliminating the dirt and gravel, and earning the speedway its nickname, "The Brickyard." The project was completed in time for races to resume Nov. 1. The addition of the bricks brought the total cost of the track to about $700,000.

Only seven people were killed on the new track over the next decade, and the brick surface endured for a half-century before giving way to asphalt.

Tourists travel across a rocky mountain road near Soda Springs, Calif., northwest of Lake Tahoe, during a trip on the Lincoln Highway in 1915. *Effie Price Gladding*

## Coast-to-Coast Rock Highway

Fisher had proved he could sell bicycles, cars, headlights and even a speedway. But his biggest challenge lay ahead. He would try to sell a highway.

The National Old Trails Road had been established in 1912, but Fisher wanted something more reliable, more impressive, more permanent. In his mind's eye, he saw a "coast-to-coast rock highway" from Times Square to San Francisco, that would "stimulate as nothing else could the building of enduring highways everywhere." Such roads, he said, would "be a credit to the American people," and a boon for commerce and agriculture.

One incident, in particular, helped spark his interest in such a project. He and two companions had traveled nine miles outside of Indianapolis, "and being delayed, were overtaken by darkness on the return trip," he recalled. "To complicate matters, it began to rain pretty hard, and you know automobiles didn't have any tops on them in those days, so we all three got pretty wet."

The travelers tried to find their way back, making their best guesses about the proper way home until they came to a three-way fork in the road.

"It was black as the inside of your pocket," Fisher recalled. "We couldn't see any light from the city, and none of us could remember which of the three roads we had followed in driving out; if indeed we had come that way at all. So we stopped and held a consultation.

"Presently, by the light of our headlamps, reflected up in the rain, one of us thought he saw a sign on a pole. It was too high up to read, and we had no means of throwing a light on it, so there was nothing to be done but climb the pole in the wet and darkness and see if we could make out some road direction on the sign."

When they held a contest to see who would climb up and see, Fisher got the short end of the stick. He got halfway up the pole and realized he'd forgotten his matches, so he had to clamber back down and retrieve them. Eventually, he made it back up to the sign and struck a match. Before the wind blew it out, he saw what the sign said:

"Chew Battle-Ax Plug."

When Fisher built the Lincoln Highway, it had its own signs on telephone poles, painted with a red stripe at the top, a blue one at the bottom, and a big blue "L" against a white background in between.

At this point, however, the road — still known informally as the coast-to-coast rock highway — was still just an idea.

Fisher was rich, but not rich enough to fund it all by himself. He and fellow investors pledged $1 million to start, but he estimated it would cost $10 million in all. Goodyear Tire co-founder Frank Seiberling and Henry Joy, president of Packard Motor Cars, were squarely behind the project, with Goodyear pledging $300,000 and Packard $150,000. But another Henry — Henry Ford — declined an invitation to join them, arguing that the government should pay for highways.

Ford's lack of interest was a huge setback, as his company was producing three-quarters of the nation's automobiles at the time. Fisher knew that if Ford got on board, others would follow, so he made one final pitch. Boarding a train to Detroit, he waltzed into the company offices ... only to be told that Ford was out at the state fair. The story goes that Fisher followed him there and found him in the livestock exhibit, looking at a bunch of pigs. Fisher presented his proposal again, and appeared to have Ford convinced.

"Come to my office tomorrow and bring your papers, and I will sign up," Ford reportedly told him.

But after sleeping on it, Ford apparently changed his mind, and when Fisher showed up the next day, Ford's secretary told him so.

Ford was, of course, in a good position to say no: He'd continue to sell cars with or without a coast-to-coast highway.

Ford's decision to pass on Fisher's invitation was a major blow, but it wasn't enough to discourage Fisher. He knew more roads meant more sales overall, and that was a big deal in a business where companies often came and went in a few short years. As he put it, "The automobile won't get anywhere until it has good roads to run on."

## Mapping the Road

Fisher called supporters together for their first meeting to plan the highway in September of 1912. Before they could do much else, a name was needed. Among the possibilities bandied about were "The American Road," "Jefferson Memorial Highway," and a name that would have paid tribute to Fisher himself — an idea he rejected. It was Joy who came up with the idea of a "Lincoln Highway" after Congress shot down a proposed Lincoln Road from Washington to Gettysburg and chose to build the Lincoln Memorial in D.C. instead.

Next up, a route had to be selected. In the east, it would follow some existing roads, including the nation's first major turnpike: the 62-mile Philadelphia-to-Lancaster Pike in

Pennsylvania, which dated back to 1796. Another section went along an old Native American trail known as the Ridge Road through Ohio.

That was only a minor dustup, however, compared to what the Lincoln Highway Association had to put up with from towns on other portions of the route.

It all started when Fisher organized a pathfinder expedition, or "Trail-Blazer" tour, as he called it, to head west from Indianapolis on July 1, 1913. He was worried that the tour would create expectations that the route he chose would be the eventual route of the Lincoln Highway. As a result, he only agreed to the tour if it wasn't connected to the highway itself. Instead, it was sponsored by two Indiana groups.

But it didn't matter. Word got out anyway, and towns began to clamor for a place on Fisher's itinerary. In one day, he received 100 requests via telegram, and some hopefuls even went so far as to make a personal trip to Indianapolis. Price Canyon in Utah sent a delegation, but W.S. Gilbreath of the Hoosier Motor Club — who was helping to organize the tour — told him it wouldn't work, because there wasn't a road through Price Canyon from the east.

No problem, said the mayor, "We'll build one then."

They went back and hired a contractor to do the job, and when it looked like the road wouldn't be done in time for the tour, he recruited men from the town to finish it up themselves. They brought out everything from shovels to crowbars to dynamite and finished by 10 o'clock at night.

By the time everything was said and done, Fisher estimated that towns had finished about $500,000 worth of road work to prepare for the tour. Nevada kicked in $25,000 of that to improve the road between Utah and California, while Colorado overhauled a 60-mile stretch over Berthoud Pass, at 11,300 feet above sea level west of Denver.

When the trip finally got underway, 17 cars and two trucks set out for San Francisco. They received warm greetings and requests for speeches at every stop along the way, with the governor of Kansas meeting them in Topeka and joining the tour to speak out in favor of highway improvements for three whole days. The governor of Colorado did the same, and in Grand Junction, near the Utah State line, they received a greeting Fisher called "the largest yet received." Four-thousand people turned out to meet them, roughly half the city's population.

The governor boasted of plans to make the highway 16 feet wide, with a 4-foot shoulder and walls to serve as guardrails around sharp turns; the maximum grade would be 6%. Fisher was duly impressed and seemed ready to invest in the project: "If we can allow him $1,000 per mile in material, we will get a $5 million road across Colorado," he enthused.

Perhaps Fisher had forgotten, in his excitement, that the Lincoln Highway route had yet to be decided. Or perhaps he simply was expressing his overall enthusiasm for good roads. Either way, the governors of Kansas and Colorado were left with the distinct impression that they were all but guaranteed spots on the highway once it was built.

Unfortunately for them, it didn't turn out that way.

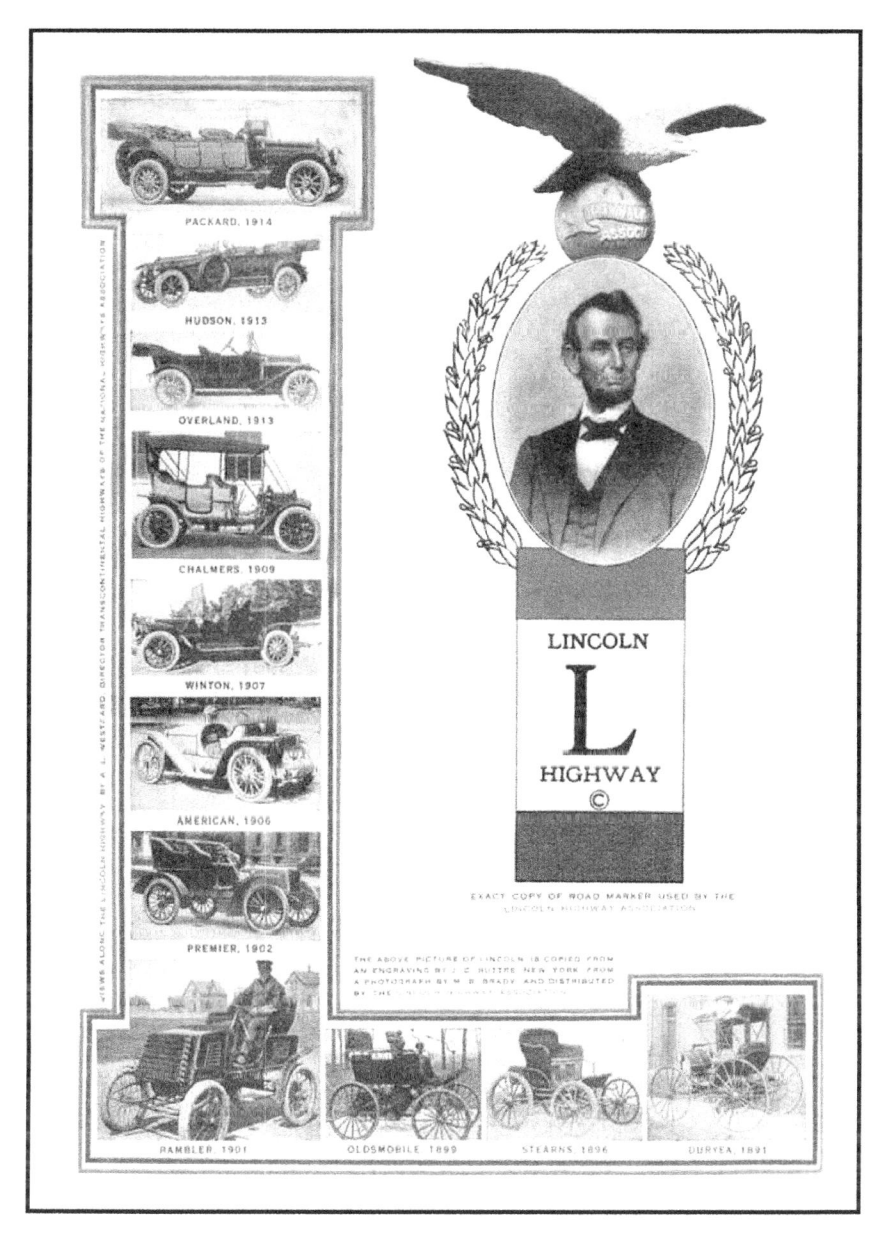

The Lincoln Highway magazine, published in 1914, featured a number of different cars from the era, with Henry Joy's Packard at the top and other companies supportive of the project also featured. Noticeably absent: Ford. *Library of Congress*

Varying conditions during early trips on the Lincoln Highway. **Top:** the Lincoln Highway's official Stutz car on tour in 1916. **Above:** A year earlier, A.F. Bemont and Lincoln Highway Association President Henry Joy got stuck in the mud somewhere in Nebraska. *University of Michigan Library (Special Collections Research Center, Transportation History Collection) photos*

The scenery a few miles from Berthoud Pass, where Colorado improved a 60-mile segment of road in the hope of bringing the Lincoln Highway through the area. Highway organizers opted for Wyoming instead, but today there are two major roads in the area: U.S. 40, which traverses the pass, and Interstate 70 just to the south. *Author photo*

One reason for the confusion over the highway's ultimate route is that Fisher wasn't the one who ended up making that decision. The task fell instead to Joy, who took over the lead role from Fisher as time went by.

Arthur Pardington, a longtime good roads champion who became secretary of the Lincoln Highway Association, said the route should be determined by three factors:

- Its directness between New York and San Francisco.
- "Points of scenic interest and centers of population."
- The level of support communities on the route could offer.

But Joy didn't care much about the second and third points; he was focused almost solely on the first. This made sense from a financial standpoint: The less ground they had to cover, the less expensive the project would be. Sidney Waldon, a member of the highway association's board of directors, put it this way: "Our idea was to get a continuous route traversable through the largest portion of the year at the least cost. On that basis we selected the route."

More northerly and southerly routes were also considered — and rejected. The northern option, following the so-called Emigrant Trail, would have put the highway's endpoint in Portland or Seattle. The association, however, felt it was crucial that the road end in San Francisco, which was then the largest city on the West Coast (although Los Angeles would soon overtake it).

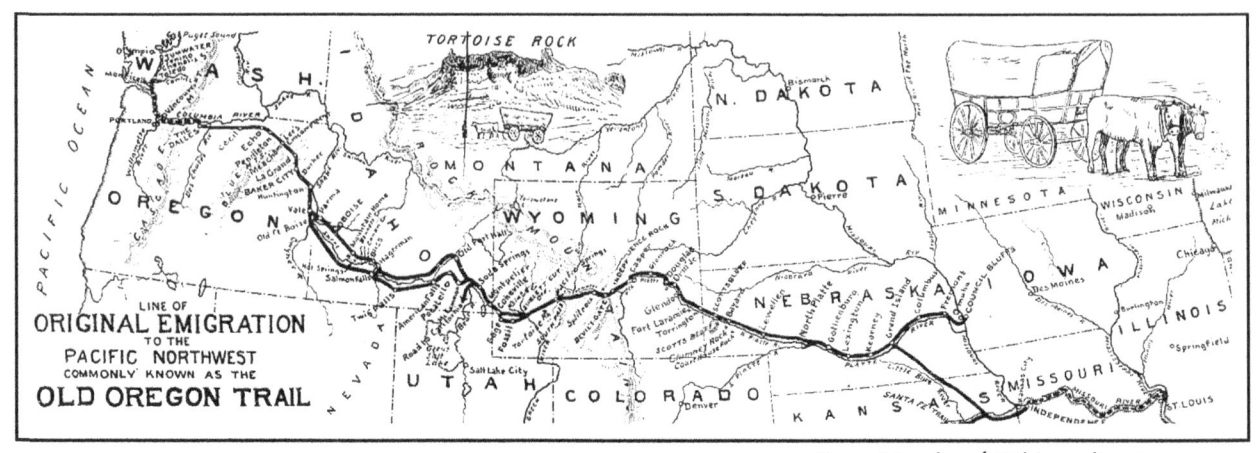

*Ezra Meeker/Wikimedia Commons*

A southern option, through Arizona, would subject motorists to extreme heat during the summer; then, there were all those shifting sands and windstorms around Yuma. And, at the time when the route was being considered, the plank road across the dunes in Imperial County hadn't yet been built.

Waldon concluded: "All things considered, I believe the Lincoln Memorial Highway should run from New York to San Francisco; that it should touch Chicago. From Chicago, there are no two questions in my mind about the Omaha-Cheyenne-Salt Lake-Reno route being the shortest and offering the least possible trouble to the tourist."

That meant Colorado was out. In Waldon's words: "The route through the center of Colorado, of course, offers wonderful scenic beauties. This, however, introduces difficulties not experienced on the road through Wyoming."

So, Wyoming it was. And Kansas was also left off the route, in favor of Nebraska.

The governors of the two bypassed states, who had lobbied so heavily on behalf of the highway during Fisher's earlier tour, were beside themselves. They felt as though they'd been misled and threatened to withdraw their support from the project entirely

Beside the Lincoln Highway in the Badlands, 12 miles west of Granger, Wyo., in 1926. *William Clinton Alden, U.S. Geological Survey*

unless they were included.

The association tried to placate the Colorado group by adding an alternate dogleg route south from Big Springs, Neb., to Denver — roughly along the path of today's Interstate 76. But when word of it got out, all sorts of other towns left off the main road started clamoring for the same treatment.

The route to Denver was quietly dropped from Lincoln Highway maps around 1915, and travelers were advised to ignore signs placed by Coloradans directing them toward the Mile High City.

A rivalry between the two biggest cities on the West Coast caused a similar set of headaches.

San Francisco preferred the northern Wendover Route through Utah, heading west out of Salt Lake City, because it was more likely to send travelers toward the Bay. Los Angeles, meanwhile, favored a more southerly route known as the Goodyear Cutoff. That road gave travelers the option of continuing toward San Francisco or switching to the Midland Trail in Nevada and heading to L.A., which at that point was about the same distance away. The Goodyear Cutoff, however, was unimproved and needed to be paved properly to serve as a viable highway.

The Lincoln Highway Association wanted to do just that, and for good reason. It preferred the cutoff to the northern Wendover Route, because the latter road headed west through a 40-mile stretch of salt flats and desert that was under as much as 2 feet of water for three months every year.

The Wendover Route experiences some of its famed flooding in 1922. *University of Michigan Library (Special Collections Research Center, Transportation History Collection)*

Despite those logistics, the Lincoln group found itself at odds with the state of Utah, which wanted motorists to stay (and spend money) in the Beehive State for as long as possible. If they were headed to Los Angeles, Utah wanted them to follow the Arrowhead Route, which the state was intent on improving instead of the Goodyear Cutoff, because it kept travelers in Utah for hundreds more miles as it wound its way diagonally to the state's southwestern corner.

That was bad enough, but the state of Utah wasn't the only obstacle for the Lincoln Highway. It was also up against the Victory Highway Association, which had attached its name to the northern route. (The Victory Highway was established that same year, in 1921; it went from New York to San Francisco just like the Lincoln road did; but it followed a different route, largely mirroring the eastern segment of the National Old Trails Road.)

# AMERICA'S FIRST HIGHWAYS

**Left:** A driver shows how badly the Goodyear Cutoff was in need of repair in this 1922 photo taken in Utah.

**Below:** Driving the Midland Trail in 1917.

*University of Michigan Library (Special Collections Research Center, Transportation History Collection) photos*

San Francisco and other cities in Northern California put their money where their mouth was by donating $50,000 toward construction of the Wendover Route in Utah and the same amount toward the project in neighboring Nevada. H.G. West, president of the Victory Highway Association, called it "the first instance in which one state has helped a neighboring commonwealth with its road work." It certainly needed the money to create a highway across a flatland the was under water three months of the year.

"The water apparently rises from the ground itself," he wrote in an article for *The Highway Magazine*, "and in the vast desert which comprises the western portion of the state, becomes an inland sea of no appreciable depth but of seemingly limitless expanse."

Winds stirred up saltwater waves that made crossing the desert even more difficult. In response, highway builders added a "sea wall" of planks on either side of a raised embankment wide enough for two cars to pass across it. West boasted that photos were being taken of the project, which would "show a road building operation unique in the history of the country."

Northern California wasn't the only source of funds for the Wendover Route.

The Victory Highway came along just in time to compete for funds newly approved under the Federal Highway Act, a situation that must have made the Lincoln folks grit their teeth. They'd been working on their road for the better part of the decade, and here were these upstarts going head-to-head with them for money the government planned to spend on one east-west road in Utah.

One, but not the other.

Much to the Lincoln Highway backers' chagrin, the feds chose the northern route and gave the money to the Victory Highway — despite its obvious disadvantages. The planned Goodyear Cutoff never improved, leaving that portion of the Lincoln Highway as a bumpy, less-than-adequate road.

## Raising Money

If mapping the highway was difficult, raising money to pay for it was even more problematic. Fisher's initial goal was to raise $10 million to build the road, but he also needed money for operating expenses to keep the Lincoln Highway Association up and running.

Road work on the Lincoln Highway, 1916. *Northern Illinois University, Creative Commons CCBY2.0*

The early response was encouraging. The cement industry committed to contributing 2.3 million barrels of cement, worth about $3 million. That was on top of the nearly half-million dollars pledged by Goodyear and Packard between them. Fisher solicited donations from well-known men like President Woodrow Wilson, who donated $5 and received, in return "Highway Certificate #1." Fisher's friends Thomas Edison and Teddy Roosevelt contributed, too. Even a group of "Esquimaux" children from Alaska rounded up 14 pennies, sending them along with a letter to the Lincoln Highway Association that was disseminated far and wide.

But despite the publicity, donations of 14 cents or $5 wouldn't buy Fisher a new road. After the initial excitement died down, contributions slowed to a trickle as the big donors tightened their purse strings. The association contacted 3,000 millionaires for help, but the results were disappointing. It became clear that the group would have to rely more heavily on contributions from those along the road.

It became equally clear, however, that many small towns had adopted an "only in my backyard" policy: They wouldn't pay for construction beyond their city limits.

Needless to say, this created a problem. City roads might need improvement, but there was far more empty space *between* the towns that needed to be paved. That was where most of the expense lay. Besides, the whole point of the project was to connect towns to one another by building roads across countryside that separated them. If no one was willing to pay for that, the entire project could come undone.

Even with a few hefty donations from the auto industry like a check for $25,000 from Willys-Overland in 1917 and a $100,000 cash infusion from GM two years later, it was becoming clear private donations wouldn't pave the entire road.

A Lincoln Highway seedling mile in Grand Island, Neb. *Author photo*

Organizers needed a way to keep the idea alive — at least in the public consciousness. To do so, they came up with the idea of "seedling miles." The association might not have enough money to complete the entire road, but it could build short sections to demonstrate what the finished product would look like. By showing the public what was possible, the association hoped to "crystalize public sentiment" for "further construction of the same character."

The first seedling mile was built in the fall of 1914 west of Malta, Ill., a town of just 415 people roughly 70 miles west of Chicago. The next year, one Fred W. Aston donated more than $1,100 to have a seedling mile installed in Grand Island, Neb. It's the only one still visible today that hasn't been covered by asphalt or widened.

# AMERICA'S FIRST HIGHWAYS

**Top:** The Lincoln Highway in 1920. *Library of Congress*

**Above:** Looking west along Lincoln Highway in DeKalb, Ill., 1922. *Northern Illinois University, Creative Commons CCBY2.0*

## The Lincoln Highway Guide

The tourist on the Lincoln Highway could get a 168-page comprehensive guide to the road for just $1. It contained pretty much everything a cross-country traveler could ask for, from mileage between key cities to licensing regulations for each of the dozen states through which the road passed.

It told you what you could plan on seeing, including five state capitals, 76 county seats and more than 4,000 towns in all. It helped you tally up costs, plan what to take along and know what to expect:

*"REMEMBER: In Illinois, Iowa and Nebraska, after heavy rains, that if the tourist will remain over in the community which he is stopping for five or ten hours, it will enable him to proceed with comfort, as the roads are well graded and dry very rapidly. Such a delay will, in the end, save time and will save your car, your tires and your temper, and make your trip more enjoyable."*

The guide counseled that the entire cost, for a car with four passengers traveling from New York to San Francisco, shouldn't exceed $5 a day — excluding "tire expense and unforeseen accidents." Of course, this could vary depending on the quality of provisions and accommodations. As the guide pointed out, "even a party which is camping out entirely across the country wants to stop at a hotel" now and then. Although side trips and longer stops were possible, "the usual pleasure party" could make the trip in 20 to 30 days, traveling, on average, 18 mph.

Provisions were a must, and the guide provided a complete list of car equipment: 4 extra inner tubes, 3 cans of oil, 2 jacks, 2 sets of tire chains, a shovel, an ax and a good pair of cutting piers, among other things. Top of the list: a Lincoln Highway radiator emblem and two LH pennants. Lists of personal provisions, food and camp equipment were also supplied. What more could you ask for?

**Top:** Hefty checks from General Motors and Willys-Overland helped fund the Lincoln Highway. **Above:** The Lincoln Highway touring car in 1916. *University of Michigan Library (Special Collections Research Center, Transportation History Collection) photos*

In addition to the seedling miles, other progress was being made, as well. By 1917, Pennsylvania boasted a 380-mile stretch of improved road, the longest such segment along the highway, with only 12 miles of dirt road remaining. Only five miles of dirt road remained out of 153 miles in Indiana. Meanwhile, in Ohio, a 4½-mile segment in Wayne County had just been laid, completing a 37-mile stretch of uninterrupted brick between Wooster and Canton. Work on "eliminating the dirt gaps" in the state was continuing and had been done "as fast as funds would allow."

Unfortunately, that wasn't fast enough for the Association and Good Roads boosters. Serious gaps remained in Illinois and Iowa, which the LHA referred to as "mud" or "gumbo" states.

And things got worse the farther west you got.

The Association attributed the difficulties to "long mileage and sparse population," along with (most importantly) "the lack of sufficient funds to accomplish results." The LHA pursued federal funds to make up the difference, but those efforts came up dry — at least in Nebraska. The problem there lay in the fact that half the highway paralleled the Union Pacific train tracks, and was on right-of-way leased at a nominal fee from railroad. Federal funds, it turned out, couldn't be used on land leased by a rail company.

The result, by the Association's own admission: "Many sections of the route in Nebraska are not yet in the best possible shape." Wyoming, Utah and Nevada, with their high mountains and daunting deserts, posed challenges of their own.

However, in spite of the uneven funding — and paving — the Lincoln Highway Association declared the road a rousing success. And, in many ways, it was. H.C. Osterman, the group's field secretary, wrote in 1916: "It is true that there is a tremendous amount of work yet to be accomplished on the road, but nevertheless, the work which has been done enables any man to plan a transcontinental trip, knowing exactly what route he will follow. ..."

"If we assume that the tourist encounters perfect weather entirely across the country, absolutely no difficulties may be considered."

To be sure, that was a big assumption. Still, Osterman asserted, "practically the only difficulties at present attendant upon a transcontinental drive over the Lincoln Highway are the result of unfavorable weather conditions." There was no hiding the reason for this, either: "This is due to the fact that so much of the road is yet natural dirt highway," he wrote in *The Complete Official Road Guide to the Lincoln Highway*.

The road was, meanwhile, taking a pounding. In a sense, it was the victim of its own success, having fired the imaginations of automobile tourists to such an extent that they were turning out in droves. The summer of 1915 saw an increase of 300% to 600% in transcontinental touring, much of it on the Lincoln Highway. The Association supplied more than 4,000 people with touring information in July of 1915 alone, and the secretary of the California State Automobile Association estimated — "conservatively" that 25,000 automobile parties had toured to his state during the year.

The town of La Porte, Ind., just a few miles southeast of Lake Michigan, said 35,000 "foreign" cars had passed through on the Lincoln Highway. And LHA Secretary Austin Bement, meanwhile, declared that "thousands and thousands of tourists ... have seen their own country for the first time."

The Association had to walk a fine line. On the one hand, it wanted to encourage motorists to travel the highway by presenting it as a bold advance that was safer, more scenic and more fulfilling than any other vacation option. But on the other, they still needed to raise money to complete the project. If the public thought everything was hunky-dory, they'd stop contributing money and urging others with deep pockets to do so.

So, in the same 1916 guide that touted a trip with "absolutely no difficulties," they warned — later on — that the highway was "by no means a good road for its entire distance." While the Association was making "great strides" with each passing year, it admitted that "the task of completing, in hard surfaced material, a transcontinental road is one of tremendous difficulties and great cost."

This was where the seedling miles came in.

"These stretches of hard-surfaced roads were built ... with cement donated by the Lincoln Highway Association" at various points in Ohio, Illinois, Indiana and Nebraska, the guide explained.

"This is done with the idea of encouraging similar construction in the same and other localities along the route. It is a self-evident fact that the traveler, be he a motorist or teamster, is certain to appreciate the value of hard-surfaced roads after traveling a distance upon one of these hard-surfaced seedling miles, and then dropping off into the rough going and ordinary dirt roads.

"The wonderful increase in improvement noted on the Lincoln Highway can be more or less directly traced to the lesson which these seedling miles is teaching."

The "Ideal Section" of the Lincoln Highway is pictured at **top**, with a closeup of the sign touting it to passing motorists **above**. The sign lists officers of the Lincoln Highway Association at left. At the right, it describes the paved segment: "The finest Section of Road in the World. Cost $62,000 per Mile for the Paving. Its General Specifications were Determined by a Technical Committee of leading American Highway Engineers." *University of Michigan Library (Special Collections Research Center, Transportation History Collection) photos*

More paved sections of the Lincoln Highway appeared over the years. **Above:** A stretch of the highway in Alameda County, Calif. **Right:** Approaching a steep grade in Ohio, 1924.

*University of Michigan Library (Special Collections Research Center, Transportation History Collection) photos*

More paved sections of the Lincoln Highway. **Top:** Wayne County, Mich., in 1916. **Above:** Allegheny County, Pa., 1924. *University of Michigan Library (Special Collections Research Center, Transportation History Collection) photos*

# AMERICA'S FIRST HIGHWAYS

Contrasting good and not-so-good sections of the Lincoln Highway. **Top:** A muddy section of road in Wyandot County, Ohio, in 1924. **Above:** The brick road near Omaha. *University of Michigan Library (Special Collections Research Center, Transportation History Collection) photos*

Another section of the old highway is still visible today in Nebraska, where a three-mile section of road between Omaha and Elkhorn was paved with bricks back in 1920.

Also in 1920, the association built what it considered to be the highway's "ideal section," a 1.3-mile stretch in Lake County, Indiana that was supposed to serve as a model for road building two decades into the future. The association brought together a group of 17 highway experts to hammer out exactly what the perfect road should look like. They decided it should be a 40-foot-wide strip of concrete with guardrails, a footpath and curves designed to accommodate speeds of up to 35 mph.

The highway took shape, slowly but surely. At the end of 1913, just 47% of the road was improved; by 1918, it was up to almost two-thirds, and a year later, it was just over three-quarters.

It was straightened through the Midwest, bypassing the Ohio towns of Marion, Kenton and Lima, as well as the college town of South Bend in Indiana. Residents along the spurned Ohio section renamed their stretch of road the Harding Highway, because President Warren Harding along the then-future route in Blooming Grove. In 1921, they go the last laugh by qualifying for government money — newly approved under the Federal Highway Act of 1921 — at the expense of the "new" Lincoln Highway.

The Lincoln Highway Association, meanwhile, continued to make slow but steady progress toward its goals. It wasn't just a matter of building a highway, but showing that it could be done. By 1938, a decade after the Association disbanded, just 42 miles of the Lincoln Highway's 3,100-mile length remained dirt or gravel. Everything else had been paved.

Fisher rejoiced at the news: "The Lincoln Highway Association has accomplished its primary purpose: that of providing an object lesson to show the possibility in highway transportation. Now I believe the country is at the beginning of another new era in highway building that will create a system of roads far beyond the dreams of the Lincoln Highway founders."

Fisher, who would die a year later, once again proved prescient: The Federal-aid Highway Act of 1938 included a proposal for a national network of superhighways. Though greatly modified over time, it formed the foundation for the movement that would culminate in President Dwight Eisenhower's interstate highway system, approved in 1956.

# AMERICA'S FIRST HIGHWAYS

**Above:** A hand-painted sign along the Lincoln Highway in Nevada shows the distances to various cities in 1915. The mileage figures weren't always accurate. The 1916 version of *The Complete Official Road Guide to the Lincoln Highway* noted that "the tourist will encounter at many points on the route signs which were erected in 1913 and 1914, or even later, and which may contain mileages which do not agree with this volume. These differences... are due to the constant effort of the (Lincoln Highway) Association, the states, the counties and the people along the route in shortening the total distance between the two coasts." *Effie Price Gladding*

**Below:** The highway during a winter snowstorm that sidelined travelers in DeKalb, Ill., c. 1920. Note the "ALL ROADS CLOSED" sign at the center of the photograph. *Northern Illinois University, Creative Commons CCBY2.0*

**Top:** A road sign points the way for early travelers on the Lincoln Highway in this 1915 photo. *Effie Price Gladding*

**Above:** A DX gas station on the Lincoln Highway in DeKalb, Ill., 1934. *Northern Illinois University, Creative Commons CCBY2.0*

# AMERICA'S FIRST HIGHWAYS

The town of DeKalb, Ill., put up a pair of welcome arches over the Lincoln Highway in 1922. The first was removed about a decade later, and the second in 1942. They read "DeKalb, A Live Wire City, 10,000 Strong" and, for departing traffic, "We'll Be Lonesome Until You Come Again."

*Northern Illinois University, Creative Commons CCBY2.0*

AMERICA'S FIRST HIGHWAYS

## The Dixie Highway

A plywood camel arch spans the Dixie Highway in 1928 at Boca Raton, Fla. *Boca Raton Historical Society & Museum*

# Great Lakes to the Gulf

> Here is a Dixie Highway
> That's hard and smooth and fair,
> Would every road and by-way
> Were like it everywhere

That poem appeared in several daily newspapers back in 1896, long before the road formally known as the Dixie Highway was built. In fact, there were plans for a Montreal-to-Miami road along the Atlantic Coast that was sometimes called the Dixie Highway back in 1913. But they were more plans than anything else. As the Tampa Times put it, "As for the 'Montreal-Miami Highway ...', it's a myth — not a tenth of its length is even located."

It was left to our old friend Carl Fisher to make the Dixie Highway a reality. It wouldn't lead to Montreal, but it would share a section of the proposed Montreal route in Florida called the John Anderson Highway. (That road, which ran from Jacksonville to Miami, was paved in part with vitrified brick and became known as the Old Brick Road.)

An arch celebrating the first planned Dixie Highway in Florida, including the terminal points of Miami and Montreal. *Wikimedia Commons*

Fisher's version of the Dixie Highway was originally called the Cotton Belt Route or Hoosier Land-to-Dixie Highway. The idea came to him in a brainstorm after he purchased a big chunk of land in South Florida and became intent on developing it into a winter resort called Miami Beach.

Fisher was, in many ways, the father of modern Miami Beach: a narrow strip of land across Biscayne Bay from Miami, looking out over the Atlantic Ocean. A man named John Collins bought some land there in 1896, initially planting bananas and avocados with an eye toward eventually turning it into a resort. In order to do so, he needed to build a bridge from the mainland, a project he began in 1912.

But the company he had hired went belly-up, and he ran out of money with the bridge just halfway done.

Enter Mr. Fisher, who happened to be on vacation in Miami at the time.

Fisher liked Collins' vision and decided to invest $50,000 in the half-finished bridge. Thinking long term, he began sinking even more money into the area, dredging up earth from the bottom of the bay to expand Miami Beach and build a series of manmade islands that would form a new archipelago off the coast. He talked it up as a real-life fountain of youth: "the sort of place Ponce de León dreamed about."

The Spanish explorer had discovered Florida while searching for the legendary fountain, but Fisher aimed to create it from scratch: His vision included a string of resort hotels, golf courses and polo grounds, interspersed among palm trees and Australian pines. He incorporated the town of Miami Beach in 1915 and offering free beach land to anyone who agreed to locate there.

It didn't take off right away, but Fisher just did what he did best: He started promoting the place. He brought in a couple of elephants to pull kids in carts around the island, and he came up with the "bathing beauty" concept, photographing women in swimsuits next to an oversized thermometer. The "wish you were here" technique worked like a charm, and Fisher rubbed it in when he put up a billboard in Times Square that reminded New Yorkers, "It's June in Miami!"

Fisher was setting the stage for what would become an annual winter migration of human "snowbirds."

He just needed a way for them to get there.

The Dixie Highway, which he envisioned starting in Chicago (not Hoosier Land), was his answer.

But he'd learned a few things from his Lincoln Highway experience. Foremost among them: Henry Ford had been right about private funding. It wasn't enough to pay for a full-fledged highway.

So, he decided, this time, he'd look to state and county governments for the financial muscle he needed. Seeking to stay more in the background this time, he called upon a friend to officially head up the effort.

The plans were announced with great fanfare, and all interested parties were invited to a meeting set for early April 1915 in Chattanooga, Tenn. Hundreds of people showed up, including state governors and civic leaders from towns hoping to land a spot along the route.

Predictably, they couldn't agree on anything.

One group wanted the highway to head south through Louisville; another wanted it routed farther east into Ohio, then south via Lexington. There were three competing options through Tennessee, and three more through Georgia, too. Each had its pluses and minuses.

Fights often came down to three factors:

- Which the route was more direct.
- Whether it better served tourism or commerce — and which was more important.
- How much work local communities had done, and could pledge to do quickly, on their preferred route.

A particularly fierce battle was waged between two small towns that stood just 45 miles apart as the crow flies in northern Georgia. Rome was a town of about 12,000 people in the Appalachian foothills that had grown rapidly between 1900 and 1910. Dalton, to the north and slightly east, was less than half its size but had history as a Civil War hotbed on its side.

Marketing their corridor as the "Battlefield Route," Daltonites touted its historic significance, adding that it was flatter and more direct. Rome countered that its road was already completed and that it had, in fact, been used more by General Sherman than the Dalton route.

The two roads diverged at Chattanooga, just above the Tennessee state line, then came back together north of Atlanta before the road fractured again into three competing options farther south. The most direct route of these three might have seemed the most logical — except for the fact that it went smack-dab through the middle of a swamp.

One good thing about having so many options: With the competing factions all eager to demonstrate their superiority, they were getting a head start on improving their respective roads.

Fisher and the rest of the Dixie Highway organizers, or "founders," as they were referred to at the meeting, had just formally launched the Dixie Highway Association, with each of them forking over a $1,000 entry fee. That wouldn't pay for any actual pavement, but it would cover the cost of auxiliary materials such as mapmaking, meetings and the like.

But when the folks who would be doing the heavy lifting (paying for the road itself) got wind of it, they were indignant.

Kentucky's commissioner of roads asked sarcastically, "Why call a conference of states to organize a Dixie Highway when you have already done it before we came?"

Just like that, the power struggle was officially on.

Vintage postcard of the Dixie Highway between Asheville and Hot Springs, N.C. *State Archives of North Carolina*

The governors didn't want the decision on where to route the highway left to the founders, but they were hesitant to make the call themselves. Choosing one route over another would appease some voters but alienate others. So they did what politicians do best: They passed the buck.

They proposed that each governor appoint two "impartial representatives" to a committee that would draw the final map.

But they couldn't even agree on that.

Since Georgia had three routes vying for a space on the highway, the city of Savannah (a stop on one of those roads) insisted that each state should have three spots on the committee. Not two. An amendment was offered to that effect, but it was tabled and went nowhere.

At least that much was settled. But anyone who believed the committee, once selected, would actually *be* impartial was living a pipe dream. The size of the committee had no sooner been decided than the governors started appointing members with a vested interest in the outcome.

A prime example: The governor of Indiana named Fisher one of his two representatives.

But at least one of the "founders" wasn't happy with his influence being curtailed by the governors during the meeting.

Just a few days after the Chattanooga meeting, J.E. James of Tennessee took matters into his own hands. Declaring that his state's governor had been too slow to name its two committee members, he announced that the founders had chosen one of the three competing Tennessee routes as the winner. That route, it just so happened, went right past Signal Mountain, where James owned a large plot of undeveloped land.

Citizens along the two rival routes, of course, cried foul, calling James' announcement "a slap in the face" to the governors and the committee — which quickly reasserted its authority. Nothing, it insisted, would be decided until a May 20 meeting in Chattanooga, and all the rival factions would have to make their cases, in writing, before that.

When the time came for that meeting to take place, everyone expected fireworks.

**Top:** Downtown Dalton, Ga., today. **Above:** A curve on a rural stretch of U.S. 70, the old Dixie Highway, between Knoxville and Chattanooga in Tennessee. *Author photos*

The delegation that arrived from Nashville, which has been bypassed in James' premature "announcement," expressed confidence it would prevail. Having secured the necessary funding for their route, they marched from their hotel to the courthouse meeting site, a brass band leading the way.

Indeed, the meeting was preceded by a gala parade of more than 400 vehicles, with the *Chattanooga News* reporting that "all of Chattanooga turned out to witness the spectacle."

Dalton and Rome both sent large delegations to the gathering, with tiny Dalton entering more cars in the parade than any other town. Rome, for its part, sent an eight-car trainload of 1,000 supporters along with a car caravan of its own. Dalton even declared it a city holiday.

The two towns made their arguments that afternoon, with the *News* calling their confrontation "the real sensation of the day."

Near the end of the session, the paper said, "the meeting became pandemonium."

The chairman of the meeting introduced the two sides by saying, "Now, ladies and gentlemen, we have come to the real oratory of the day. You who have tears, prepare to shed them now."

The News reported that "great crowds of supporters from each town vied ... to make themselves heard," even as the chairman continually called for order. "Organized cheering and individual shouts filled the air" with "each side supporting its own speakers and even going so far as to try to discomfit the advocates of the other side."

In the end, however, it was all for naught.

The committee, unable to make up its mind about anything, ultimately chose the path of King Solomon and cut the baby in half. Instead of a single highway from Chicago to Miami, it opted to create a network of roads, circled roughly by an outer oblong ring. Both the middle and eastern Tennessee routes got to be on the network, which ultimately was extended up over the top of Michigan to Sault Ste. Marie.

Dalton and Rome each got their own routes, and "crossbar" roads were sanctioned to connect the main north-south highways. Everyone, in fact, pretty much got what they wanted ... except that it was going to take a whole lot more money to find an entire system of roads than it would have to pay for a single highway.

A car stops by the side of the Dixie Highway outside Tampa in 1923. *Flickr/public domain*

## Mapping the Dixie

Carl Fisher is better known for founding the Lincoln Highway, but the Dixie Highway was really his baby.

After Fisher's trailblazing tour west, Henry Joy had become the driving force behind the Lincoln group. Fisher was still involved, but he was no longer calling the shots. It was Joy who decided that the Lincoln's route should be the most direct possible, even if it bypassed big cities and scenic wonders.

But whereas Joy's priorities won out for the Lincoln, Fisher's vision carried the day on the Dixie — which was anything but direct. That was good for Fisher, who wanted as many people from as many places as possible to find their way to Miami Beach. So the meandering grapevine of a highway network served his purpose just fine.

Indeed, the Dixie Highway network was an often-shifting maze of main arteries, connector roads and alternate routes that looked a little like braided hair.

After adopting the two main north-south routes at the outset, organizers were continually fielding requests for further expansion. At the same time, they were tweaking the route in response to promises made — and broken — by towns on poorly maintained sections.

In 1918, a "Carolina Division" was added along the Atlantic coast, heading up from Jacksonville through Savannah, Ga., where it veered slightly inland. From there, it headed north to Augusta, passed through Greenville, S.C., and cut across the edge of North Carolina at Asheville before rejoining the main eastern route at Knoxville.

The addition of this route gave the Dixie Highway three separate north-south arteries through Georgia.

Meanwhile, other sections of highway were being revoked.

The original route from Atlanta to Macon was changed because the road was so poor, and other counties were put on notice that they risked losing their spot on the highway if they failed to improve their sections. The list of broken promises grew so long that, in 1923, organizers stopped accepting any new segments that weren't already built.

Even before that, they were getting more selective.

In 1921, a group emerged with a plan to create a new road through Kentucky and Tennessee. Unlike Carl Fisher, they preferred a more direct route: The Cincinnati-to-Lookout Mountain Airline Highway would be a straight shot from the Ohio River south to the popular tourist spot just south of Chattanooga. The *Chattanooga Daily Times* described it as "almost a direct line between the two points" and "a considerably shorter channel than either the eastern or western division of the Dixie highway system."

Organizers asked that their new route, which largely followed the Cincinnati Southern rail line, be included in the Dixie Highway's official network, but they were rebuffed. Still, they continued their work, and the resulting road eventually became part of U.S. 27.

## Long Way to Go

In 1917, with the United States poised to enter World War I, it was clear there was a lot of work to do on the Dixie Highway.

A supplement in *Scarborough's Official Tour Book* proclaimed that the past year had seen "wonderful improvements all along the Dixie Highway and its connecting lines throughout the South," with steady work being done on the sections linking Lexington to Knoxville, and Nashville to Chattanooga.

Over the former stretch, the supplement authors had to admit that the road was in such bad condition, they couldn't even hazard a guess as to an accurate routing. It hastened to add, however, that this was due to extensive work being done to upgrade the road through the Cumberland Mountains, thanks to a $400,000 bond supplemented by state aid.

Over the Nashville-to-Chattanooga section, the tour book boasted, an entirely new road was being built, "with the exception of about 50 miles." (It didn't bother mentioning that those 50 miles constituted more than one-third of the segment.) The rosy portrait couldn't hide the fact that, despite the progress, road conditions were far less than optimal. The supplement even acknowledged as much: "The work of road building in the South is really just starting" and "the fact that these roads are still uncompleted speaks volumes for the terrible condition they have been in."

One section, from Jacksonville to Tallahassee in Florida was described as "mostly sand in its present condition and difficult to travel."

"While the counties are very emphatic in their promises to improve it, and one or two counties have started the work, a year will probably be required to get the counties in line to make the necessary improvements."

Despite such limitations, the authors tried to put the best face on things by maintaining that tourists could travel the entire length of the highway "by making well-selected detours." Doing so, it said, would lead to only "slight inconvenience" — and, apparently, minimal repairs: "An example of what is possible in making such a trip is the wonderful record of a car traveling last fall from Goshen, Ind., to Bartow, Fla., and having to expend only 11 cents in repairs."

But that was a best-case scenario. Left unsaid was the fact that repairs would likely cost a good deal more, and that the not-so-well-selected detours might well send you into a swamp.

Staying on the established route, where it was free of detours, was a challenge in its own right. The tour book offered an extensive, step-by-step guide on where to turn that ran a few dozen pages of small print (albeit liberally sprinkled with ads), offering drivers a detailed list of landmarks to look for so they could stay on the beaten path. It wasn't as though they had those big, green traffic signs above the highway in those days. Before the age of GPS, drivers often found their way by consulting paper maps they picked up at their favorite service stations. And using a tour book in the age of the auto trail was even more of an ordeal. On the one hand, you had to pay attention to a one- or two-lane road that might be dirt or gravel; on the other, you had to keep consulting the book to make sure you hadn't strayed off the route. New instructions appeared every few tenths of a mile.

As an example of just how complicated it could get following a guide book's directions, consider this stretch of just a few miles on the Dixie Highway between Ocala and Gainesville, Fla.:

| | |
|---|---|
| 20.6 | White church on left. |
| 21.5 | Turn left at big oak tree. Pass Evanston Station. |
| 25.2 | Micanopy. Turn right on main thoroughfare. Turn left. Turn right, then left, passing Tuscawilla Hotel. |
| 26.0 | Cross railroad and turn right around corner of fence. |
| 28.0 | Turn left. Follow railroad, pass Kirkwood and Claytts. |
| 30.9 | Flewellen Station. Cross railroad. |
| 32.7 | Cross railroad. |
| 33.3 | Pass Wacahoota Station. |
| 37.1 | Turn left at corrugated iron store house. |

It wasn't until 1920 that even one entire county had a fully concrete section of the highway. That was Spalding County, Ga., which had whetted residents' appetite with the first paved section of concrete outside a city — a demonstration strip beyond the Griffin city limits.

It so impressed county residents that they approved a $350,000 bond to pave their entire section of highway.

The irony was that, even though roads in the South were among the nation's worst, the section of Dixie Highway in Georgia accounted for nearly a quarter of its total mileage.

A further irony: Even though the roads were, by today's standards, primitive, they were built for the well-to-do: tourists who could afford an adventure vacation to Florida, with its tropical climes and sandy beaches.

The switchback road up Signal Mountain is seen in this c. 1930s postcard. *Digital Commonwealth*

## Along the Dixie

There was no doubt that the Dixie Highway was built for tourists. The majority of northerners were bound for sunny Florida, just as Fisher had intended. But there were plenty of attractions along the way, too, and more were popping up almost daily. There were tourist camps and eateries and filling stations, to be sure. Among them were a motel village in the shape of wigwams in Cave City, Ky., that served as a model for several more across the nation, and a filling station shaped like an airplane in Powell, Tenn.

There was a big hotel at Signal Mountain just north of Chattanooga, which served as the center of the Dixie Highway, both geographically and politically. It marked the beginning of a short stretch where the highway's eastern and western branches shared the same road. And it was also a nexus for several other major roads: The Lee Highway, Airline Highway, and several other, lesser highways all came together there.

Coming in from the north, you'd reach a bottleneck at the two-lane Stringers Ridge Tunnel, built in 1909 on a road that would become a section of the Dixie Highway (now known as State Highway 8). A number of early businesses, such as the Cherokee Tourist Camp and service station, clustered around the tunnel entrance, collecting customers as they slowed on their way into the city. Motels lined Cherokee Boulevard until it became Market Street, crossing the Tennessee River via the Walnut Street Bridge and entering downtown.

That's where you'd find the Hotel Patten, headquarters to the Dixie Highway Association and AAA. It advertised itself as being "where the highways meet," at the junction of road that would become U.S. 27, 11 and 41.

It was a suitable location for the Dixie Highway's base of operations.

But highways weren't just booming with services. There were big attractions, too. By 1928, the *Appalachian Journal* was crowing that the tourist industry had become "the largest industry in America, with a 'payroll' of three and a half billion dollars this year." That payroll was funded by tourist money, and the factory was "the national system of hard surfaced highways."

No wonder everyone wanted in on the action.

Enterprising investors flocked to the roadside, each searching for an angle to exploit. Near Dalton, Ga., roadside residents started displaying colorful chenille bedspreads for sale along the roadside. They were such a hit that demand began to outpace supply, and local factories set up shop to keep pace. Because the most popular style was a peacock pattern, that area of the highway became known as "Peacock Alley."

(The term was also a derisive term that originally referred to hotel corridors, where the wealthy would strut along, showing off their elegant attire on their way to the dining room. It later came to be used for auto trails frequented by rich tourists who could be seen showing off their expensive cars as they passed through town. These tourists — critics said — took money that might have been used for local, working roads and spent them on vacationers' through-ways. The bedspread-makers were earning some of that money back.)

Other roadside businesses were more ambitious.

Lookout Mountain became a draw because you could supposedly see mountain peaks in seven states from there. An entrepreneur named Garnet Carter opened a hotel on the site, and his wife created a whimsical rock garden populated by fairy-tale statues. Another attraction: the first-ever miniature golf layout, which he called "Tom Thumb Golf." It proved so popular that thousands of them opened in the late 1920s.

Carter had hundreds of barns along the highway plastered with the painted message "See Rock City," drawing even more motorists to Lookout Mountain. Other signs went up, too, many of them directing tourists to caves and caverns that had been converted into roadside attractions.

They weren't just places to tour, either. Often, they were event venues, hosting hundreds or even thousands for picnics, concerts and dancing. Lost River Cave on the highway in Bowling Green, Ky., was an alleged hideout for Jesse James and, later, housed the Historic Cavern Nite Club. Its natural air conditioning 75 feet underground kept visitors cool as they heated up the dance floor to the sounds of Jazz all the way up until the 1960s.

It was one of many caves along the Dixie, the most impressive of which was Mammoth Cave. The name is appropriate, because it really is mammoth: In fact, it's the world's longest known cave system at more than 400 miles, and it was already famous before the age of the automobile. Early road builders created the Louisville and Nashville Turnpike, a macadamized toll road for wagons and stagecoaches, between 1837 and 1849. It took about three days to get from Louisville to Nashville, during which you'd pass a toll booth every five miles.

Mammoth Cave lay about 85 miles south of Louisville, and it became a tourist stop long before the L&N Pike became the Dixie Highway. When the highway was built, however, and vacationers started driving by in droves on their way to Florida, copycats began springing up everywhere. There were plenty of caves in the area, and savvy entrepreneurs quickly lay claim to them, one by one: Colossal Cave, Crystal Cave, Indian Cave, Great Onyx Cave and others. Mammoth Cave was the most impressive, so its competitors had to find a way to divert business away from it and to their own attractions.

What ensued was something called the Kentucky Cave Wars.

Different caves started posting signs on the roadside ... and competitors would tear them down. They might even burn down another cave's ticket booth. Then one of the caves might send someone out onto the road, dressed in a cap like a police officer — earning them the nickname "cappers" — to convince passing motorists to stop. They might say Mammoth Cave was closed or flooded. Drivers shouldn't bother stopping there and should go to (fill in the blank cave) instead. Some of these tactics resulted in violent confrontations.

Not content to merely compete using their own caves, some owners looked for alternate entrances to Mammoth Cave itself after an explorer discovered it was connected to Colossal and Salts caves. Where such entrances didn't exist, a few unscrupulous types even tried to dynamite their way through solid rock to gain access to Mammoth Cave itself.

Tourists boating on Echo River in Mammoth Cave c. 1891. *Library of Congress*

## AMERICA'S FIRST HIGHWAYS

Nearby Cave City grew up as a resort town tied to Mammoth Cave, incorporating in 1866. There, one entrepreneur got the idea to capitalize on the popularity of the place by building a motel with individual rooms in the shape of teepees. His first Wigwam Village, as he called it, had been up the road in Horse Cave, another "cave town," and had done well enough that he decided to build a second.

Between 1933 and 1949, he built seven of them across the country, with the others going up in New Orleans; Orlando, Fla.; on U.S. 11 in Bessemer, Ala.; and on Route 66 in Holbrook, Ariz., and San Bernardino, Calif. As of 2020, only three remained standing: in Cave City, Holbrooke and San Bernardino.

**Above:** The Wigwam Motel in Holbrooke, Ariz. *Author photo*

**Right:** Postcard advertising the Kentucky "cave" Wigwam Villages.

**Above:** The Tin Can Tourist Camp of Gainesville, Fla., welcomed tourists who traveled to the Sunshine State via the Dixie Highway.

**Left:** Herbert Fuller stands next to a sign for the Altamonte Hotel that was erected in the 1920s along the highway. *Florida State Archives/ Wikimedia Commons*

## Postscript

Not everyone approved of Fisher's grand schemes. Some saw the Dixie Highway as nothing more than a driveway to the doorstep of his resort boomtown. These critics decried interstate highways as "peacock alleys" where the rich strutted their stuff as they drove to frolic in playgrounds the poor could never visit in cars the poor could never afford.

Tour companies such as Scarborough gave guided tours, complete with official pilot cars. These weren't excursions for the working class; they were adventures for the wealthy, the elite.

In fact, the entire Good Roads movement was split in two over the issue. On one side were auto companies and developers of vacation spots that catered to the wealthy "auto tourist" set. On the other were farmers and rural residents who wanted money spent on local roads and couldn't have cared less about cross-country excursions.

This conflict came to a head, in one example, in 1919, when Tennessee voted down a $50 million bond that would have helped fund work on the Dixie Highway. Michael Allison, head of the Dixie Highway Association, had lobbied hard for the bond, only to see it derailed by advocates of local roads.

The Roman Pool at Miami Beach, seen here in 1926, was emblematic of the resort community Carl Fisher and his successors built in South Florida. *Library of Congress*

The bill that ultimately got through, Allison complained, "fails to provide for any permanent or through highways."

He continued: "The road tax is apportioned out to all the counties in the state and will result in building a few miles of road in each county which cannot be connected up."

Despite the naysayers however, the Dixie Highway did exactly what Fisher had hoped it would do. By 1917, Miami Beach was already being called "America's Winter Playground."

And people weren't just going for the summer, they were staying in South Florida year-round.

Also in 1917, Fisher built a swanky hotel in his newly made paradise.

The founder of the Lincoln Highway didn't forget the 16th president when he opened it: He called it the Lincoln Hotel, built on the corner of Drexel Avenue and (naturally) Lincoln Road. It was the third building on Lincoln Road, after Fisher's own house, built in 1915, and his sales office.

President-elect Warren Harding lunched there in 1921, although he stayed at a newer hotel — also owned by Fisher — the Flamingo. "The only fault I find with it is that more people haven't got time for winter play," Harding said.

"Because of the attractiveness of Miami and Miami Beach, I hope to come here again.

"This beach is wonderful," he enthused. "It is developing like magic."

With a little help from Carl Fisher.

A lot of other people shared the soon-to-be-president's sentiments.

In 1900, just 5% of Florida's population lived in the southern third of the state; three decades later, the number had risen to more than 17.5%. Two-thirds of the population at the turn of the century was in northern Florida, close to the Georgia state line; but by the time the Depression came along, those numbers had flipped: Nearly six in ten Floridians lived south of that northern third.

Almost everything Fisher touched seemed to turn to gold ... until the very end, that is. His final project was an odd miscalculation: In the late 1920s, when the Florida land bubble burst, he sought to replicate what he'd achieved in the Sunshine State with a new resort on Long Island called Montauk.

But Fisher's "Miami Beach of the north" was in direct competition with the *real* Miami Beach he'd already helped build. He'd created place for his human snowbirds to "fly" south for the winter, and he'd given them a migratory route — the Dixie Highway

— to get them there. Why would they want to stay in the bitter cold when they had the option of escaping to sunny Florida?

They didn't.

Even if they had wanted to invest in Fisher's latest scheme, however, they lacked the money to do so. Before they the great promoter's project at Montauk was completed, the Great Depression hit.

It wiped out Fisher's $100 million fortune.

He returned to Miami Beach, where he lived on $500 a month he received from his former partners to do promotional jobs. In 1938, a year before he died, he undertook his final project: a "poor man's retreat" called the Caribbean Club on Key Largo. Exterior shots from the place were used in the 1948 film, also called *Key Largo*, starring Humphrey Bogart and Lauren Bacall.

Carl Fisher's Miami Beach dream had been more than realized by the time this 1965 photo was taken. *Florida State Archives*

## AMERICA'S FIRST HIGHWAYS

## The Army Convoy of 1919

Lt. Col. Dwight Eisenhower in 1919, when he would take part in a transcontinental Army convoy that would leave a lasting impression on the future president. *National Archives*

# Eisenhower's Eye-Opener

What the Good Roads Movement, the rise of the automobile and even the great Carl Fisher couldn't do, World War I did. It showed the nation just how much it needed highways. As the nation mobilized, it became clear that the railroads weren't equipped to handle the sheer volume of traffic needed to supply the war effort.

And neither were the roads.

Even before the U.S. formally entered the war, it was sending supplies overseas. Hostilities broke out in 1914, and railroad freight volume spiked by 43% in the summer, taxing a system designed for peacetime travel and commerce. Three years later, when the U.S. declared war, it couldn't get its troops to the East Coast for deployment fast enough:

There simply weren't enough rail cars to accommodate them.

For the railroads, the timing of the war couldn't have been worse. The once-mighty industry had entered a period of decline, begun when the government granted itself the power to set rates in 1906. Rate restrictions on one end and rising taxes on the other put a financial squeeze on railroad companies. And enforcement of union demands for an eight-hour work day following a strike by engineers, conductors and other rail workers in 1916 only made matters worse.

Major carriers like the Rock Island Line (Chicago, Rock Island and Pacific) and the Wabash Railroad were struggling just to stay afloat.

At Christmastime in 1917, President Woodrow Wilson took the unprecedented step of seizing control of the nation's railroads and suspending civilian passenger service to focus on the war effort. It wasn't a pure nationalization effort; rather, it was something more like eminent domain, as the rail lines received compensation for their services. The government purchased 100,000 new rail cars, most of them boxcars, along with 1,930 steam engines at a cost of $380 million, and took over routing and scheduling.

A law passed in 1918 specified that the government would remain in control of the railways until 21 months after a peace treaty was signed, ending the war. Under that law, private control was restored on March 1, 1920.

But much changed in the intervening period.

Good Roads advocates had used the war to point up the inadequacy of the nation's highways to meet the needs of the military.

Proclaiming good roads to be "a military necessity," AAA called for "a highway following roughly the borders of our country, and connecting various coast points with a road over which military supplies could be quickly mobilized." The 1917 proposal addressed the problem of supplies being tied up on rail lines and backed up at ports along the North Atlantic coast.

That same year, the Massachusetts Highway Association also pointed out the limitations of the nation's rail system: "Railroads cannot always be depended upon, and especially in war time, they are subject to congestion, and shortage of rolling stock. They must be supplemented by highways. ... Success in war, wholly like success in business, depends on mobility. And mobility depends on good roads."

And a similar argument was made by the National Highways Association — a group formed by backers of the Jefferson, Lincoln and Dixie highways, among others — which penned an open letter to President Woodrow Wilson in 1917. In it, they declared "transportation is the rock upon which battles are won or lost" and argued that "there can be no real preparedness for war, for defense, for peace without national highways and good roads everywhere."

Meanwhile, nearly 1.4 million more cars and trucks were registered in 1917 than the previous year, making the need for better roads even more acute, regardless of the war.

The problem was all the more acute in the South, where able-bodied men were often responsible for working a certain number of days each year to maintain local roads. But many of those men were being shipped overseas to fight in Europe, leaving no one behind to ensure the roads were in adequate conditions. Meanwhile, the number of car registrations nearly doubled in Arkansas, Florida, Oklahoma and South Carolina.

A 1918 editorial in *Motor Age* magazine proposed a solution: letting captured enemy soldiers do the work. The magazine argued that enemy aliens were "a drain on our resources when the should and could be made an asset":

"Not only will it provide the necessary labor but to a great extent it will overcome the one great objection to wartime road building, that of the transportation of road materials over our already over-burdened railroads. In practically every locality, road material of more or less value is present, and if this labor can be used in developing local road material resources, we can get the road work done without calling on the railroads."

## Ike's Rough Ride

Despite such calls, little was done to build or maintain roads during the war. Money and resources were being sent overseas, and fears of an attack on American shores never materialized.

Everything changed, however, once the Treaty of Versailles was signed in June of 1919. The ink was barely dry on the document when, a week and a half later, a convoy of U.S. Army trucks and other military vehicles rolled out of Washington, D.C., on a cross-country trip to test the mettle of American's roads — specifically, the Lincoln Highway. Among the officers making the trip was a 28-year-old lieutenant colonel named Dwight David Eisenhower, who joined the expedition "partly for a lark" and would later describe it as "a great adventure."

Photos from the 1919 Army convoy across the continent, from top: traveling between Bedford and Greenburg, Pa.; Eisenhower's photo of the 1½-ton Packard in the convoy; pulling a truck through the mud during the journey.
*National Archives*

# AMERICA'S FIRST HIGHWAYS

Soldiers build a wood-plank bridge across a gully, top, then drive across, above, in a photo Eisenhower captioned, "Hoping it will hold." *National Archives*

Two dozen officers and 250 enlisted men took part in the 1919 Army convoy, crossing Nebraska here on the Lincoln Highway. *National Archives*

Anyone who expected a smooth ride probably hadn't read the 1916 *Complete Official Road Guide to the Lincoln Highway*, which remained quite accurate.

It warned prospective travelers that "a journey from the Atlantic to the Pacific by motor car is still something of a sporting proposition. It differs from a tour of the Berkshire Hills or any of the other popular, extensive drives in the northeastern part of the United States."

The guide listed what it called "a few" things to be avoided — actually a lengthy list — when traveling the highway:

- Don't wait until your gasoline is almost gone before filling up. There might be a delay, or it might not be obtainable at the next point you figured on. Always fill your tank at every point gasoline can be secured, no matter how little you have used from your previous supply.
- Don't allow your water can to be other than full of fresh water, and fill it whenever you get a chance. You might spring a leak in your radiator, or burst a water hose.
- Don't allow the car to be without food of some sort at any time west of Salt Lake City. You might break down out in the desert, and have to wait some time until the next tourist comes along.

- Don't buy oil in bulk when it can be avoided. Buy it in the one-gallon original cartons.
- Don't fail to have warm clothing in the outfit. The high altitudes are cold, and the dry air is penetrating.
- Don't carry loaded firearms in the car. Nothing of this kind is in the least necessary except for sport, anyhow.
- Don't fail to put out your camp fire when leaving.
- Don't forget the yellow goggles. In driving west you face the sun all afternoon, and the glare of the western desert is hard on the eyes.
- Don't forget the camphor ice. The dry air of the west will crack your lips and fingers without it.
- Don't build a big fire for cooking. The smaller the better.
- Don't ford water without first wading through it.
- Don't drink alkali water. Serious cramps result.
- Don't wear new shoes.

There wasn't much of a road near Cheyenne, Wyo., as members of the Army convoy discovered. *University of Michigan Library (Special Collections Research Center, Transportation History Collection)*

The guide allowed that even those who made it all the way across the country often chose not to return the way they'd come; many, in fact, opted to return by train and ship their car back home as freight. The businesses advertising in the guide included quite a few hotels, but even these were outnumbered by ads for garages along the route.

Translation: "There's a very good chance your car *will* break down, and you *will* need our services."

The guide sought to present the hazards of the journey as delicately as possible: "You must cheerfully put up with some unpleasantness, as you would on a shooting trip into the Maine woods, for example," it cautioned, adding that "those who want luxury and ease on a transcontinental trip should take a de luxe train."

Eisenhower and his fellow soldiers weren't interested in creature comforts. Still, two dozen officers and 250 enlisted personnel probably weren't prepared for what awaited them as they guided their two-mile line of vehicles "through darkest America," as the future president described it. The convoy included ambulances, field kitchens, tanker trucks and a five-ton trailer hauling a pontoon boat they called the Mayflower II. Their journey went relatively smoothly, if slowly, on the paved section of the Lincoln Highway east of the Mississippi, where cheering crowds lifted the soldiers' spirits as they passed through each new town.

But the farther west the trucks traveled, the worse the road got. Scouts on motorcycles rode ahead to be sure the trucks continued on the proper course — which was necessary not only because the road was poorly marked, but because it was hard to see. As the pavement gave way to dirt and gravel, dust billowed up over the plains when it was dry, making it hard to see. And when it was wet, they got stuck in the mud.

Along the way, some of the rickety bridges built to carry automobiles failed to stand up under the weight of Army transports. When a span gave way beneath them, soldiers found themselves up to their knees in muddy water, from which they had to extricate not only themselves, but their vehicles. If a truck or other conveyance really got stuck, they could call on a towing tractor called a Militor, equipped with a power winch, to pull it out.

One on evening, the Militor rolled into camp towing four vehicles. But on another, the rescue vehicle itself was one of 25 trucks that wound up in a ditch outside North Platte, Neb.

# AMERICA'S FIRST HIGHWAYS

Locals give soldiers in the 1919 Army convoy some free lemonade at an undisclosed location during their journey across the country. *National Archives*

Things got even worse in Wyoming and Utah, where the "highway" was nothing like what that word suggests today and few vehicles had even dared to traverse it before. For a good portion of the way through Wyoming, the trucks didn't even use a road at all: Instead, they traveled across a former Union Pacific right-of-way that the railroad had abandoned in favor of a more direct route. On arriving in Cheyenne, they were greeted by a wild west show, a dance and refreshments. In return for its hospitality, the town asked that the convoy display posters touting the fact that the state was spending $7 million on roads.

It needed every penny.

As the trucks moved west from Cheyenne past the town of Rawlins, Eisenhower remarked on the "bad, sandy trail" that was "very rough, with drop-offs over shelves of rock just below (the) surface." Four-wheel-drive models, he noted, were far better suited to this seven-mile stretch than were other vehicles.

And things didn't get any better in Utah. Eisenhower called the Lincoln Highway through that state a "succession of dust, ruts, pits and holes" where a number of vehicles got stuck in the salt flats. The area was in the midst of 4½-month dry spell, and soldiers had to remove sand that swirled and drifted in dunes across the roadway.

The convoy finally reached San Francisco, its destination, 62 days after it had set out, having covered more than 3,200 miles and 11 states.

The trip left a lasting impression on Eisenhower, who would sign a bill creating the interstate highway system as president nearly four decades later. But fortunately for the army and, more immediately, for civilians traveling U.S. highways, roads would start getting better a whole lot sooner than that.

Dwight Eisenhower, right, with three unidentified men in 1919. *National Archives*

In 1921, two years after the convoy's cross-country trip, Bureau of Public Roads Director Thomas MacDonald asked for the Army to list roads it considered to be of "prime importance in the event of war."

Gen. John "Black Jack" Pershing would deliver the results to Congress in 1922: the first official topographic map of the United States, featuring a 78,000-mile network of roads and highways. The document, which came to be called the Pershing Map, set down the twin priorities that would guide the creation of Eisenhower's interstate system in the 1950s: carrying commercial and industrial travel during peacetime, while accommodating the military's needs during wartime.

Pershing, who had commanded the American Expeditionary Forces on the Western Front during World War I, was already something of a legend. He was one of only two service members to attain the title General of Armies, and the only one to do so while still on active duty. (The title, equivalent to that of a six-star general, was also bestowed posthumously on George Washington in 1976.)

By the time he delivered the map, Pershing already had at least three major U.S. roads named after him. A larger-than-life figure was making his mark on an informal network of highways that was itself becoming larger, almost by the minute.

## Auto Trails Everywhere

Rand McNally auto trail maps are displayed at a booth, time and location uncertain. By the 1920s, motorists had 18 transcontinental routes from which to choose. *Wikimedia Commons*

# Land of Confusion

By 1926, more than 440 named highways had been plotted out across the country, many of them sharing the same roads for at least a portion of the way. Lincoln Highway sponsors weren't too happy when the Victory Highway piggybacked on some of their route, then grabbed federal funds they felt should have come their way and used them on the Wendover Route.

It didn't matter that the Victory Highway had a high-minded and heroic-sounding name that commemorated the allies' World War I triumph. The Lincoln organizers had been in the trenches — some of them literally — building their highway long before the Victory Highway came along. And the VH wasn't the only Johnny-come-lately seeking to hijack a portion of the Lincoln route.

When the Lee Highway Association formed in 1920, it tried to do the same thing with the Lincoln road through Pennsylvania, before splitting off and heading southward through Virginia.

According to S.M. Johnson, leader of the Lee Highway effort, he had the backing of AAA, which naturally put the Lincolnites on the defensive.

Johnson took great pains to placate the Lincoln Association, stating that he had no interest in placing Lee Highway signs along the older route. He called it "a bad policy to have one route marked with several different kinds of markers," which he said were "unnecessary, misleading and ... (could) result in half a dozen or more different kinds of markers along various identical sections of road."

He said he preferred to simply tell travelers to "follow Lincoln Highway markers" between New York and Philadelphia, criticizing another newer highway for "simply taking about three-quarters of the Lincoln Highway and sections of other well-known roads, and designating them as 'Pershing Highway.' "

The Lee Highway had "strenuously objected" to that, he said.

It wanted no part of any such tactics.

In short, the Lee Highway was on the Lincoln Association's side.

But the Lincolnites wanted there to be no misunderstanding. They had no intention of sharing their highway with the Lee folks, and they resented being called "difficult." So, they fired off an open retort to the *Sunday Times*, defending their position.

A.V. Bemont, vice president of the Lincoln Association, noted that "while we are cooperating in every way possible with the Lee Highway Association and are in full sympathy with its plans, we do strenuously object" — there were those two words again — "to sections of the Lincoln Highway being taken over 'piecemeal' by other organizations and named as parts of other through trans-continental routes."

He concluded: "There is no sense in doing so, and no good can be accomplished, and much confusion can result."

Still, it happened all too frequently.

A section of the Lee Highway in its early years lives up, or down, to its name as an auto trail. *Library of Congress*

A similar dispute arose between the Dixie Highway and the Old Spanish Trail, which shared a section between Tallahassee and Jacksonville in Florida. OST leaders argued that they were there first, with the DH using the road as a connector between its eastern and western branches. The Dixie Highway Association agreed to abandon the route, and in exchange, the OST relinquished its claim to a shared section of road between Jacksonville and St. Augustine.

Elsewhere, one trail overlapped with as many as 11 others. Another road carried eight different trail makers, and 70% of another trail overlapped with various marked routes.

A segment of road in New Mexico was part of the Apache Trail, the Atlantic-Pacific Highway, the Evergreen Highway, the Lee Highway, and the Old Spanish Trail, all at the same time, and it carried their markers to prove it. Complicating things even further, there was a New Santa Fe Trail dreamed up in 1910 to follow the Atchison, Topeka & Santa Fe line, and an Old Santa Fe Trail — which was conceived, oddly, a year *after* the "new" one, but which followed a route that was closer to the actual old trail. Then, there was a Jefferson Highway running north and south, and a Jefferson *Davis* Highway that ran east to west.

Of course, they were named after two very different men.

The Valley Pike in the Shenandoah Valley of Virginia, seen in 1922, was the foundation upon which the Lee Highway was built. *Library of Congress*

## Lee Highway

The Lee Highway was actually the second road proposal to pay tribute to Civil War Confederate Gen. Robert E. Lee.

A project to have been called the Washington and Lee Highway was floated by an engineer named Charles Thatcher, who called himself the "Apostle of Good Roads." Thatcher's proposal was an ambitious one: build a highway that would run from Quebec, Canada, south through Boston and New York to New Orleans, then westward all the way to Los Angeles.

One of the places he visited while promoting the project was Gaffney, S.C., which received a letter in advance of his arrival in 1918. In it, he boasted: "I have been arranging details and laying the foundation of this great project for fifteen years. Hundreds of miles are now paved."

Five years earlier, he'd been calling the project the Magnolia Highway and had proposed a route from New York to Atlanta, then west to New Orleans and L.A.

Both the name and the route had changed since.

According to Hammond, he had recently secured funds to pave a section of road from Hammond, La., to New Orleans, shortening the route by more than 60 miles. He was coming to town with a mule team he claimed to have driven more than 40,000 miles in support of good roads.

"The wagon is now rickety and covered with western curios," he wrote. "It draws like a circus. Advertise it's coming, and the people will crowd to town to see it. My visit can be a monster boost for good roads in your section.

"We are planning that the Washington and Lee Highway be lined with shade and fruit trees along with roses and other beautiful flowers. It will elevate the standard of living. By bringing prosperity, peace, and joy, more of heaven will reign. The passing of the world's war brings a new epoch to our lives. All should rise to the situation and take advantage of the great opportunities. We owe this to civilization."

That was in 1918.

Three years later, Thatcher had put 10,000 more miles on his mule team and was promoting a highway with a slightly different name: the Washington Highway. He died in 1927, and what became of his various proposals is hard to say. He had promoted himself to the press as the "father of the Jackson Highway and the Dixie Highway" — at the very least an exaggeration, and at worst an outright lie. So it's no surprise that the Washington and Lee Highway apparently vanished without a trace.

Meanwhile, however, an actual Lee Highway was taking shape, independently, in the minds of two different men: S.M. Johnson and David Humphreys.

Johnson lived in New Mexico, but his family had roots in Virginia; Humphreys was a professor of engineering at Washington and Lee University in Roanoke, in the eastern part of that state. Humphreys had published some articles proposing that the Shenandoah Valley Pike be extended south to Chattanooga and New Orleans, under the name "Battlefield Highway," "Lee Highway" or, as it was already known, "Valley Highway."

Johnson heard about Humphreys' work and contacted him about joining forces to create such a highway that would span the nation, ending on the West Coast. They were two of 14 men who gathered for a preliminary meeting to discuss the project on Feb. 22, 1919.

An early photo taken along the Lee Highway. *Library of Congress*

AMERICA'S FIRST HIGHWAYS

**Top:** A section of the Lee Highway today between Salem and Roanoke, Va. *Author photo* **Above:** Members of the Lee Highway Association set off on a cross-continent tour. *Library of Congress*

With the exception of Johnson, all those in attendance were from Roanoke, where the meeting was held. Ten months later, in December, the situation was far different: A larger group of some 500 men came from across the country met at the Roanoke Hotel to form the Lee Highway Association.

D.D. Hull Jr., another Roanoke man, was named president of the group, while Johnson was named general director.

For the time being, the Association scaled back the coast-to-coast idea and mapped out a highway that would run from New York to New Orleans (which seemed to be where most of the north-south highways wound up). The following year, the route was extended again, to San Diego, and the Association decided to market it as "The Backbone Road of the South.

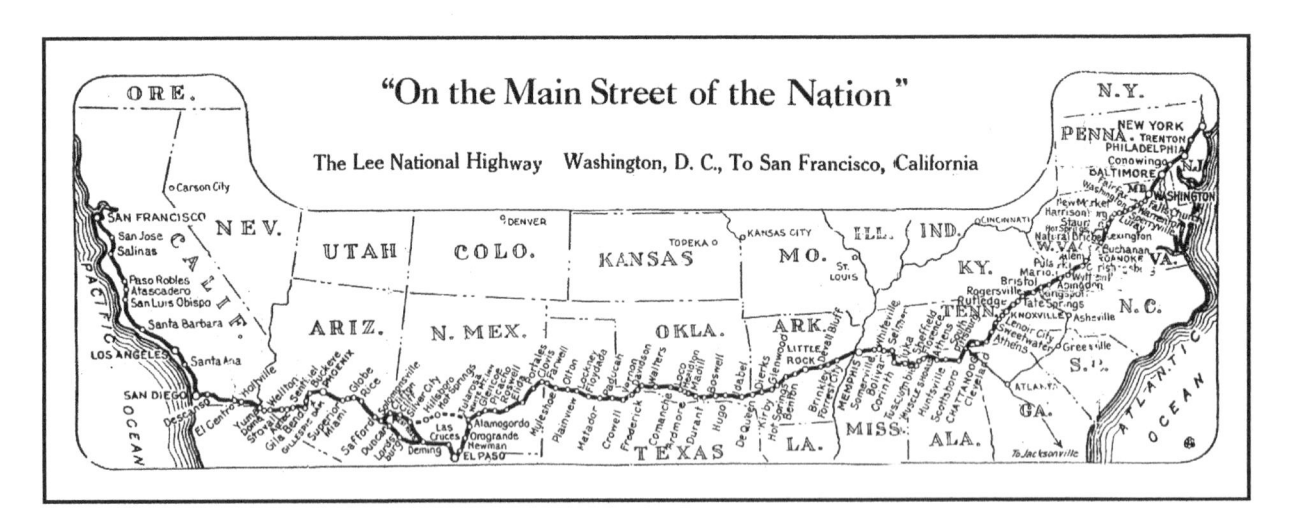

Then in 1921, a year further on, the New Orleans stop was abandoned, because San Antonio and Houston to the west wanted no part of yet another highway: "All feasible routes" through New Orleans and west of that city had already been "preempted by other highways."

The highway ran into the same problem across the Southwest, where there were few roads, so it wound up following portions of the Apache Trail, Atlantic-Pacific Highway, Bankhead Highway and Old Spanish Trail, among others.

In its final form, it ran from Roanoke south through Knoxville and Chattanooga; across an upper sliver of Alabama to Memphis; through Little Rock. Then it progressed across southern Oklahoma and northern Texas to Johnson's town of Roswell, New Mexico, before dipping south to El Paso. From there, it went through Phoenix and Yuma to San Diego (and, according to some maps, up to San Francisco from there).

Ironically, considering it was named for a Southern general, the highway became the first to be marked through Washington, D.C. Johnson oversaw a project to install a zero milestone for the road — and for all other roads leading out of the capital — which took the form of a 4-foot-high pink granite marker placed on the Ellipse behind the White House.

Johnson's daughter later wrote that he considered "promoting a coast-to-coast highway across the southern tier of states as a memorial to General Robert E. Lee ... his crowning achievement."

## Jefferson Davis Highway

The Jefferson Davis Highway was created in 1913 by the United Daughters of the Confederacy as a sort of southern east-west counterpart to the Lincoln Highway in the north.

It made sense, from a Southern point of view, to honor the president of the Confederacy with a coast-to-coast highway. It certainly did to Mrs. Alexander B. White, who envisioned "a big fine highway going all the way through the South."

When she shared the idea with her cousin, she was told there was already a Lincoln Highway.

But it wasn't the same. The Lincoln Highway prided itself in "teaching patriotism (and) sewing up the remaining ragged edges of sectionalism." That's how one motorist put it.

An author in the *Confederate Veteran* responded that northerners didn't have a monopoly on the subject: "The South should not be less patriotic or enterprising than the north," and that creation of the Jefferson Davis Highway would be proof of this fact. And history was just as important to the South as to the North. The United Daughters of the Confederacy argued that, by placing historical markers, they were creating "history for the tourist."

But there was still tension between preserving the South's history while, at the same time, healing the wounds of a war that was then less than a half-century past. Many people were still alive from that time, with vivid and sometimes bitter memories of a bloody and heated conflict.

Besides, history and pragmatism didn't always mix.

In addition to the main route, it wasn't uncommon to designate spur roads with historical significance as part of a named highway, as was the case with the Jefferson Davis road. The UDC created one such road from the main Gulf Coast highway in Beauvoir, Miss. — where Davis settled more than a decade after the Civil War — northward to his birthplace in Fairview, Ky. A second spur, meanwhile, headed north to Irwinsville, Ga., along the route Davis took at the end of the war before he was finally captured.

The decision to create these offshoot roads was not uncommon among auto trail organizers eager to please as many communities as possible. The Lincoln Highway and, to a far greater extent, the Dixie Highway had done the same thing. But it would come back to haunt JDH organizers in later years, when they petitioned the federal government to create a single numbered route from the Jefferson Davis Highway. Such a move would have been unusual: When designating numbered routes for the federal highway system created in 1926, old auto trails weren't typically left intact. Instead, they were splintered up into several different numbered routes.

When the Jefferson Davis Highway group protested this, E.R. James from the Bureau of Public Roads responded that it couldn't make sense of where the route was supposed to be.

He wrote: "A careful search has been made in our extensive map file ... and three maps showing Jefferson Davis highways have been located, but the routes on these maps are themselves different, and neither route is approximately that described by you, so I am somewhat at a loss as to just what route your constituents are interested in." One of the routes he specifically mentioned was the Fairview spur.

But this wasn't the real reason James demurred.

After the UDC protested further, he said plainly that the government had "never officially recognized any of the named trails by various civic organizations." And it did not intend to do so now.

Still, Jefferson Davis Highway advocates were nothing but persistent, continuing to argue that the maps were clear, even as the government repeatedly denied their claims. Years after the routing numbers were in place, they expanded the scope of their highway to include U.S. Highway 99 up the Pacific Coast all the way to Washington state, where the UDC placed a monument near the Canadian border in the 1940s identifying it as such.

It was one of the first things travelers from the north would see upon entering the United States.

But outrage that a champion of the slaveholding South should be so honored led to the state to remove the marker in 2002. As Washington state legislator Hans Dunshee put it, "In this state, we cannot have a monument to a guy who led an insurgency to perpetuate slavery and killed half a million Americans."

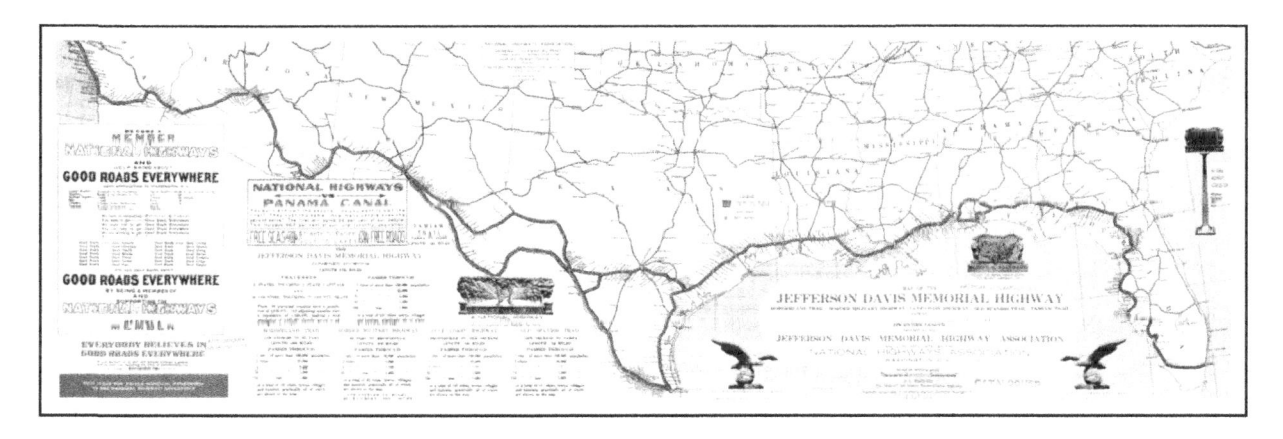

The monument was taken down and eventually moved to a park on private land just north of Portland, Ore. In 2017, a plaque that marked San Diego's Horton Plaza as the highway's original terminus was removed in response to a petition. The monument had been approved, initially, by the mayor and the Park Commission, but the state of California had never been consulted.

There was a similar backlash in Virginia, where the General Assembly had voted in 1922 to designate U.S. Route 1 as the Jefferson Davis Highway in response to a petition by the UDC. The name remained for nearly a century, until a white supremacist's deadly assault on a black church in South Carolina led to calls for an end to memorials glorifying the Confederacy — calls that intensified after George Floyd's brutal death at the hands of a Minneapolis police officer. In a unanimous 2019 vote, Virginia's Commonwealth Transportation Board changed the road's name to the Richmond Highway. Perhaps oddly, calls for a similar name change on the Lee Highway weren't as vocal.

It cost $17,000 to remove the old Jefferson Davis signs. But the Lee Highway signs remained in place, despite the blood on the general's hands in defense of slavery.

# Jackson Highway

Women's groups were frequent sponsors of auto trails, with organizations like the UDC and Daughters of the American Revolution (DAR) coming up with ideas for routes and placing historical markers to help identify them. Often, but not always, they commemorated heroes of wars past and traced the routes those heroes used to march into battle.

- In 1911, Elizabeth Gentry of the DAR founded a publication called *The Old Trails Road, The National Highway*. Bess Truman, the future first lady, became president of that group in 1926, and Mrs. John Trigg came up with the idea of placing ten-foot-tall "Madonna of the Trail" statues in the 12 states through which it passed. (The New York chapter of the DAR similarly marked the Old Post Road to honor writer Washington Irving.)
- As we have seen, Mrs. Alexander B. White of the UDC came up with the idea of the Jefferson Davis Memorial Highway in 1913.
- And the Jackson Highway was the brainchild of a Birmingham woman named Alma Rittenberry, who belonged to a group called the Daughters of 1812.

Rittenberry envisioned a road from Chicago to New Orleans via Alabama that would honor President Andrew Jackson (who, ironically, once vetoed a bill that would have provided money for the National Road). It would be, she said, "a grand road (that) goes through the grandest country on the face of the globe."

She floated the idea at the 1911 National Good Roads Convention in Birmingham and received an enthusiastic response. She was the logical choice to chair of the Jackson Highway Committee of the Alabama Daughters of 1812.

Rittenberry believed so strongly in her cause that she made it her life's mission. In 1912, she and Alabama's first female lawyer, Maud McLure Kelly, spoke to a group of 2,500 delegates at a meeting of the Alabama Good Roads Association in Selma. At a meeting in Pine Hill, Ala., she addressed an even larger crowd of 3,000.

But more importantly, she took her show on the road, traveling up and down her proposed route, touting her plan to chambers of commerce and county commissioners

By 1915, she had made two trips along the entire length of it. She paid her own way on the first trip by selling copies of *Southern Good Roads Magazine*, for which she also wrote articles. On her second journey, she sold postcards of Andrew Jackson.

The response was largely enthusiastic, but also noncommittal.

"In all patriotic work of this kind, with no financial backing ... you always meet with more or less indifference and more or less opposition," she said. "As chairman I have tried ... to interest the various commercial bodies in the different cities through which the Jackson Highway passes. They all endorsed the proposition and assured me of their hearty support and cooperation. But, oh, they seem so long in giving it."

But Rittenberry soon learned that, despite her key role in organizing and promoting the highway, it was still, in this era before women's suffrage, very much a man's world. Although she had been named chair of the Daughters of 1812 highway committee, she'd been relegated to the status of vice president in the Jackson Highway Association, which made the actual decisions.

Before she knew it, members of the JHA had altered her suggested path through Alabama south of Nashville, so that it passed through Mississippi instead. The updated highway was more direct but less historical: Jackson's troops in the Creek War of 1813-14 had marched along the route Rittenberry had suggested, not through Mississippi.

Not only Rittenberry, but the state of Alabama were up in arms.

The majority tried to placate them by proposing a spur route through Alabama, which would be called the Alabama-Jackson Highway. But Rittenberry was having none of it. She stormed the dais, declaring that "if Andrew Jackson knew the unchivalrous act of you men, he would turn in his grave; he at least was courteous to women." Whereupon she resigned as vice president of the group and immediately set about forming a rival association to create a competing National Bee Line Highway along the route she'd originally proposed.

Like the Jackson Highway, it would come down from Chicago to Nashville, but there it would continue through Birmingham, Montgomery and Selma to the Gulf Coast at Mobile, where it would split in two, heading west to New Orleans and eastward into Florida.

The competing and overlapping trails that resulted typified the chaotic nature of auto trails during the 1910s and '20s. New ones emerged, seemingly every week, and there was no central authority to decide where they should be placed, what they should be called or who should run them. It was pretty much a free-for-all.

Even before Rittenberry formed her rival Bee Line Route, the Jackson Highway itself was a model of confusion. A map of the highway and its proposed spur, the Alabama-Jackson Highway, shows two alternative routes in the north as well. The main line envisioned by Rittenberry began in Chicago, but an alternate route is also depicted coming down from Buffalo. It bisects the state of Ohio and heads south into Kentucky, turning west at Lexington, and hooking up with the Chicago route around Louisville.

## Jefferson Highway

The phenomenon was hardly limited to the Jackson Highway.

The Lee Highway not only shared portions of the Lincoln Highway and Old Spanish Trail, when it hit California it veered north up the coast along El Camino Real.

If you wanted to travel north and south through the nation's midsection, you could choose from a handful of different highways with a northern terminus in Winnipeg, Canada. Among them, the King of Trails, Mississippi River Scenic Highway, Meridian Highway, and Blue J Highway.

Foremost among them was the Jefferson Highway, conceived by Edwin T. Meredith of Iowa. Meredith, who served as secretary of agriculture under Woodrow Wilson, founded the Meredith Corporation when he began publishing a magazine called *Successful Farming* in 1902.

Another magazine proved more successful: First published in 1922 under the name *Fruit, Garden and Home*, it was rebranded two years later with its more familiar title: *Better Homes and Gardens*. As of 2020, the company founded by Meredith owned an array of newspapers, websites and magazines, along with television stations that reached 11% of U.S. households.

As an advocate for farmers, it was natural for Meredith to become a champion of better roads, as well. *Successful Farming* ran articles lamenting that bad roads left farmers "imprisoned in mud," echoing the arguments presented in the *Gospel of Good Roads* a decade earlier. The economic and social costs of failing to maintain and improve rural byways were laid out in its pages.

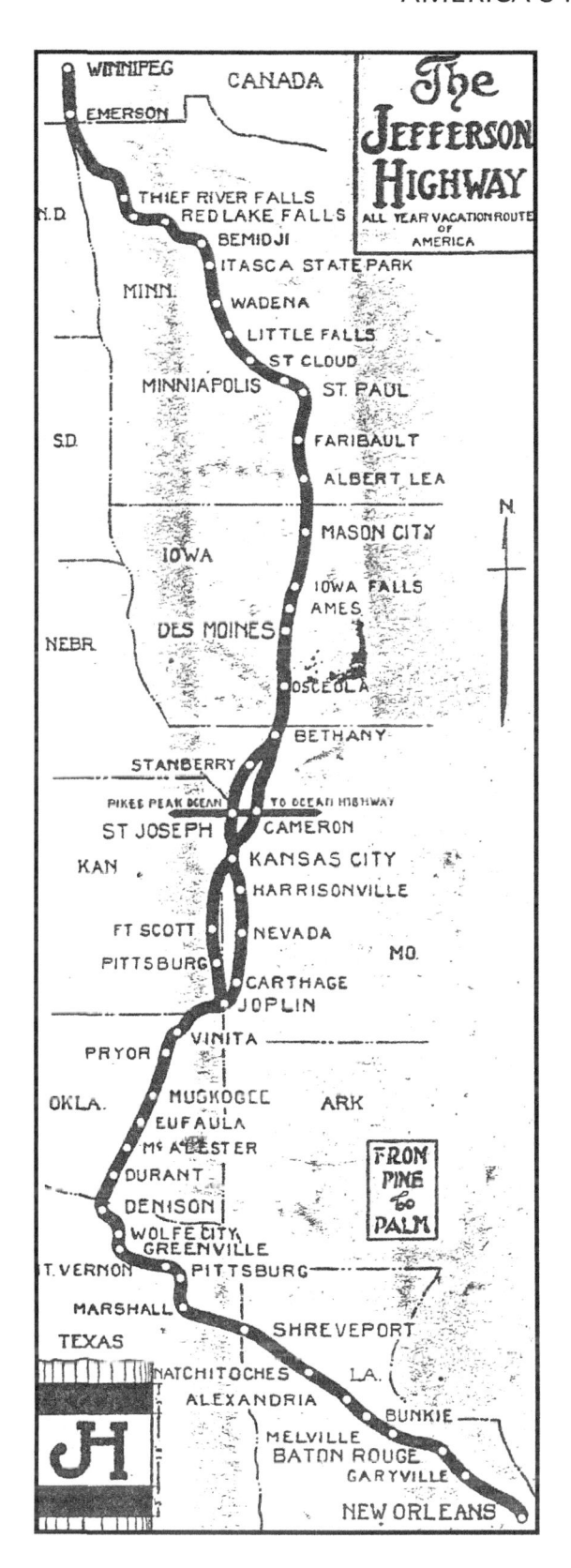

In 1915, however, he embraced a grander vision: a north-south highway from "pine to palm" that would complement the Lincoln Highway. In fact, the two roads would cross paths in Meredith's home state of Iowa, creating a great central intersection for the North American continent. Meredith chose the name Jefferson Highway for his project because most of it would pass through lands that formed part of the Louisiana Purchase engineered by Thomas Jefferson. Unlike the Lincoln Highway, it would be an international road, commencing beyond the Canadian border in Winnipeg and running all the way to New Orleans.

The question was what route it would take.

One idea was to build on the Interstate Trail, a more modest highway that linked Des Moines with Kansas City. The trail, founded in 1911, was later extended northward to St. Paul, Minn. Its supporters felt it was natural to use it as the foundation for Meredith's longer highway. But when delegates to the newly formed Jefferson Highway Association gathered for their first meeting in mid-November of 1915, they brought with them a slew of diverse and competing ideas.

As was often the case at such meetings, every city and chamber of commerce wanted a place by the roadside, and they weren't shy about airing their demands.

At the outset, seven options were set on the table:

- The Meridian Route through Texas, Oklahoma, Kansas, Nebraska and the Dakotas.
- The Parsons Route through different cities in those same states.
- The Eastern Kansas Route, through Arkansas and up across eastern Kansas.
- The Ozark Trail, which followed the Eastern Kansas Route up from New Orleans, then passed through several counties in western Missouri.
- The Interstate Trail.
- The Omaha Route from Kansas City through Sioux City, Iowa, South Dakota and on to Winnipeg.

After two days of heated debate, it was decided to agree upon a series of "cardinal points" — major cities through which the highway would pass — and save a decision on the precise route for later.

In other words, they kicked the can down the still-unbuilt road.

| Cardinal point | State or province | 1910 population |
| --- | --- | --- |
| Winnipeg | Manitoba | 136,035 (1911) |
| Minneapolis | Minnesota | 301,408 |
| St. Paul | Minnesota | 214,744 |
| Des Moines | Iowa | 86,368 |
| St. Joseph | Missouri | 77,403 |
| Kansas City | Missouri | 248,381 |
| Joplin | Missouri | 32,073 |
| Muskogee | Oklahoma | 25,278 |
| Denison | Texas | 13,632 |
| Shreveport | Louisiana | 28,015 |
| Alexandria | Louisiana | 11,213 |
| Baton Rouge | Louisiana | 14,897 |
| New Orleans | Louisiana | 339,075 |

# AMERICA'S FIRST HIGHWAYS

A stretch of Jefferson Highway near Leon, Iowa, in 1917. *Wikimedia Commons*

But the choice of so many cardinal points (there were 13 in all) solidified the position of the Interstate Route as foundational for the new highway, and effectively eliminated several cities from consideration because they were too far off to one side or the other. One of those cities was Chillicothe, Mo., which was due south of Des Moines but about 75 miles east of St. Joseph — one of those "cardinal points."

With a population of just over 6,200 people, Chillicothe was smaller than any of the cities guaranteed spots along the highway. It was less than one-tenth the size of St. Joseph, which would become the Jefferson Highway's headquarters. Size was important, because it made sense, for several reasons, to run the road through major cities. For one thing, big cities attracted more visitors; for another, they contributed more revenue.

This second factor was a big deal, because if the highway association ran into financial trouble, it would need the cities to bail it out. In 1918, that very thing happened, and the association's general manager responded by putting the cities on the spot. If the cities failed to pay their assessments, he reserved the right to kick them off the highway and reroute it somewhere else.

This actually happened five times.

Whether Chillicothe was bypassed because of its small size or for some other reason, native son Harry Graham was furious that his town had been slighted. Graham had touted the Chillicothe Route as the best and most direct, and had been led to believe that it was still under consideration. According to his hometown paper, the *Chillicothe Constitution*, an initial caucus of delegates had agreed unanimously not to favor one route over the other; but after officers were elected, the decision was reversed, with the Chillicothe route being cast aside.

Graham responded by calling a meeting of his own that very night, to which he invited delegates from central Iowa and Missouri whose towns and counties had been shunted aside. Together, they organized what they called the Jefferson Highway-Blue J Route, adopting a blue "J" on a white bar sandwiched between two red stripes as their marker.

According to the *Constitution*, Graham then hopped aboard a train and went to Jefferson City, where he registered the highway name and marker — a step he repeated in other states along the route. The newspaper reported that Graham's breakaway group caused the delegates who had supported the St. Joseph route "no small amount of worry (because) they could not use the letter, blue J." Instead, the settled on a logo that merged the letters J and H in a black monogram set against 12-inch white band and sandwiched between two blue stripes.

Bad blood boiled on both sides.

*The Constitution* said the main group held "indignation meetings condemning Graham for his action, published him as a robber and finally hung him in effigy."

Graham wasted little time in producing a promotional map for the Blue J Route that urged motorists to "follow the blue 'J' marker, direct as the blue jay flies," proclaiming it "The Short Way" Jefferson Highway. Graham even had the audacity to christen his new group the Jefferson Highway in Contest Association, because he was contesting the original route.

And he sent a letter to the Iowa Highway Commission seeking formal recognition.

Instead of responding immediately, however, the commission informed Meredith and his group of this new development. This was the first they'd heard of it, and they were, understandably, less than pleased.

J S Clarkson, general manager of the group, fired off a letter of protest to the commission in January of 1917. The Jefferson Highway Association, he said, "would regard the registration of the 'Jefferson Highway in Contest' (name) ... to be a decided infringement upon our rights, and as tending to confuse the traveling public, whose rights are even greater than ours."

Clarkson insisted that the JHA had "no objection whatsoever" to the rival group registering its route as simply the Blue J Trail, "as that is a distinctive mark that carries its own meaning."

He warned, however, that any claim to the Jefferson Highway name could lead to "a storm of protest" within Iowa or even along the entire length of the road from Winnipeg to New Orleans. Clarkson pointed out that there were "thousands of people" who were "taking a vital interest in the Jefferson Highway." He implied that these people could be counted on to support the established highway, fiercely and vocally. But it didn't have to come to that. Clarkson trusted the commission to do the right thing and support the JHA.

That trust turned out to be well placed.

Less than a month later, the commission sent a letter to the spinoff group denying its request as "a decided infringement on the rights of the Jefferson Highway Association." In a stinging rebuke that amounted to stating the obvious, it declared that "the law which provides for the registration of highway routes was intended to prevent just such conflicts as this would bring about."

It enclosed a new, blank application, along with a bit of advice: "As your route seems to be very widely known as the Blue J Trail, it occurs to us that this would be a very good name under which to register your association in this state."

That wasn't the end of the matter, though. In April, just two months later, a sign mysteriously appeared at the Blue J's junction with the Jefferson Highway south of Des Moines. The sign referred to the upstart highway by the Jefferson name, and the entire controversy was rebooted: The JHA contacted the Iowa commission, which investigated and sent a cease-and-desist letter to the Blue J leaders. They, in turn, insisted they'd done nothing wrong. The sign, they said, "must have been placed there by Missouri men while marking the route to Des Moines and boosting Excelsior Springs."

Left unexplained was what "Missouri men" had been doing so far from the town outside Kansas City they were allegedly promoting. However it might have gotten there, the Iowa Blue J promised to send a crew out to remark the highway as soon as weather permitted. Even so, the *Chillicothe Constitution*, Harry Graham's hometown newspaper, continued to insist on calling the route through its town the "Jefferson Highway-Blue J Route" as late as 1921.

In 1925, Graham got a call from W.M. Jardine, the man who held Meredith's old job as secretary of agriculture. According to the *Constitution*, Jardine was calling in order to congratulate him and his Blue J Highway on "winning out" in the federal transition from trail names to numbered roads. As a result of that conversion, Chillicothe wound up on not one but two federal highways: Route 36, an east-west section of the former Pikes Peak Ocean to Ocean Highway, and Route 65, running north and south.

Although most of the new numbered highways didn't follow the old auto trails exactly, it was 65 — which traced the old Blue J through Chillicothe — that most closely approximated the route of the old Jefferson Highway.

Harry Graham's insurgency had worked.

He had won, after all.

## Competitive Spirit

Graham wasn't the only one who spent considerable effort jockeying for a spot on the highway.

In 1918, Platte County in Missouri, just north of Kansas City, voted down $1 million in bonds to build a countywide system of roads. It wasn't close: The bond failed by a 2-1 margin. But less than a year later, a crowd of county residents gathered at the county seat to use their might and muscle in an effort to improve a section of road they hoped would be part of the Jefferson Highway.

The winter's worst blizzard had just passed through, and the snow had melted, leaving the road a mucky mess. But that didn't stop farmers and townsfolk from gathering to build a road through their community.

"I've seldom seen a crowd so large as this," one restaurant owner remarked. "Even in dry weather I don't remember having such a crowd as we have had for dinner today. There's some sort of road meeting going on. I think it's something about this Jefferson Highway."

The leader of the effort, a man by the name of C.V. "Charley" Hull, said the Jefferson

Highway's general manager had held five meetings in Platte County, but the highway itself had chosen a different route.

He wanted to change that.

"The Jefferson Highway missed us, and we want it to come over to our road," he explained. "I had previously filed a contest, showing that the distance would be shortened over two miles between St. Joseph and Kansas City."

Hull went around talking up the Jefferson Highway Association, asking his neighbors to join. But if the county didn't even have a road yet, how could it lure the highway folks? That's what at least one of those neighbors, a certain John S. Williams, wanted to know before he signed on the dotted line — and ponied up a membership fee. "What good will memberships do if we don't have a road?" he asked.

Hull retorted: "What good will the road do if we don't get the highway?"

Williams found the argument persuasive enough to donate $500, a far from paltry sum that would amount to nearly $7,500 in 2020.

In all, the campaign raised $17,000.

Other cities left off the approved route took a different approach. Instead of trying to earn a spot on the Jefferson Highway, they followed the Blue J Route's example and formed their own competing lines. Towns that failed to make the cut for the Jefferson route banded together in the aftermath of that vote and formed rival highways such as the Mississippi River Scenic Highway and Pershing Way. Both shared the Jefferson's northern terminus of Winnipeg and passed through Iowa on their way south to New Orleans. Another highway founded in 1917, the King of Trails, also started in Winnipeg but took a more westerly route, following the Missouri River in Iowa and winding up in Galveston, Texas.

But New Orleans was perhaps the most popular stop on American auto trails. In 1919, no fewer than 13 highways passed through it, according to one count. The city's association of commerce even adopted the slogan: "As the highways in Europe led to Rome, so the highways of the United States are leading to New Orleans."

The Jefferson Highway branded itself as the Vacation Route of America, touting the fact that it offered different climates as one traveled from north to south (or vice versa). Of course, it was not always advisable to do so — especially in the dead of winter. But that didn't stop the Jefferson Highway Association from organizing another in a series of "sociability runs" in 1926, a decade after the first one.

A hotel and café along the Jefferson Highway in Melville, La., is flooded after the Atchafalaya River in St. Landry Parish overflowed its banks in 1927. *Library of Congress*

By this time, roads were becoming good enough to host social trips rather than the "reliability runs" of the past. In the words of JHA President Hugh Shepard, the runs were organized to promote "an interchange of friendly relations between the communities along the highway."

They were also a chance to promote the highway: On the first tour in 1916, a participant from the New Orleans Association of Commerce reported giving 60 short speeches lauding his city. Nearly 2,800 cars took part in that first tour, with every stop along the way getting into the spirit of things. At each town, Jefferson Highway signs spanned the road, and enthusiastic crowds greeted the cars on their arrival.

By the time the 1926 run came along, work on the highway was nearly complete. The section through Louisiana was finished, and the final section of an 835-mile stretch between Winnipeg and Des Moines was scheduled to be wrapped up by the end of the season. It seemed the perfect time to show off all that had been accomplished.

Well, not *quite* perfect.

There was this small matter of a blizzard that was moving across Iowa.

Fred White, chief engineer of that state's highway commission, warned the JHA that a sociability run might not be the best idea under the conditions. If they chose to pass through Iowa during January, he said, they'd be "taking a big chance."

"The highway may be in perfect condition one day, and the next day it may be hopelessly snowbound," he cautioned. The winter season had already produced a lot of snow, and roads had frequently been blocked by the white stuff. He concluded that "personally, regardless of whether the roads are surfaced or not, I would not undertake a drive at this season of the year from Winnipeg, Canada, to St. Joseph, Missouri."

But the run not only went ahead as scheduled, the cars even managed to reach New Orleans on time.

## Pike's Peak Ocean to Ocean Highway

For a time, the Jefferson Highway formed a partnership of sorts with a unique east-west auto trail called the Pike's Peak Ocean to Ocean Highway. If you think that's a mouthful, its full name for a time added the moniker "The Pershing Transportation Route." Which was not to be confused with the Pershing Way, a north-south auto trail that ran from Winnipeg to New Orleans.

There was also a Pershing Highway in Florida, a red-brick road that ran east from the state's interior to Daytona Beach.

In response to the Pike's Peak tribute, Gen. Pershing wrote: "Appreciate the honor Missouri pays her gallant troops in wishing to call that part of the Ocean to Ocean highway, which passes through the state 'The Pershing Transport' Route. Am pleased to accept the compliment in their name."

The name never became commonly used for the highway, though, which seemed to be continually undergoing one sort of change or another throughout its history. Although it was one of the most picturesque of the national auto trails, it's also one of the least widely remembered today, for reasons that will become clear.

The PP-OO, as it was known for short, was formed in part as a reaction to the Lincoln Highway's decision to bypass Colorado. Highway boosters there, who had invested a lot of time and money in pitching their state to Carl Fisher during his pathfinding tour of 1913, felt jilted and began casting about for other prospects. The PP-OO fit the bill perfectly. It had already formed an association of its own a year earlier, and it was based in Colorado Springs.

The PP-OO was planned initially as a continuation of the so-called Golden Belt Route through Kansas — another state left off the Lincoln Highway's map. But the centerpiece of the highway was Pikes Peak (the mountain's name had officially been modernized to remove the apostrophe, but the highway retained its original spelling). The highest peak in the Front Range of

A car makes its way through Ute Pass, the focal point of the Pike's Peak Ocean to Ocean Highway, in this vintage postcard.

the Rocky Mountains at more than 14,000 feet, the snow-capped summit would tower over the planned highway as it made its way through the Ute Pass to the north.

The pass, which ranges in elevation from a little more than 6,000 to above 9,000 feet, began as a buffalo trail used by bison and Native Americans. By the 1860s, it had become a wagon road, which was in turn used by motorists with the arrival of the automobile age.

> **The Cross Roads of the Nation Serve all Latitudes and Longitudes**
> They Intersect all North and South, East and West Transcontinental Routes
>
> **THE JEFFERSON HIGHWAY** and **PIKES PEAK OCEAN TO OCEAN HIGHWAY**
>
> The Avenue from the Bread Basket of the World to the Land of Cotton, Palms and Romance.
>
> **Winnipeg—2300 Miles—New Orleans**
>
> The Jefferson Highway traverses the heart of the richest country on the globe, and one filled with romance and sentiment. It connects Acadia, the Land of Evangeline, with the lake region and pine forests of the great North-land; the land which stretches away across lake and plain, through forests and over mountain tops, to the Hudson Bay country. It extends through the cotton plantations of the South and the oil districts of Louisiana and Oklahoma, across the great corn belt of the trans-Mississippi country, through the zinc mining districts of Missouri to the vast wheat fields of Minnesota and Canada.
>
> The Street from Hell's Gate to the Golden Gate.
>
> **New York—3564 Miles—San Francisco**
>
> The Pikes Peak Ocean to Ocean Highway is the superlative scenic route. Leading to places of beauty and grandeur, it gives expression to the "See America" idea. But it is more than a sight-seer's road—it binds together the work shops of the industrial centers with the treasure chests of the mountains. It is an artery of travel that gives life to the commercial, industrial, agricultural and mining districts of the first magnitude.
>
> **For Touring Information Address Either Association at St. Joseph, Mo.**

In 1919, the Pike's Peak Ocean to Ocean Highway formed a partnership with the Jefferson Highway, moving its headquarters to St. Joseph, Mo., where the two roads met. The Jefferson group had recently adopted a financing plan patterned after the U.S. government's war-bond effort. The idea was to sell individual memberships for $25 apiece to rural residents, to go with "club memberships" in the seven largest cities along the route. The concept impressed the PP-OO Association so much that it pursued a de facto merger with the Jefferson Highway group.

Not only did the two associations share the same headquarters, they also jointly published a magazine called *The Modern Highway*. The Jefferson Highway Association's general manager, meanwhile, took over the same duties for the PP-OO group.

But the Pike's Peak Ocean to Ocean Highway never seemed to know exactly what it wanted to be. Historian Richard F. Weingroff of the Federal Highway Administration would call it "the highway that couldn't make up its mind."

The Association styled itself as the "Appian Way of America," after the famous

Roman road to the Adriatic Sea, and touted its central path across the continent: between the Lincoln Highway to the north and the National Old Trails Highway to the south. But whereas its original route took travelers through several major cities between the two coasts, organizers gradually adopted a more rural, scenic focus.

In a way, the PP-OO pioneered the concept of the bypass. West of New Jersey, the biggest city on the route was Harrisburg, Pa.

The shift was explained in a 1924 article for the *Citizens Good Roads Association* magazine. "When the ... route was first laid out in 1913, the principal cities in the central part of the United States were included." Among them: Philadelphia, Pittsburgh, Columbus, Indianapolis, Denver and Salt Lake City. But "the demand of the tourist that he be given a route eliminating the larger cities, because of delays, traffic ordinances, etc., caused this to change."

The result: "The tourist can make the best time to the territory where he wants to spend his vacation, instead of spending his vacation in getting there."

The article insisted there were enough hotels, garages and eateries along the way to serve the motor tourist, and it also declared that "you can't get lost on the Pikes Peak Highway," because it was so clearly marked. The problem, though, was that the route itself seemed to change so frequently. The highway originally went through Reno to San Francisco, but in 1924, it shifted its western endpoint to Los Angeles, leaving northern Nevada out of the loop. The decision would spark a bitter backlash from the press in Reno, as we shall see.

Three years later, it adopted new alignments in three different locations: in Colorado's Eleven Mile Canyon, through the Mojave Desert in California, and heading out of New York City to bypass Newark. This last change was made in keeping with its goal of "avoiding all large cities where traffic congestion retards the progress of the through motorist," the Association said. At least, it was being consistent in that.

But by this time, the new federal highway system was already in place, and although the PP-OO Association stayed active into the 1930s, the writing was on the wall. In late 1931, it celebrated the completion of a new paved section in Missouri, leaving just a 300-mile section of Kansas unpaved along the entire length of the highway.

The association's insistence on taking the scenic route, however, all but guaranteed it would fade into obscurity.

# AMERICA'S FIRST HIGHWAYS

## Major Auto Trails

| Name | Starting point | Destination |
| --- | --- | --- |
| **Atlantic Highway** | Fort Kent, Maine | Miami |
| **Bankhead Highway** | Washington, D.C. | San Diego |
| **Dixie Highway** | Sault Ste. Marie, Mich. | Miami |
| **Dixie Overland Highway** | Savannah, Ga. | San Diego |
| **El Camino Real** | Mexican Border | Sonoma, Calif. |
| **Jackson Highway** | Chicago | New Orleans |
| **Jefferson Davis Highway** | Arlington, Va. | San Diego |
| **Jefferson Highway** | Winnipeg, Manitoba | New Orleans |
| **King of Trails** | Winnipeg, Manitoba | Galveston, Texas |
| **Lee Highway** | Washington, D.C. | San Diego |
| **Lincoln Highway** | New York | San Francisco |
| **Meridian Highway** | Winnipeg, Manitoba | Mexico City |
| **Midland Trail** | Washington, D.C. | Los Angeles |
| **Mississippi River Scenic Hwy.** | Winnipeg, Manitoba | Port Arthur, Texas |
| **National Old Trails Road** | Baltimore | San Francisco |
| **National Park to Park Hwy.** | Loop | 12 National Parks |
| **New Santa Fe Trail** | Kansas City | Los Angeles |
| **Old Spanish Trail** | St. Augustine, Fla. | San Diego |
| **Ozark Trails** | St. Louis | El Paso, Texas |
| **Pacific Highway** | Vancouver, B.C. | San Diego |
| **Pershing Way** | Winnipeg, Manitoba | New Orleans |
| **Pike's Peak Ocean to Ocean Hwy.** | New York | Los Angeles |
| **Theodore Roosevelt Int'l Hwy.** | Portland, Me. | Portland, Ore. |
| **Victory Highway** | New York | San Francisco |
| **Yellowstone Trail** | Plymouth, Mass. | Seattle |

## Yellowstone Trail

If you didn't want to cross the Arizona desert or the Utah salt flats, you had a third option for crossing the continent: You could take the Yellowstone Trail. Like the Pike's Peak Ocean to Ocean Highway, it tied its identity to that of a scenic natural wonder: in this case, the first U.S. national park.

The trail began as a more modest effort to build a road in South Dakota between the booming city of Aberdeen, which had more than doubled in size to 10,000 residents from 1900 to 1910, and the town of Ipswich, less than 30 miles to the west. Aberdeen made sense: At the time, it was the second-biggest city in South Dakota, trailing only Sioux Falls (it's since fallen to third behind Rapid City).

Ipswich, by contrast, was about one-tenth that size. The city proper had barely 800 residents, but one of them was a man named Joseph William Lincoln Parmley, a lawyer and, later, a judge who had been elected to the state legislature in 1905 and re-elected two years later.

Parmley's big passion was the automobile. He bought his first car the same year he joined the legislature, and his grandson would later recall that he always had at least two cars "during his prosperous years." He had the wheels. But like other car owners of the period, he lacked a good road upon which to drive, so he introduced a bill that would have allowed counties to collect money for road development.

It failed.

Farmers weren't convinced it would improve rural roads and thought all the money would be used for major thoroughfares that would just bring more traffic into town.

One farmer, a certain W.H. Wenz, told the *Aberdeen Democrat* that "if the bill should unfortunately become a law ... it would be 15 to 20 years before any work would be done on any lateral or less traveled roads, the entire fund being devoted to work on the main highways of the county, over which the principal automobile traffic would naturally go.

"Although most of the money would be expended on these main roads, as Mr. Wenz views it, few farmers, much less their wives or daughters, would dare venture on them with the autos scorching every few minutes one way or the other over them." Wenz told the newspaper that the farmers' wives would rather order from catalog houses than "brave the autos," and that the result would hurt local merchants' business.

But Parmley was undeterred. It wasn't long before he began promoting the idea of a graded road between his hometown and Aberdeen. The main problem was Helgerson Slough, a spot in the road where cars habitually got bogged down.

Literally.

"We want your help to put a grade across Helgerson Slough," Parmley told a group of businessmen, "so that when our people want to buy their spring millinery of your merchants, they can do so without getting stuck in Helgerson."

Parmley had clearly learned his lesson. By appealing to local businesses — the very group that the Farmer Wenz had complained would suffer as a result of better cross-country roads — he turned the old argument on its head. As a result, he won enough backing to build a graded road between the two towns and render the slough irrelevant to travelers.

In the meantime, farmers who were bringing in good crops earned enough money to purchase cars of their own, and began to look more favorably on the idea of better roads.

By the fall of 1910, Parmley had been named president of the South Dakota Good Roads Association, and had begun pushing for a convention of road boosters to be attended by delegates from every town in the Dakotas. Around the same time, the Minneapolis Tribune sponsored a two-day reliability run from its own city to Aberdeen. The pace car went 18 miles off course just before Aberdeen, but the event was judged a success and heightened interest in better roads across the region.

Parmley and others took hold of that momentum.

Also in 1910, Parmley led a pathfinding caravan over the rugged country between Aberdeen and Mobridge on the Missouri River, more than 100 miles to the west. His vision soon expanded from that of a road linking his hometown to Aberdeen, to one that traversed almost half of South Dakota.

The Aberdeen-to-Ipswich road had begun to attract attention, and a friend of Parmley's named F.A. Finch from Lemmon (a small town near the state line between the two Dakotas) headed down to Ipswich for a chat. After checking out the new road, Finch was duly impressed and had a proposition for Parmley: "We want to hitch onto this," he said.

"We'll come in on this. Bet Mobridge, MacLoughlin, and some of those other towns will jump in."

Aberdeen, S.D., as seen in 1910, when it was the state's second-largest city. *Library of Congress*

"Sure," Parmley said. "We'll just hook up—"

Finch finished his sentence: "Minneapolis with the Yellowstone National Park. What do you say?"

Parmley thought the idea was a good one, and the two started ticking off names of movers and shakers who might be interested in supporting such a project.

A lot of people wanted to call it the Parmley Highway, but Parmley himself wasn't too keen on that idea. He started thinking about extending the trail past Yellowstone and all the way to the West Coast. As the concept grew, so did the name, morphing into the unwieldy Twin Cities-Aberdeen-Yellowstone Park Trail. In 1912, Parmley called together a group of boosters in Lemmon, and they formed an official group to promote the project, which ultimately expanded eastward, as well. The concept became a transcontinental highway across the northern reaches of the United States "from Plymouth Rock to Puget Sound."

A 1920 map showed the highway traversing Upstate New York to Buffalo from the east, then following the southern contours of Lake Ontario and Lake Erie to Toledo, Ohio. From there, it hooked down to Fort Wayne, Ind., and up through Chicago and Milwaukee into northern Wisconsin before heading west again toward Minneapolis.

Long before that map was made, they had started calling it simply the "Yellowstone Trail," a road marked with yellow bands and black arrows painted on trees, telephone poles and (in Montana and the Dakotas) sandstone pillars 6 to 10 feet tall. The only example of this last kind of marker remaining today is an obelisk in Hettinger, S.D.

It was one thing to have a name and trail markers, but quite another to have a road all the way to Yellowstone and beyond, especially when Helgerson Slough wasn't the only obstacle — or even the most formidable one. Enthusiasm was high among those along the proposed route, and on May 22, 1912, thousands of farmers turned out, businesses closed up shop, and residents grabbed shovels, picks and other tools to help improve the road.

It was one of several such "trail days" at which residents of various towns along the route donated their labor to the cause of better roads. And they weren't just held in the western wilderness, either. Among trail days held in 1915 was one at Marshfield, Wis., in June and another about 50 miles east in Amherst the following month. The *Amherst Advocate* urged its readers to "bring your shovels, spades, hoes, rakes, picks and whatever other implements you have that could be made to do some good road work and come out with the Trail Builders."

More than 100 men came out in Amherst, Wis., in July, and a second trail day was set for the following month. With many farmers occupied by harvest season, the turnout for this second event was slightly smaller, at 80 men, but the enthusiasm remained.

But sheer manpower alone couldn't create the road, which had to cross the Little Missouri River in Eastern South Dakota and the Powder River in Montana. The area around the Powder was so sparsely populated that the new $40,000 bridge that was needed to cross it "didn't serve a dozen local people," according to an article by F.L. Clark in the May 1917 *Road-Maker*. Unfortunately, that didn't make it any less necessary.

The Little Missouri was an even bigger problem, Clark wrote, because it was highly unpredictable: It might be "a purling brook today and tomorrow a torrent a quarter mile wide." The Trail Association built a temporary wooden bridge over it — only to see it washed away downstream. And when a steam ferryboat was tried, it broke down. County commissioners tried to raise money for a concrete-and-steel span using a levy, but the project was delayed for a year when taxpayers obtained first one injunction and then another.

The highway bridge across the Missouri River at Mobridge, S.D., after it opened in 1924. *Bridgehunter*

Of course, the biggest obstacle was the Missouri River itself, which crossed paths with the Yellowstone Trail at the ironically named Mobridge. The town had been christened based on the fact that a *railroad* bridge had been built there in 1906 — the year the city was founded as a stop along the Chicago, Milwaukee, St. Paul and Pacific line. It lacked, however, a highway bridge. From 1907 to 1922, motorists could cross the frozen river in winter, but had to hope the ice would hold. In spring, they could take the ferry, but that could be just as risky because the melting ice raised the water level and made crossing a tricky endeavor at best.

Meanwhile, traffic was increasing as more people bought cars, and more drivers started using the Yellowstone Trail. Seven-hundred cars used the ferry in all of 1913, and a year later, Parmley visited the area to see about having a bridge built there. But his efforts came to naught, and the ferry remained the only option: By 1922, traffic had grown so heavy that 700 cars crossed via the ferry in the span of just 15 days.

Part of the reason was Yellowstone Park itself, which was opened to automobiles for the first time in 1915. This, of course, led to an increase in cars on the trail. The following year, more than 4,100 automobiles went 1,100 miles or more on the still-largely gravel and dirt highway.

A pontoon bridge opened in 1922, but it was supported by 52 boats so it had to be taken down before the river froze over. It wasn't until late 1924 that a permanent bridge finally opened.

The bridges were necessary, but not sufficient, to make a highway.

The YT's main competition was the Lincoln Highway, which ran parallel but a little south and got started a year later — but had a lot more financial backing. The Lincoln was also much more centrally planned. Whereas it had been mapped out in advance by Henry Joy, the Yellowstone Trail left that task to various county leaders.

As with all the highway boosters, the Yellowstone stalwarts touted their highway as the best, especially when compared to the alternative.

"From Minneapolis to Aberdeen, S.D., over two-thirds of the road is graveled," Clark enthused in *The Road-Maker*, leaving aside the fact that the distance between these two cities was just 17% of the way to the Pacific Coast.

As for the western part of the road, Clark put the best face on this, as well: "Through the Dakotas and Montana, the road has been graded, bridged and provided with hundreds of cement culverts, and some graveling has been done."

Of course, the word "some" might have meant anything.

Boosters always put the best face on such descriptions — especially in trail association journals, which downplayed the negative aspects of taking a favored route. The same was true of trade magazines, many of which accepted articles directly from trail boosters and which, in any case, wanted to promote auto touring in general. Individual tourists had their favorites, as well.

A writer named Frederic Van de Water discovered this firsthand when planning a trip west with his family — an adventure he recounted in his 1927 book *The Family Flivvers to Frisco*.

When inquiring about which road was most reliable, he was told, "You'll do much better to take the Yellowstone Trail."

"Beware the Lincoln Highway," he was warned. It was supposedly torn up, "filled with detours" and "deep in dust." Van de Water later reflected on this less-than-reliable advice, musing that it seemed customary to badmouth the Lincoln Highway, even though it was "undoubtedly the best of the transcontinental roads."

"Why it is decried," he wrote, "we never discovered. Probably because it is the best."

Or perhaps because someone was putting him on.

Or maybe, just maybe, he'd unwittingly taken advice from a Yellowstone Trail booster.

Once he got on the trail, however, he realized that his chosen route would be no Sunday drive through the park. Yes, meadowlarks serenaded his family, but the sweet sound of their call soon gave way to fits of hacking at the dust kicked up as his car "rattled along on dust and gravel."

"We sneezed and coughed in its billowing dust clouds and thought, poor gullible innocents that we were, how much more those who traveled on the Lincoln Highway must be suffering. Our acquaintance with road liars had just begun."

Still, for many auto tourists, the adventure of "roughing it" was part of the charm. They had become tired of train travel and wanted to see the wonders of America on their own terms. Many of those wonders — Yellowstone, Yosemite, the Grand Canyon, the Rocky Mountains and more — were in the great untamed West. They didn't want the scenery to whizz by at 60 mph the way it did aboard the train. They wanted to take their time and soak it all in.

And they definitely were tired of cities. Sure, you might get some dust in your eyes, but was that so much worse than soot and ash from a smokestack? You might break get stuck crossing a slough, but at least it was a change of pace. Then there was the scenery. The only time a train slowed down was when it was coming into a city. Then, you could finally see something. But that "something" was a cluttered landscape of tall, drab buildings that looked like soulless giants frozen in place by the lethargy of their humdrum existence. Posted bills, frayed at the edges; smoky skies; and gray-garbed men scurrying about like so many rats in search of crumbs. That wasn't scenery. It was a tableau of life at its grittiest and most mundane.

The contrast was presented in stark detail by two writers of the era.

On a train, Julian Street wrote in 1914, "towns and cities flash by, one after another, in quick succession, as the floors flash by an express elevator." Then, when you get to the city, "outside are factories and railroad yards, and everywhere tall black chimneys vomiting their heavy, muddy smoke."

Motorcyclist R.S. Spears, meanwhile, wrote in 1916 about his time on the Yellowstone Trail: "When I pulled west, I began to pass little lakes, surrounded by woods and patches of reeds and grass through which muskrats had cut their swimways and where the mink hunt. There were gray squirrels in the trees and along the roads. It was a land of knolls, and the road ran with short turns and sharp pitches, with villages here and there, and between farms of undeniable prosperity."

Then, there was the lure of the breathtaking scenery beyond, contained in the name of the highway itself.

*J.Ridge, Creative Commons CCBY2.5*

Yellowstone was a name that fired the imagination for tourists eager to throw off the iron shackles of rail-bound transportation and set out exploring on their own. And most tourists who set out on the Yellowstone Trail expected to find adventure, not luxury. Spears described how he come across the trail on a large map: "The black letters caught my eye," he wrote, "as the name catches the attention, or the psyche, with the promise of something new and remarkable."

And, it seems, hard to find: Spears set out from Minneapolis, but had a hard time locating exactly where the trail began.

"People," he lamented, "could not give me understandable directions." One person referred him to a doctor "two blocks up and one block over" who had (supposedly) been on the trail when it was laid out. Another told Spears he'd have no problem finding it once he got to "the Lakes, or Lake Avenue, or something like that." A third said, "You can't miss it! Not after you turn to the right, go around the lake, and hit, let's see, one, two, three — three or four blocks out, and then you're all right!"

He finally just headed west by southwest until he stumbled upon a "fine, broad way" lined with poles that carried a three-banded marker: a white stripe sandwiched between two yellow ones. The Yellowstone Trail.

## Ozark Trails

Although they didn't span the United States, the regional Ozark Trails (plural) were an interesting phenomenon — and a precursor, as we shall see, to Route 66.

The network of trails was centered on Oklahoma and spread west as far as New Mexico and El Paso, while branching east as far as St. Louis. There were no fewer than 11 branches, covering some 1,500 miles, but like many other early trail projects, the network was more concept than reality.

"No effort will be made at present to grade the roads," the *Afton American* reported in May of 1913 when it announced the project. "But the route is carefully selected over the best roads, and it is certain that the dwellers along the line selected will take pride in the fact and a better thoroughfare will be gradually stimulated."

This was no Field of Dreams.

The process went more like this: If we announce it, they will pay for it... and *then* we (or they) will build it.

The route would be marked initially by white rings on telephone poles, trees and bridges. This would be followed only later by copyrighted signs bearing the green letters O.T.

If towns didn't get behind the effort, they'd be scratched off the map and replaced before the white paint dried, trails founder W.H. "Coin" Harvey warned.

The routing was being set, he explained, "as early as possible to avoid unenterprising towns." As for those towns that *were* included but refused to pitch in, "should they continue to sleep on their opportunity, the route will be changed. The white markings will be tentative, so that the route can be changed easily before the green marking goes on. In the meantime, their county will suffer from loss of reputation by not being enterprising people" if they don't contribute.

Harvey was a colorful character to say the least. A lawyer by training, he eventually quit practicing and went into real estate, after which he began taking an interest in politics. The issue that drew his interest was "free silver" — the unlimited coinage of silver into money.

Such a policy would have expanded the amount of money available beyond the then-current gold standard. Under that standard, federal currency was backed exclusively by gold, and creditors retained the right to demand payment in gold. The U.S. would eventually abandon this policy during the Great Depression, but at the turn of the 20th century, a number of populist politicians wanted to create a "bimetal" economy based on gold *and* silver.

Critics said this would flood the market with cheap money and drive up inflation, but Harvey and others — most notably Democratic presidential candidate William Jennings Bryan — argued that, while this was true, it would also stabilize the economy and make it easier to pay off debt. Coin published a pamphlet in 1894 called *Coin's Financial School*, which sold about a million copies, and was a supporter of Bryan's failed campaign two years later.

Afterward, Harvey left politics and built a resort hotel on land he had purchased near Rogers in northwest Arkansas, naming it "Monte Ne" (which he said meant "mountain of water" in a combination of Spanish and Native American tongues). Harvey, of course, wanted to promote his resort, so he added two more hotels, a tennis court and the state's first indoor swimming pool as attractions. He then built a railroad spur line linking it to the St. Louis and San Francisco Railroad line, and bought a gondola from Italy to ferry tourists from the depot across a lagoon to the hotels.

But Harvey knew the railroad couldn't be the only point of access for his resort. He felt the winds of change rising and saw the need to attract tourists by automobile, as well. So, he made Monte Ne the starting point for his new Ozark Trails, with branch lines bringing in visitors from large cities in the region like Kansas City, Tulsa, Oklahoma City, St. Louis, Memphis, El Paso, Wichita and Amarillo.

This was, without question, a money-making proposition for "Coin," and he wanted to make sure people knew how to get to Monte Ne. He even admitted as much: "My personal interest in the Ozark Trails is that they all lead to Monte Ne," he wrote in 1913.

Among the most distinctive aspects of the Ozark Trails were the trail markers built at key junctions along the way. These were far more than painted telephone poles or tree trunks; they were concrete pillars 20 to 24 feet high, in the shape of obelisks — like smaller versions of those in ancient Egypt (or the Washington Monument), with pyramid capstones at the top. Each obelisk was marked on its four sides with the names of towns along the trail, together with the distances to each location. Four or five electric lights in globes at the top provided illumination for drivers passing through at night.

Pillars were placed in the following locations (though there may also have been others):

- Anadarko, Okla.
- Artesia, N.M.
- Buffalo, Mo.
- Clovis, N.M.
- Dimmit, Texas
- Farwell, Texas
- Junction of Jefferson Highway, near Bluejacket, Okla.
- Lake Arthur, N.M.
- Langston, Okla.
- Miami, Okla.
- Quitaque, Texas
- Romeroville, N.M.
- Silverton, Texas
- Stroud, Okla.
- Tampico, Texas
- Tulia, Texas
- Wellington, Texas

A 1919 article in the *Chanute Daily Tribune* described the decision to place an Ozark pillar in that Kansas town, at a cost of $125.

"The base is four feet square and four or five feet high, with a shaft rising from it three feet square where it joins the base, and tapering to dimensions of 18 inches at the top. The base will be protected by a beveled bumper."

Harvey initially proposed erecting a dozen such obelisks, and putting up a towering 50-foot version at the junction with the Santa Fe Trail.

At least one of them didn't last long.

Despite the lights and base bumpers, the pillar built at Main and Central in Miami, Okla., was decried as a "menace" in the local newspaper in 1919. At the time, it was the custom to place stop signs at the center of intersections, and that's where the pillars were, too. This made it imperative that drivers pay attention in order to navigate around them. If they didn't, well, a young man discovered the consequences when he was on his way home from seeing a show with his girlfriend one February evening. His car plowed directly into the obelisk, which moved about a foot as a result. The car was in worse shape, having suffered a cracked windshield and broken spring.

The driver's excuse was that "closed curtains" had interfered with his visions. The article failed to explain what curtains had been doing in the car or why they were closed while it was being driven.

But it wasn't just the unfortunate motorist who didn't like the pillar. The fire and police chiefs both spoke out against it the following month, saying its base was so large that accidents were inevitable. The police chief added that pedestrians were at risk because drivers might not be able to see them, thanks to the obelisk. In the event of a crash, he said, the city would be liable for damages.

In an odd display in April of 1919, a tank "bucked the Ozark Trail road marker" three times, "climbed the base and left its marks, but the Ozark Trails monument refused to go over."

This seems to have been done on purpose, as part of a war-related demonstration, but whether it was intended to knock the pillar over is

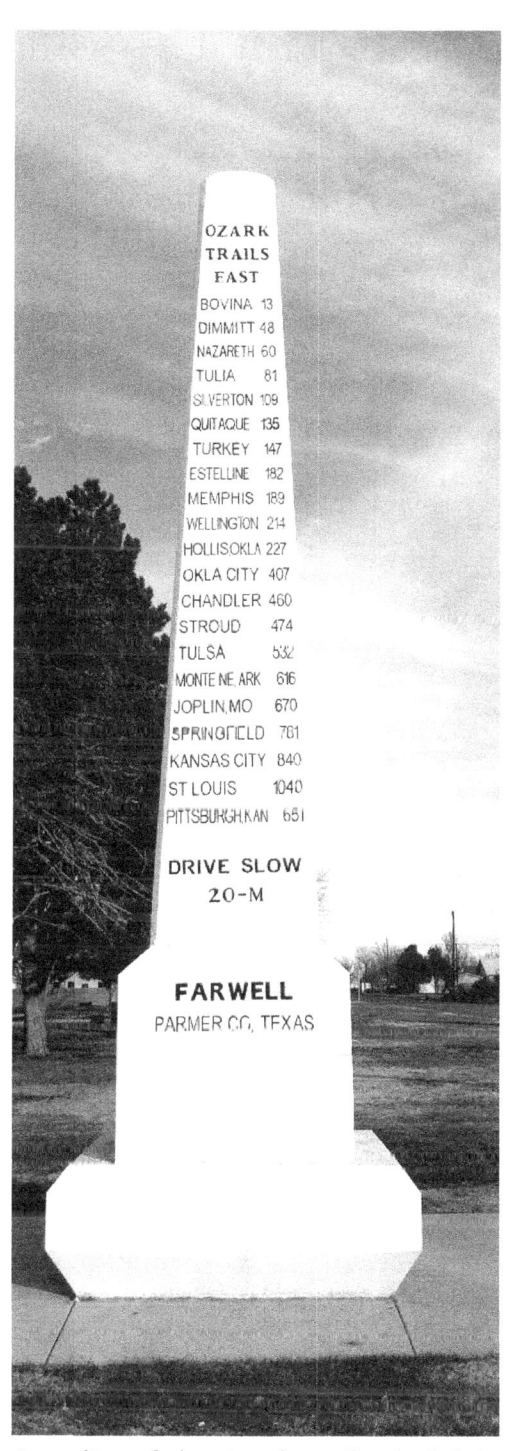

A replica of the Ozark Trails obelisk in Farwell, Texas, photographed in 2013 by Pete Unseth. *Creative Commons CCBY3.0, via Wikimedia Commons*

unclear. Whatever the driver's intention, "the tall shaft refused to go over." It was pushed along but would not fall over, its base being far heavier than its shaft.

The pillar was never put back in its proper place. Instead, a little more than two weeks later, a city wrecking crew tore it down, with a tractor engine hauling away the heavy base. The police and fire departments had won their argument. The obelisk lost.

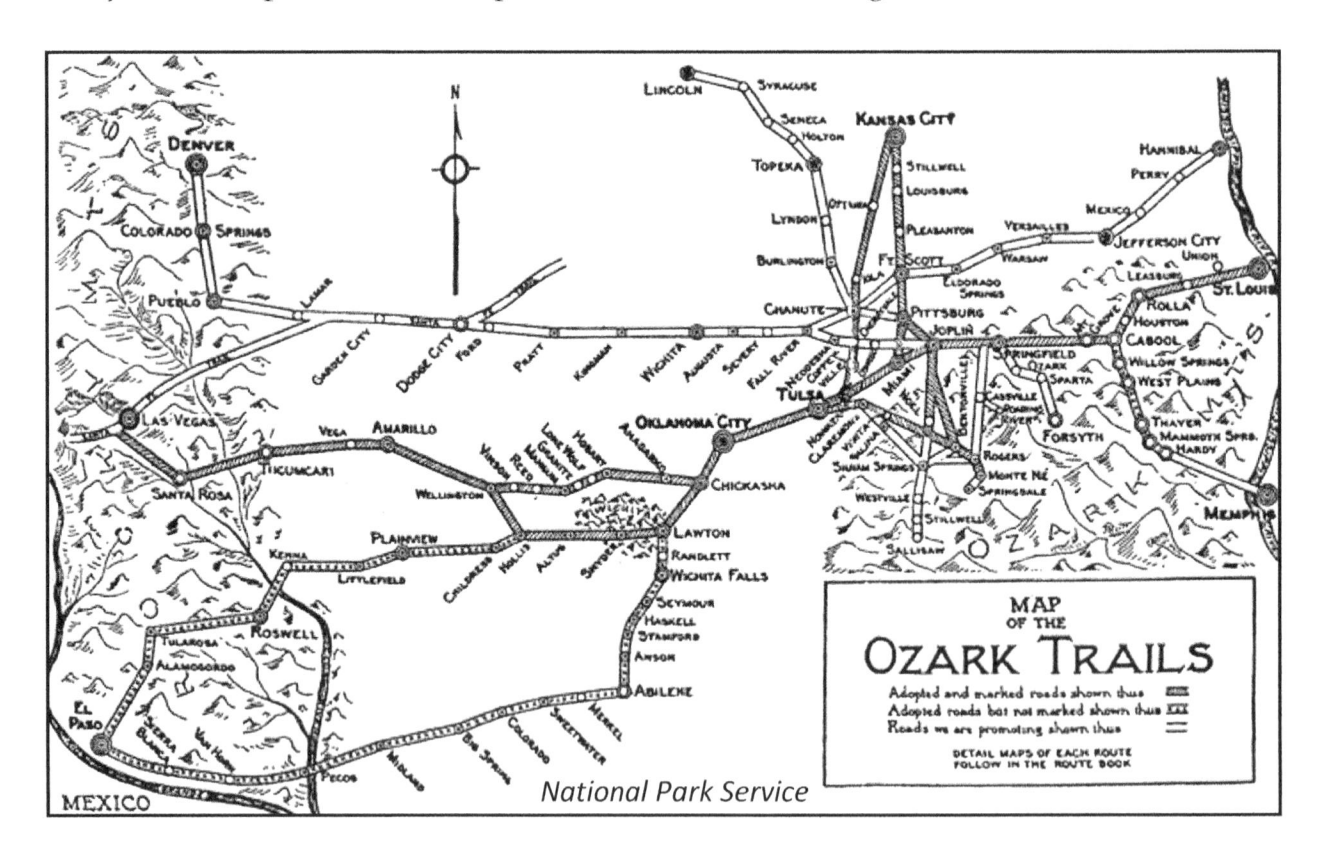

*Map of the Ozark Trails — National Park Service*

The obelisk in Artesia, N.M., was taken down in the late 1920s because it, too, was deemed a road hazard. Others, such as the Dimmitt and Wellington markers, were moved from the center of the road to near the curb. Silverton's obelisk was originally placed at the junction of the Amarillo and Silverton highways, but when the highway alignments changed, the pillar was left out of the loop (so to speak). It was apparently used to help fill a roadside ditch during a World War II paving project. The Quitaque marker, similarly, was toppled and buried in another road-construction effort.

The Clovis, N.M., monument was also torn down.

Meanwhile, an obelisk in Stroud, Okla., that was covered in graffiti was cleaned up in 2019 — although it had been so badly defaced that the towns once inscribed upon it

The retaining wall for "Coin" Harvey's planned pyramid at Monte Ne was constructed, but the pyramid itself was never built. *Wikimedia Commons*

had been forgotten.

The Tulia, Langston, Lake Arthur and Tampico pillars remain at their original locations. A replica of the original obelisk in Farwell, Texas, also stands, complete with mileage distances to 21 different locations. (For the record, the closest is Bovina, Texas, just 13 miles away, and the farthest is St. Louis, 1,040 miles distant.)

And whatever became of "Coin" Harvey and Monte Ne? Unfortunately, all Harvey's efforts to connect tourists with his resort didn't work. His rail spur and auto trails failed increase business at the resort, which was mostly sold or foreclosed in the 1920s. Even the 10,000 copies of an *Ozark Trails Route Book* he mailed in September of 1920 alone didn't help.

Harvey, meanwhile, became increasingly convinced that the fall of civilization was just around the corner, and wanted to do something to leave a monument of what American culture had achieved at its zenith. His choice was, naturally, a pyramid, which he planned to build on the property he still owned at Monte Ne.

He started the project with an amphitheater, but before he could do much work on the pyramid, he lost most of his fortune in the stock market crash of 1929. As a result, the pyramid was never built.

Harvey did make one final run at politics, launching a new party called the Liberty Party and running as its candidate for president in 1932 at the age of 80. His party gave him the nomination at its convention (held, naturally, at Monte Ne), and he wound up finishing sixth in the overall balloting with 53,000 votes. He died four years later, and much of Monte Ne disappeared in the 1960s beneath the surface of Beaver Lake, which was created with the damming of the White River.

But the true legacy of the Ozark Trails was their role in paving the way for Route 66. One of the Ozark Trail branches became the lynchpin between the two main sections of the road: the one running south from Chicago, and the other heading toward the Pacific across the Southwest.

This 2014 photo shows Rock Creek Bridge, which was built in 1921 as part of the Ozark Trails west of Sapulpa, Okla., and became part of Route 66 when the federal highway was dedicated five years later. Today, it's only open to pedestrians, having been placed on the National Register of Historic Places in 1995. *Carterse, Creative Commons CCBY2.0*

# AMERICA'S FIRST HIGHWAYS

**Top:** A monument sits beside Georgia State Route 3, the former Dixie Highway. *Michael Rivera, Creative Commons CCBY3.0*

**Left:** A Madonna of the Trail statue placed in Albuquerque by the Daughters of the American Revolution c. 1928.

**Above:** A monument erected by the United Daughters of the Confederacy, erected in 1928, stands alongside a section of the Lee Highway between Roanoke and Salem, Va. While many Confederate monuments such as this have been justifiably condemned as offensive for honoring defenders of slavery, this one still stood in 2020.

**Right:** One of 3,000 concrete posts set up along the Lincoln Highway by the Boy Scouts of America in 1928. *Author photos*

# AMERICA'S FIRST HIGHWAYS

**NEBRASKA HISTORICAL MARKER**

**THE SEEDLING MILE**

Here is a section of an original Seedling Mile on the Lincoln Highway. It was completed November 3, 1915. Grand Island was the second city in the United States to build such an example of concrete roadway. The original Seedling Mile extended from the corner of Willow Street one mile east, ending near the Seedling Mile School.

By 1913 the route of the Lincoln Highway had been chosen and dedicated nationwide by the newly formed Lincoln Highway Association. The association's main goal was to develop a paved, toll-free, transcontinental highway from New York City to San Francisco. To help meet this goal, the association conceived the Seedling Mile program. Seedling Miles would be the "seeds" from which paved roads would extend across the nation.

The Seedling Mile was constructed with locally donated cement and funds. Fred W. Ashton of Grand Island raised $1,170 for the project. Realignment of the highway in 1931 allowed this section to be preserved. It is the only remaining original section of a concrete Seedling Mile that has not been widened or covered with asphalt.

Nebraska Department of Roads    Nebraska State Historical Society, 2010

**Above:** A marker at a Lincoln Highway seedling mile in Grand Island, Neb., the second such demonstration section ever built on the highway, in 1914.

**Left:** Nearly 400 bells were installed in the early 20th century to mark the path of El Camino Real in California. This one is at Mission San Miguel. *Author photos*

## Tourist Auto Camps

A camper in Yellowstone National Park, c. 1920. *Library of Congress*

# Primitive Cool

The popularity of the Jefferson Highway Association's sociability runs was just one sign that Americans were warming to the idea of exploring the country in their cars. Automobiles were getting faster, more reliable and more user-friendly every year. Carl Fisher's Prest-O-Lite headlamps had made it possible to drive at night. Cars now came equipped with spare tires, so motorists could change them on the road if one of their regular tires went flat.

Tires themselves were improving, too. Frank Seiberling of Goodyear had invented grooved tires in 1908 to improve traction, and more durable tires kept hitting the market in the decade that followed. Meanwhile, the hand crank, that frustrating, back-breaking method of starting your car, disappeared after Cadillac introduced the electric starter in 1912.

A Model T only got 13 to 21 miles to the gallon, but it didn't matter because fuel was cheap and gas stations were sprouting like weeds beside the highway. The average price for a gallon of gas actually fell during the 1920s from 30 cents at the start of the decade to 21 cents by 1929. In the first decade of the 20$^{th}$ century, you had to get gas at a garage or drugstore, but "filling stations" started arriving in 1913, when Gulf Oil opened the first drive-in location in Pittsburgh. By 1920, there were 15,000 service stations nationwide, a number that mushroomed to nearly 124,000 in the space of a decade.

Cars were more available and affordable, too. A Model T Runabout cost $900 in 1910, but more efficient production cut the price to $350 six years later and even further, to $260, by the mid-'20s. A Model T came off of Ford's assembly line every 24 seconds, which helped explain the rapid growth in the number of cars on the road. When the Lincoln Highway was conceived in 1912, there were fewer than a million of them. By the end of World War I, that figure had soared to 7.5 million.

All these cars needed (and their drivers wanted) somewhere to go, and like frontier explorers, their natural instinct was often to "Go west!"

The end of the "war to end all wars," as they called it, had unleashed a pent-up wanderlust among the nation's rapidly growing population of car owners. They wanted to see the great outdoors.

National Parks were, understandably, a popular destination. Yellowstone had been founded first in 1872, and the National Park Service had been established in 1916.

The National Park to Park Highway wasn't far behind. It followed a giant, broadly circular route that took visitors to a dozen national parks, including Yosemite, the Grand Canyon, Yellowstone, and Mt. Rainier. Only about a third of it was paved, however: the section that followed the Pacific Highway along the West Coast. Road organizers beckoned travelers with the inviting slogan, "You Sing 'America' — Why Not <u>See</u> It?"

Tourists were, in fact, a big part of the reason highways were changing ... and had to continue doing so. Yellowstone, the first national park, was established in 1872, and the National Park Service was founded in 1916 after a campaign by conservationist and borax company president Stephen Mather.

A Ford on a mountain road near Idaho Springs, Colo., c. 1910. *Library of Congress*

A year later, Mather became the Park Service's first director, and one of his goals was to make it easier for Americans to see the natural wonders they were preserving. A primary means of doing so was the National Park to Park Highway.

In 1920, Mather set out with AAA pathfinder A.L. Westgard and others on a 60-day tour to dedicate this new loop highway, which passed through nine states and spanned nearly 5,000 miles. When it was completed, Warren E. Boyer wrote for *Western Highways Builder* magazine, "twelve major Federal playgrounds in the West, as well as many national monuments and forests" had been "lassoed by a scenic running noose, known as the National Park-to-Park highway."

It was, Boyer wrote, the longest continuous scenic motorway in the world.

It had the added advantage of crossing "every major transcontinental trail," allowing motorists easy access ... even if they did have to contend with long stretches of gravel and dirt road once they got there.

A Detroit Electric car took a promotional tour through the mountains from Seattle to Mt. Rainier in 1919. The Anderson Electric Car Company built 13,000 electric cars from 1907 to 1939. The top speed was only about 20 mph, enough for a leisurely outing. *Library of Congress*

One could arrive in Cheyenne, Wyo., on the Lincoln Highway and head south to Rocky Mountain National Park, then continue to Mesa Verde National Park, just north of the New Mexico State Line. A detour at Flagstaff, Ariz., took travelers north on a spur to the Grand Canyon, and a longer spur from Needles, just inside the California state line, wound its way back northeast to Zion National Park in southern Utah.

California itself offered the twin Sequoia and General Grant (now Kings Canyon) national parks on the Sierra Nevada's western slopes, along with Yosemite farther north and Lassen via a short detour at Red Bluff. The Pacific Northwest beckoned with Crater Lake in Oregon and Mt. Rainier in Washington state. Then it was back east again to Glacier Park in Montana, near the Canadian Border, and down to Yellowstone in northwest Wyoming before completing the loop.

"More than ever before there exists a real inclination among our people to see America first," Mather said. "Where for years the lure of Europe has caught their fancy, the eyes of all those countries are now directed to the most spectacular world aggregation of scenic wonders, set apart for the enjoyment and recreation of a free people."

It wasn't Mather's first big project opening the parks to automobile traffic. At the beginning of 1915, while serving as assistant to the secretary of the Interior, he'd set his sights on opening up Yosemite to automobile traffic. The timing couldn't have been better: California was playing host to two international expos that year — one in San Diego, and the other in San Francisco — to celebrate the opening of the Panama Canal.

But reaching the Golden State from east of the Sierra Nevada range could be a dicey proposition. There were only a couple of options, 270 miles apart: Sonora Pass, south of Lake Tahoe, and Walker Pass east of Bakersfield. Mather wanted to create a middle way, and recalled a poorly maintained trail through Yosemite National Park called the Tioga Road. Unfortunately, others reminded him, the 56-mile road in question was privately owned.

No problem, Mather maintained. "I'll buy the road, have it repaired myself, and donate it to the government."

But there *was* one problem: The government wouldn't accept a donation from one of its employees. It had to come from somewhere else. So Mather enlisted the help of two private donors, the Sierra Club and the Modesto Chamber of Commerce, who together raised $8,000 of the $15,500 purchase price. Mather supplied the rest, but enlisted the help of a fellow Sierra Club member to actually transfer the property. The United States bought it from him for $10.

A second problem: The road was in terrible shape. It had been constructed for a specific purpose, but when that purpose had been served, it was all but abandoned. "The Tioga Road was built in 1881 by eastern capitalists to reach a mine which soon after failed," said Mather's boss, Interior Secretary Franklin Lane. "In the years since, it has fallen into complete disuse."

Even so, Mather was able to have the road repaired and formally opened to traffic in late July, more than two months before the Panama-Pacific International Exposition in San Francisco. (The San Diego expo was already underway, but it would continue for another year and a half.) During 1915, a total of 190 cars entered Yosemite via

Tourists take in the scenery at Tioga Pass in California in 1926. *Library of Congress*

Tioga Pass, with 578 entering the following year, each paying a $5 entrance fee.

That was quite a hefty price tag, considering it would amount to about $120 in 2020. For their money, they got access to a road that allowed them to go as fast as 20 mph on straightaways but not more than 8 mph going uphill and 12 mph on descent. Some of those hills were mighty steep, too: According to one guidebook, there was even a 20% grade near May Lake. The road was in continual need of repair and reconstruction, as trees fell across it and severe storms undid improvements, washing out huge sections of road "faster than we could keep up with repairs," Yosemite trail-builder Gabriel Sovuleski lamented.

Fall River Drive at Rocky Mountain National Park was one of the new, but still unpaved, roads for auto tourists in 1917. *Internet Archive*

Plans were made for a complete realignment of the road in the 1920s, but they wouldn't be finished until 1961.

Still, the road became increasingly popular, with 50 to 60 cars a day traveling the road in 1918, and traffic only increasing after that.

Tioga Pass wasn't on the National Park to Park Highway: It accessed Yosemite from the east, while the parks loop jogged in from the west. But the two routes met up, giving motorists more access points than ever to the park's scenic wonders.

Either way you traveled, you'd be roughing it.

A park road wasn't your typical highway. For much of its length, there weren't any gas stops or hotels on the National Park to Park Highway — not that there were many such conveniences west of the Mississippi in those days, anyway, but there were even fewer along this wilderness route. The only concrete roads apart from the Pacific Highway were very brief stretches in Denver and Spokane. There was some gravel from Caspar, Wyo., south to just past Colorado Springs, with shorter sections near Great

Falls, Yellowstone and Flagstaff. Otherwise, though, it was dirt road all the way, some of it improved, a lot of it not.

For vacationers, though, that was part of the charm. Who needed a hotel when you could pitch a tent and sleep out in the desert, with a million stars all around? Who wanted four walls separating you from the majesty of the Grand Canyon or Half Dome in Yosemite Valley?

Campgrounds at national parks are popular today, and they were back then, too. But they weren't the only places tourists were pitching their tents. Entire cities had been built around the railroads, with hotels setting up shop within walking distance of depots. But motorists didn't need to head into town for accommodations, nor did many of them want to. Hotels weren't just out of the way, they were expensive.

A picture in a 1917 tour book shows an idealized version of what automobile touring was like.

Some Americans got around this by booking group auto tours. But most wanted a way to explore the country on their own terms, without having to pay an arm and a leg. Not only had they grown tired of the cookie-cutter railroad experience, they'd had enough of hotels, too. Most hotels were creatures of the railroad, anyway, stacked up one on top of the other in city centers near the depot. They served train passengers, so they treated their guests much the same way the railroad treated its customers.

It almost felt like an assembly line, for instance, when hotels began substituting card indexes for old-fashioned registers. The *San Francisco Examiner* mused in 1929: "The guest feels that he is applying for a job to the personnel director of a big corporation or asking for admission to a clinic. ... The guest enters his name on the card, which is then whisked away to the electric icebox where heartless efficiency experts keep their statistics."

Trains ran on schedules. So did hotels. Their dining rooms were only open at certain hours. Nearby restaurants, meanwhile, were jammed when the trains came in. If you wanted to be sure of your accommodations, had to make reservations, too, and as more people started traveling in the 1910s, you had to make them further in advance, because hotels filled up more quickly.

If you traveled by car, on the other hand, you could take your hotel with you.

What did it matter, author Elon Jessup asked, "if night finds you in the center of an expansive desert miles from the nearest hotel? In five minutes, you could set up a hotel of canvas that is much more satisfying than any builded of brick and stone. You discover wonderful byways which he who travels by rail will never know and over which the motorist who depends upon hotels dares not venture."

Camping out was also a lot cheaper than staying in a fancy hotel, where bellhops and waiters demanded tips — an expense you didn't have to deal with if you could manage your own baggage and had brought your own food. One traveler expressed his displeasure at tipping practices in a 1917 letter to a hotel chain. "People in hotels want a cordial welcome, a kindly atmosphere and human warmth," he wrote, "which you do not give them." Instead, he found "obsequiousness and indifference."

"The porter was very anxious to carry my little valise that weighed ten pounds. The cloak room girl insisted on checking my hat and cane which I could easily take care of myself. The waiter manifested a lively interest in my wellbeing only at the crucial moment when I was counting my change. ... I was not a guest, I was prey."

Auto camping offered no such awkward interactions.

Mary Crehore Bedell wrote in 1924 of a 12,000-mile motor camping trip that took her through Florida, across the South, up through California and back via Glacier Park and Yellowstone. "If one has the time," she wrote, "a trip such as ours should cost no more than station at home. To be sure, there is the expense of the automobile, but food and clothing cost less, and with no rent, fuel or electricity to pay for, one should be able at least to come out even."

There was no doubt that auto camping was cheaper than staying in hotels: A newspaper piece in 1922 estimated that a family of four would pay $200 for a two-week road trip compared to $310 at a summer resort.

Tin Can tourists camp out at De Soto Park in Florida, 1920. *Florida State Archives*

Some tourists even insisted that going on the road was less expensive than staying at home. But it all depended. Sure, you saved a lot on rent and utilities, but the farther you went, the more you paid for gas and oil. The more distance you put between yourself and the major cities, the more expensive gasoline got: It could be twice as much per gallon on the frontier. Oil had to be replenished often, and it wasn't cheap, either. On top of that, the worse the roads were, the more often you had to change the tires.

But that didn't encourage these modern adventure-seekers. They loaded up their cars with camping supplies and tents — which they pitched by the side of the road, in farmers' fields, pretty much anywhere they happened to be when the sun went down. Some farmers welcomed them initially as a source of income. Fruit stands, anyone? (In fact, some early fruit stands blossomed into major businesses in the years following the age of auto trails; among them, Knott's Berry Farm in Southern California). Some enterprising farmers charged motorists $1 a night to camp out.

AMERICA'S FIRST HIGHWAYS

But some of the uninvited visitors picked the farmers' fruit without asking, and others left trash strewn about in their fields. "Tin can tourists," as they were sometimes called, ran the gamut from middle-class families out for an adventure on the open road to hobos and tramps who needed a place to sleep for the night. During the glory days of America's auto trails, there were more of the former; it was only during the Depression that many auto camps out west became havens for migrant farmworkers taking refuge from the Dust Bowl.

Camping by the side of the road became all the rage in the second half of the teens and into the early 1920s.

In 1912, just a dozen tourists managed to complete a trip across the continent. Nine years later, 20,000 Americans did so. And the *New York Times* estimated that nearly half of the 10.8 million cars on the road in 1922 would be used for camping.

Needless to say, it was big business. Sporting goods retailers stocked up on outdoor stoves, tents, cots and folding tables. A company called Schilling's created a fold-out bed with tarp awnings that could be attached to the side of your car. "Live in the Big Outdoors independent of hotels — free from the worry of the summer cottage or the cumbersome unwieldy 'camping outfit,' " a Schilling's ad from 1917 proclaimed. "Stop where you like and stay as long as you want."

That was the essence of auto camping.

Shilling's offered a 48-by-78 double bed that could be fully enclosed in a waterproof tarp-tent. The canvas could be affixed to any standard car, while the bed's steel frame extended out from the running board and could be folded up and stored easily there when not in use. It weighed 60 pounds in all, and could create not one but two bedrooms: one on either side of the car. The company also offered other products, such as a touring trunk for storage and "tents, tarpaulins and covers of all sizes and descriptions to order."

Other companies offered similar products, such as the A.B.C. Sleeper and Stoll's Auto Bed.

Hoping to keep travelers close to town (where they could boost the local economy), some cities started clearing fields for motorists who wanted a place to pitch their tents. One of the most popular municipal camps on the Jefferson Highway was in Muskogee, Okla. That made sense because Muskogee was a relatively small town along a sparsely populated section of the highway. The closest large towns were Joplin, Mo., nearly 120 miles to the north and Denison, Texas, almost 160 miles south.

The Muskogee Kiwanis Club built the camp at Spaulding Park in 1921, offering electric lights, a dozen gas plates for cooking and four tables with benches. There was space for 200 cars, and campers could swim in a pond on the property while a brass band provided entertainment.

A night's stay would cost you a quarter.

Frank Smith, president of the Dallas Chamber of Commerce, was impressed with his visit to the park in 1921. His comments were duly carried in the local newspaper, the *Muskogee Democrat*:

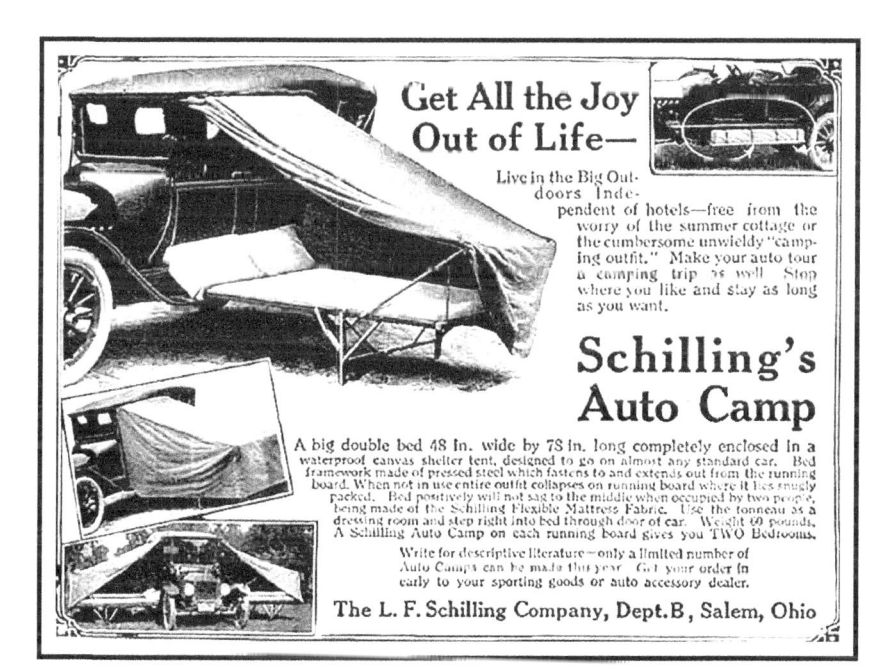

"When we reached the park, we hesitated to go in, as the lawn and everything about it was so well kept we thought we must have made a mistake," he said. After an officer invited his party in, however, they were directed to "a large building where we found bath rooms, reading and rest rooms, and also a place to cook meals." The camp, he said, was "highly praised during our trip, and every tourist has a good word for the city on account of the excellent arrangements made for their comfort."

Some municipal camps allowed visitors to stay for free, reasoning they would spend money in town. Others charged a small fee and offered a degree of protection from undesirables, such vagrants and hobos. A 1926 article in the Omaha-based magazine *Trade Exhibit* outlined the dilemma facing the camps and those who stayed in them.

"There is no question but that a nice camp makes a favorable impression on the large number of tourists who are not of the 'tramp' variety," the article said. "The majority

A large auto camp, probably in Yellowstone National Park. *Library of Congress*

reciprocate by making purchases in the town — gasoline and oil, if nothing else, but usually groceries as well. Some (camp visitors) would rather pay and have the benefit of added protection. Others would rather seek the free camp."

Municipal auto camps were quickly joined by privately operations, which similarly offered basic amenities like running water and toilets, while charging a modest fee.

One of the earliest auto camps, Denver's Overland Park, opened in 1915. It was conveniently located on the Park to Park Highway, near Rocky Mountain National Park and just south of where the Lincoln Highway fed the parks loop. Its expansive 160-acre property along the Platte River was divided into 800 lots, with room for more than 2,000 auto campers. It offered running water and electric lighting, with a central clubhouse that sold groceries, a grill and kitchen, a lunch counter, a barbershop, laundry room, and showers.

Some tourist camps even offered gasoline service. Shupp's in Columbia City on the

Lincoln Highway, for instance, offered Red Crown gas for sale.

The camps were so popular the Jefferson Highway Association published a tourist camp manual in 1923 that listed more than 100 camps up and down the highway. AAA came out with a manual of its own the following year that featured nearly 2,000 sites, many of which were "equipped with every facility for the motor tourist's comfort and convenience." California had the most, followed by Wisconsin, Michigan and Illinois.

As time passed, fewer campgrounds were run by municipalities, and more were private enterprises. Fifty-five of the 64 campgrounds in Colorado were publicly run in 1925; but just three years later, the balance had flipped, with 65 private campgrounds among the state's total of 85.

In Oklahoma, the Kiwanis closed the Muskogee camp and gave the main building to the Girl Scouts during the 1930s. By that time, there were eight privately run camps in town, all of them offering private cabins, not just a place to pitch your tent.

Cabins served two purposes: They offered guests a measure of privacy, but they also offered added protection from bad weather — as well as from other "undesirable" elements, like the mad dog that paid a visit to the Highbridge Park tourist camp in Spokane, Wash. The dog, which was foaming at the mouth, appeared out of nowhere just after dark and made mad dashes at some of the visitors. They were forced to take refuge in their cars and wait for police, who found the dog and put it down.

Such dangers were less frequent than the vagabonds, beggars and grifters who showed up, especially at the free municipal camps.

The *Trade Exhibit* article mentioned such auto camp visitors in the following poem:

He owns a dented tin machine
A roll of ragged bedding
Perhaps sufficient gasoline
To last to where he's heading

Some pots and pans, a dirty tent
Some rusty spades and axes—
He needs no home, he pays no rent
He never heard of taxes!

> The Flivver Hobo is a tramp
> I met in hordes last summer,
> At many a town's Free Auto Camp—
> A most accomplished bummer

In the West, especially, auto camping became a way of life for the less fortunate and displaced during the Depression, with Dust Bowl migrants loading all their belongings into their cars and pitching their tents (if they had them) at camps or under billboards by the side of the road. The auto courts or motor courts sprang up to serve the tourists, primitive motels that largely supplanted the camps after the age of the auto trail had run its course. Private campgrounds later enjoyed a minor resurgence, with the founding of Kampgrounds of America in 1962, and Good Sam Club parks, which opened in 1966.

Although auto camps became less popular after the 1920s, the Minneapolis Municipal Tourist Camp was still operating in 1937. *Library of Congress*

## Suggested Provisions

The 1916 Lincoln Highway Association guide contained a comprehensive list of provisions for intrepid auto camper. A sampling is presented here:

**Optional Camp Equipment**

5-gallon milk can with stay straps
2-quart canteen
Frying pan (10 inches)
Campfire grate
2-quart coffee pot
4 large cups
4 knives
6 forks
6 teaspoons
2 cooking spoons
1 dipper
8 planes (8 inches diameter)
2 stew pots
1 butcher-style carving knife
1 cooking fork (3 prongs)
3 bars Ivory soap
6 dish towels
1 can opener
1 bread pan (for dish washing)
1 bucket with lid
1 can for pepper
1 patent egg carrier
Air-tight coffee and tea cans
1 corkscrew

**Personal Equipment**

Lincoln Hwy. Assn. member card
Lincoln Highway lapel button
Waterproof sleeping, duffel bags
1 pair light moccasins
2 pair khaki riding trousers, belt
1 pair lightweight shoes
2 pair wool, 3 pair medium socks
2 suits heavy wool underwear
2 bandana neck handkerchiefs
6 pocket handkerchiefs
White, yellow goggles
1 canvas coat high collar
1 stick camphor ice
2 dozen "cathartic tablets"
1 package gauze
3 rolls gauze bandages
Toothbrush, toothpaste comb
Strong knife (2-3 blades)
Pocket compass, inexpensive watch
Razor, shaving soap/powder, brush
Small mirror
Needles and thread
"Bachelor buttons"
Mosquito netting

**Top:** On the Lincoln Highway near Colfax, Nev. **Above:** A campground on the Lincoln Highway near Aurora, Ill. *University of Michigan Library (Special Collections Research Center, Transportation History Collection) photos*

## The Federal Highway System

A sign in Key West, Fla., welcomes motorists to U.S. Highway 1, much of which traced the old Atlantic Highway auto trail up the coast to Maine. *National Archives*

# End of the Trails

Just as they were hitting their stride, America's auto trails found their days were numbered.

And so were the roads.

Auto trails had been born in a time when the government refused to spend money on interstate highways. The Good Roads movement had pushed for such funding, but had been rebuffed at every turn, so highway advocates had taken matters into their own hands. Through private donations and a little sweat equity, they had begun to build a system of highways that crisscrossed the nation. It was, in places, rudimentary. It was chaotic. But it was far more than the government had managed to accomplish, or even cared to pursue.

But now that the auto trails were making real progress, elected officials decided to dip their toes in the water.

The states were already taking action.

In 1917, Wisconsin became the first state to create a numbered highway system, at the same time banning any trail associations from posting markers in the state without its permission. Two years later, only one interstate auto trail (the Yellowstone Trail) was marked within the state. The law also set forth a plan for a state highway system covering 5,000 miles.

State highway engineer Arthur Hirst seems to have viewed the numbering system as an antidote to fly-by-night auto trail associations. They were, in essence, all style and no substance: "The ordinary trail promoter has seemingly considered that plenty of wind and a few barrels of paint are all that is required to maintain a 2,000-mile trail," Hirst quipped.

## Taxes and Tussles

Despite this criticism, however, the state itself didn't actually set up a fund to pay for its highways until 1925, when it adopted a 2-cent-per-gallon gas tax.

It was, if anything, behind the times. Oregon had been the first state to levy a gas tax — a penny a gallon — to pay for roads in 1919. New Mexico and Colorado followed suit the same year. Two years later, the Georgia General Assembly adopted its own penny gas tax to fund road building; it tripled the tax two years after that. Three cents may not sound like a lot, but adjusted for inflation, it would amount to 45 cents a gallon in 2020.

Despite the cost, the taxes were popular. Gasoline taxes were far better than property taxes, the thinking went: The amount of gas a vehicle consumed was a fair method of determining how much it used, and damaged, the road.

"Who ever heard, before, of a popular tax?" Tennessee's gas-tax collector exclaimed in 1926.

Years later, historian John C. Burnham looked back and declared that "never before in the history of taxation (had) a major tax been so generally accepted in such a short period of time." It was remarkable, he added that Americans were so "willing to pay for the almost infinite expansion of their automobility."

# AMERICA'S FIRST HIGHWAYS

A restored old-style cottage gas station along the Lincoln Highway in Sutherland, Neb., is typical of the kind built in the 1920s. *Author photo*

Other states soon established gas taxes of their own, with 33 having done so by 1923. Iowa set up a Primary Road Fund, to be paid for by a 2-cent-a-gallon surcharge. As part of the initiative, the state moved away from named highways and started numbering its roads. The Jefferson Highway was marked as Route 1, and the Lincoln Highway was No. 7. The Blue Grass Trail became No. 8, and the Red Ball Highway was now Route 40.

The state issued a road guide explaining it all.

Pennsylvania followed suit with a similar initiative the next year. So, it wasn't as if the federal move to exchange colorful names for more consistent numbers came out of nowhere. The states had already realized it made sense, given the proliferation of privately run auto trails. (In Iowa, for instance, there were no fewer than 64 marked auto trails during the 1920s.)

A news story in the *Harrisburg Evening News* in Pennsylvania explained the rationale as follows: "In the days when the National Pike, the Lincoln Highway and a few other well known roads were using symbols and signs on poles along their route it was not difficult for motorists to follow the main road." But things had changed in a short span of time:

"Today ... some poles where roads converge contain three four or more of these signs. But the confusion which results has been ended by the State Highway Department."

Still, the movement of some states toward numbered routes didn't end the confusion entirely, because the numbers might change (or disappear) when you crossed the state line. That's where the federal Bureau of Public Roads, an arm of the Agriculture Department, entered the picture, working up a numbering system that would apply to the entire country.

The federal government had been gradually getting more involved in making decisions about the nation's roads since 1916, with the passage of the first Federal Road Aid Act. The bill that set aside $75 million for road improvements, but the money had gone largely unspent: By 1919, only a little more than half of 1%, or $500,000, had been used, and just 12 miles of actual roadway had been built.

That same year, however, the BPR Acting Director P. St. J. Wilson hinted that, if more funding became available, it might not be spent on the growing network of auto trails.

In a memo to the secretary of agriculture, he accused the trail associations of conducting "propaganda, quite usually referring to their projects as national roads of importance ... in such ways as to lead citizens of many localities to believe that the roads in question were actually proposed by the Federal Government, to be constructed by the Federal Government, or in a few instances even to be taken over and handled exclusively by the Federal Government."

Trail promoters often went where the money was, exchanging one route for another if it looked like it might provide more financial support.

This, understandably, left citizens along the original route — who had already invested heavily in the roads — feeling used and misled. In 1924, the Pike's Peak Ocean to Ocean Highway abandoned its western endpoint in San Francisco, switching the terminus to Los Angeles.

San Francisco had been the most populous California city in 1910, with nearly 100,000 more residents than L.A., but its growth had slowed during the decade that followed, allowing the Southern California metropolis to leapfrog it: By 1920, Los Angeles had 70,000 more residents than its northern rival. Whether that was the rationale for the switch, or whether it was made for some other reason, it left those along the jilted route decidedly bitter.

The *Reno Evening Gazette* used the sourest of grapes to brew up a scathing editorial. With the exceptions of the Lincoln and Victory highways, which had "accompanied their propaganda with some real cash expenditures for road construction," highway associations were the work of flim-flam men who brought with them nothing more than noise and unending requests for money, the newspaper said.

"In nine cases out of ten, transcontinental highway associations are common nuisances and nothing else," it concluded. "And in many instances, they are organized by clever boomers who are not interested in building roads but in obtaining salaries at the expense of an easily beguiled public."

A similar situation occurred on the Jefferson Highway, which had hired a general manager named A.J. Keith with a background as a publicist and a salesman — just the sort of person castigated in the *Gazette* editorial.

The new general manager lost no time in persuading the advisory board to move the main highway into Arkansas, demoting the highway's original route (which passed through part of western Arkansas but mostly through Louisiana) to secondary "scenic" status.

Louisiana citizens were incensed.

In response, they issued an ultimatum: Their state would "have no further interest in the Jefferson Highway Association until her wishes that the marks through central Arkansas be removed and the western Arkansas marks from Joplin to Shreveport are respected."

The Jefferson Highway Association president, who had recommended Keith for the post, now sought to oust him on the grounds that he had failed to collect enough money in two months to pay his own salary during that time. The board refused to fire Keith, but the president exerted enough pressure that he finally resigned late in 1925. Still, the damage was done, though Keith's failure to collect assessment fees was not entirely his own.

The fact of the matter was that, by this time, the Jefferson Highway was mostly built. It had been easy to generate excitement — and donations — when the purpose was to build an actual road. It was more difficult, though, to collect fees for maintenance and sign-posting, which was what most of the money was going for these days. Besides, the federal government had already begun stepping up highway funds with the passage of a second Federal Road Aid Act in 1921.

Unlike its predecessor, which had led to just a trickle of federal funding, the 1921 act unleashed a torrent. The 1916 bill had contained a one-time allocation of $75 million, most of which had gone unspent. But the new and improved version set aside that same amount of money *every year* for the next decade. Just as important, it created a formula under which federal funds could only be spent on 7% of the nation's roads ... three-sevenths of which (42%) *had to be* "interstate in character."

This created no small amount of tension. On the one hand, the government was determined to spend money on interstate highways. But on the other hand, it had no love for the network of interstate roads that already existed: the national auto trails that P. St. J. Wilson had accused of conducting "propaganda" and operating under false pretenses. The solution was obvious: The government could use its vast funding resources, appropriated under the 1921 Federal Road Act, to take over those roads and break them up, destroying whatever influence they might have.

That is, ultimately, exactly what happened.

Amid such attacks from the government, the trail associations had trouble finding the money they needed to stay afloat. With state gas taxes and the federal government kicking in plenty of funds, citizens along privately funded highways saw less urgency about donating to the folks who ran them. And it didn't help that people like Wilson and Howard Gore, head of the Agriculture Department, were disparaging the associations.

In early 1925, Gore wrote to Cassius Clay Dowell, a congressman from Iowa, concerning the issue:

"The practice of promoting trails, marking highways, and making collections under the guise of membership fees" had grown "to such proportions" that his department found it necessary to intervene. Gore lamented that con men had set out to collect "large sums of money from our citizens" while "giving practically no service in return." And he warned citizens to carefully investigate any trail association asking for money before, in fact, contributing.

Gore noted that the actions of these bad apples had cast a shadow over auto trail groups in general, with "reputable trails associations" being unfairly tainted by their actions. But his warnings didn't make it any more likely that donations — even to groups that were operating on the up-and-up — would continue. Especially since, as Gore noted, he intended to name a joint board that would oversee the routing and marking of interstate highways.

If the feds were about to intervene, why should citizens keep paying assessments to the trail groups, legitimate or otherwise?

And indeed, those groups were feeling the squeeze.

By October, the Dixie Highway's Board of Directors judged the association to be in "a more or less serious financial situation." Making matters worse, ad income for the *Dixie Highway* publication was down, and the group soon had to pull the plug on what had once been an effective marketing tool.

The Dixie Highway wasn't alone, either.

The Jefferson Highway Association had already stopped producing its own magazine, back in 1923.

Now, it was having trouble finding money to pay for road markers. Communities that had willingly paid assessments for road building were less eager to shell out money for what they viewed as less essential features such as signs. Some had stopped paying their membership fees altogether.

## Signs and Seals

Still, the signs were important.

The association had placed some 20,000 pole markers and 2,000 metal signs to mark the trail. Those had to be maintained regularly, as paint became faded or worn away by the elements. In addition, the association included warning signs on poles:

- The letter "D" against a white field between two blue bars signified danger ahead.
- "R" meant the road would turn right at an intersection up ahead, and "L" indicated a similar left turn.
- Where "D" appeared beneath the "L" or "R," it meant a dangerous left or right turn was just ahead.

Those signs worked on the Jefferson Highway, but other trails had different systems.

A 40-foot sign in Tennessee warned motorists: "Drive Slow — Dangerous as the Devil." A billboard in California read: "Motorists Attention! You are on your honor. Fresno County has no speed cops. Drive so they will not be needed. Speed limit 30 miles per hour." The message was attributed to the county's Board of Supervisors. Some railroad crossings were marked with a skull and crossbones.

Clearly, a better system was needed.

AAA had been placing signs of its own for several years; in 1914, the Automobile Club of Southern California had put up some 4,000 signs between Kansas City and Los Angeles on the National Old Trails Highway. But despite such efforts, there was still plenty of confusion, so the government decided it was time to step in.

In 1923, the Mississippi Valley Association of State Highway Departments adopted a series of signs it hoped would be easier to understand. AAA's signs were diamond-shaped, whether they identified highways, warned of road hazards or marked the distance to various destinations (some speed-limit signs were triangular). The focus was on their content, but that could be difficult to determine from any distance away. To solve this problem, the MVA came up with an idea: Signs could be identified just by their content, but by their shape.

"The underlying thought was that, if each shape had a definite meaning, it would be a great advantage for night driving," said Walter Rosenwald, the Minnesota engineer who helped devise the system. "Undoubtedly," he reasoned, "the shape could be distinguished long before the words could be."

Round signs would indicate railroad crossings. Stop signs would be octagonal. "Slow" warning signs would be diamond-shaped. Square signs, meanwhile, would carry caution or "attention" messages. Rectangular signs would be reserved to indicate directions or traffic regulations, such as speed limits.

There was a method to these distinctions. Signs indicating the greatest danger were circular, which explains why they were posted at railroad crossings. Intersections where drivers would face cross traffic were slightly less dangerous, so these took the slightly less circular stop signs. Diamond-shaped signs were a step down from that.

The first stop sign was installed in Michigan in 1915. When they were standardized, the signs were originally yellow with black lettering, because red paint faded over time. The color was switched to red in 1954, to match traffic lights, when fade-resistant porcelain hit the market.

# AMERICA'S FIRST HIGHWAYS

**Left:** An unidentified man shows an old-style stop sign in 1936, with reflectors on black letters against a yellow background. *Library of Congress*

**Below:** A diamond-shaped auto club sign in Southern California carries an inspection warning. *Dorothea Lange*

**Above:** Road sign along the Lincoln Highway erected and maintained by the Duquesne Light Service in Pennsylvania.

**Right:** A mileage sign on the Lincoln Highway in New Jersey sponsored by Polarine Motor Oil shows distances to cities including Asbury Park, Newark and Trenton, 1918.

*University of Michigan Library (Special Collections Research Center, Transportation History Collection) photos*

## Secret Board

The signs were set, but the big decision still lay ahead: How would the highways themselves be marked and numbered?

It wasn't long before Ag Secretary Gore named the board he had referred to in his letter to Congressman Dowell. He appointed 24 members — three from the bureau and 21 state highway officials — to consider where federal highways should be routed and how they should be marked.

In secret.

This was crucial because the new committee didn't want to get bogged down in the outcry that was sure to erupt when its intentions became known. Fred White, outgoing president of the American Association of State Highway Officials (AASHO), put it like this: "As soon as the purpose and work of the proposed board shall become known, the infernal regions will begin popping."

The infernal regions, as he called them, were where the troublemakers lived: the people bound to oppose the committee's ideas *whatever* they might be. It wasn't a difficult prediction to make: White had watched "infernal regions" pop whenever an auto trail bypassed one town in favor of another. As chief engineer of the Iowa State Highway Commission, he'd seen it firsthand when the Jefferson Highway — which ran through his state — had become ensnared in heated debates over how it should be routed.

Similar debates, he knew, were bound to break out the minute the committee's work became public.

In fact, Jefferson Highway Association's president, Hugh Shepard, had already contacted him about the pending changes. Shepard had gotten wind of the possibility that the highway "in its entirety from New Orleans to Winnipeg" would be "taken over by the various State Highway Commissions," and that its markings would then be "kept up" by those commissions. If this were indeed the case, he wanted to know whether there was any reason for the Jefferson Highway Association to keep going, other than to preserve the highway's name.

It was a sensible question, considering the association was having trouble raising the funds needed to keep up the markers itself. Transferring this power to the states would, presumably, have taken a weight off Shepard's shoulders.

But White replied that Shepard had the "wrong impression" of what AASHO was planning. He said, correctly, that the plan was to replace the trail names with numbers. But he added that the entire Jefferson Highway would carry the same number from one end to the other — which turned out to be entirely *incorrect*.

Apparently, White himself had the wrong impression, at least in this regard. It might have been because, as the *outgoing* president of AASHO, he was no longer directly involved in the decision-making process. Perhaps, at some point, state representatives had fully intended to keep some, or even many, of the existing trails intact and merely replace or even just supplement their names with numbers.

Indeed, a similar message was sent to Dixie Highway directors. The Georgia state highway commissioner told them in the fall of 1925 that they'd be able to keep posting their signs on state routes, and that the state would even maintain them. A year later, Michigan's top highway official — who had served on the federal routing committee — said his state would continue to use the name Dixie Highway.

"So far as I know," he said, "there will be no attempt to prevent the continuance of the names of the highways." He believed, further, that the various states would permit "the name of the Dixie Highway to appear, either on the shield bearing the U.S. number or on the standard bearing the shield." All the Dixie Highway Association would need to do, he suggested, was furnish the signs. The states would be happy to put them up.

It didn't work out that way.

No auto trail name ever appeared on an official U.S. shield. And not only did various states decline to maintain Dixie Highway markers, they even passed laws outright prohibiting any signs from appearing on state rights-of-way without the state's explicit consent. In writing.

So much for reassurances.

At some point, it must have become clear that the sheer number of overlapping, conflicting and jumbled auto trails across the country would make it impossible to do so. And accommodating one trail in this manner would lead to a slew of protests from all the others. This was why, after all, White himself had suggested that the process be kept under wraps for as long as possible.

When it came to the Jefferson Highway, there was a glimmer of hope to be found in something called AASHO Resolution No. 5. In it, the group decreed that "reputable" trail associations be allowed to keep marking their roads "during their period of usefulness, pending the establishing of the proposed marking system." Such courtesy, however, would not be given to *disreputable* groups, and no new groups would be allowed to form. This language, in fact, came directly from Gore's letter to Dowell, in which he had suggested just that.

Fortunately, according to White, the Jefferson Highway was one of these reputable groups.

But did it matter?

What, in the end, did Resolution No. 5 really mean?

A highway in Benson, Ariz., show the shield for U.S. 80, formerly the Old Spanish Trail, alongside a sign for Arizona State Route 86. *Wikimedia Commons*

It was hard to imagine the so-called "period of usefulness" lasting more than a few months, since the committee would soon be unveiling the new marking system that was to replace the auto trail system. And when the new system *was* finally unveiled, it turned out that the board had thrown everything out and started from scratch. Instead of starting out with a map of the auto trails, the board had consulted a series of uniform maps provided by the Postal Service and considered three factors in deciding where the federal numbered routes should go. Those factors were county population figures; the value of agricultural produce for each of those counties; and the value of the counties' manufacturing, mineral and forest products.

The final decision would have nothing to do with the nostalgia evoked by names like Lincoln and Jackson; it would have everything to do with how many people would be served and what their economic interests were.

Gone would be the painted pole markers of the auto trail era, to be replaced by metal signs in the shape of a shield, with black lettering on a white background. Some members of the board had suggested yellow letters on a black background, arguing that this combination would be more visible during snowy weather. But that argument ultimately failed.

The style of the highway shield modified in 1961 to show a white shield on a black background, as seen in this photo showing shields for U.S. 460 and U.S. 11 (the former Lee Highway) in Virginia. *Author photo*

At first, the committee wanted to put the initials "U.S.A." at the top, but decided instead to place the state name in that position, with a black bar below it, and the initials "U.S." in the main field, just above the route number. The marker's shape was based on a spur-of-the-moment sketch by Michigan representative Frank Rogers F W James, the board secretary, recalled that, "as we discussed a possible distinctive and unique marker

… he doodled and produced a sort of shield. He handed it to me. I think I improved on his design by drawing a picture of our present shield. He took it back, presented it to the board as just what was wanted, and that was that."

A Utah road with an informational mileage sign, 1936. *Dorothea Lange, Library of Congress*

The board then tackled the issue of where they highways should go. It suggested 10 main federal highways running east and west, each of them ending in zero: 10, 20, 30, 40, and so forth. Eleven primary north-south highways would each end in 1, running from U.S. Highway 1 on the East Coast to U.S. 101 in the west. Branch highways were given three-digit numbers based on the numeral of the main road to which they were attached. For example, U.S. 299 in Northern California was a branch of the interstate highway labeled U.S. 99.

The *Cincinnati Times-Star* called the move "one of the most unique and at the same time most progressive steps ever taken with respect to our entire federal road program." Not everyone liked the idea, though.

Rep. Charles Edwards of Georgia protested: "If we are forced to drop the designation of these roads by the names of great men of the past, we lose the only means by which we can create the enthusiasm for their proper development. The very spirit of the thing is wrong, an injustice. These roads were actually built as monuments to Washington, Lincoln, Jefferson Davis, Senator Bankhead and others."

The Bankhead Highway, which ran from the nation's capital to San Diego, had been created in 1916 and named for Sen. John Bankhead of Alabama, a key figure in enacting the Federal Aid Road Act passed that same year.

J.A. Rountree, director-general of the U.S. Good Roads Association, contended that, instead of creating a "simplified system," the new numbers made everything more complicated. How did it make sense, he wondered, to go from a system of 330 named trails to 375 numbered highways? Taking the Bankhead Highway as an example, he lamented that the once-cohesive, continuous road had been broken up into 30 numbered roads under the board's plan.

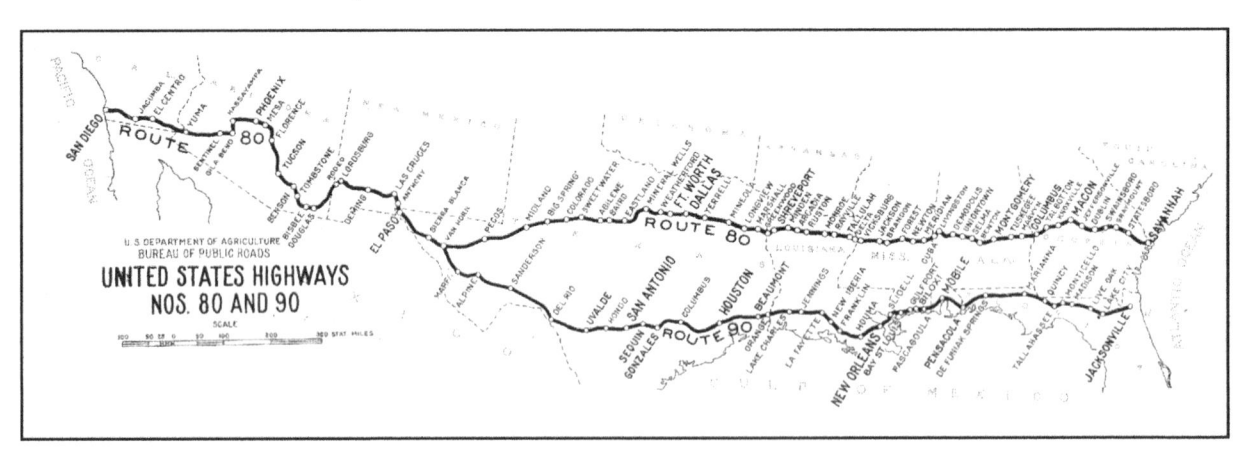

Indeed, virtually all the old interstate auto trails had been splintered into fragments of their former selves. On the West Coast, the old El Camino Real remained largely intact along what was now known as U.S. 101, while most of the former Pacific Highway lived on as U.S. 99. Two east-west Southern highways got "zero" designations and remained largely intact. The Old Spanish Trail was U.S. 90 from Jacksonville west to Van Horn, Texas, just east of El Paso, where it became U.S. 80 as it merged with the former Dixie Overland Highway (U.S. 80 from Savannah to Van Horn).

The Meridian Highway from Winnipeg to the southern border, meanwhile, was preserved in its entirety as U.S. 81.

This last must have been a bitter pill for the Jefferson Highway, which found itself broken up into more than a dozen separate federal highways. It would have been hard to assign the Dixie Highway a single number, given that it consisted of a loop road and several branches, and it was in fact divvied up among four different U.S. routes and a couple of state highways. But even the venerable Lincoln Highway did not survive the federal scalpel, which carved it up into about half a dozen different routes. (Fortunately, it was designated as U.S. 30 for most of the way, from Atlantic City, N.J., to western Wyoming.)

Lincoln Highway Association President Henry Joy sarcastically referred to "the Lincoln Highway, a memorial to the martyred Lincoln, now known by the grace of God and the authority of the Government of the United States as Federal Route 1, Federal Route 30, Federal Route 30N, Federal Route 30S, Federal Route 530, Federal Route 40 and Federal Route 50."

Joy's diatribe was part of a letter he considered sending to President Calvin Coolidge and the members of Congress protesting the decision.

He ultimately thought better of it.

The poet Ernest McGaffey used his mastery of the language to poke fun at the entire idea, suggesting that the idea of numbering highways might be applied elsewhere, too. Why not number senators "according to seniority, with a judicious sprinkling in of ciphers where necessary"? And why not replace the names of rivers, mountains, states and oceans with numerals: "Logarithms will take the place of legends, and 'hokum' for history."

## Rooting for 60

The new system led to protests, not just from the dismantled auto trail associations, but also from those simply unhappy with how things had come out.

Perhaps the most famous dispute involved the decision to label the proposed federal highway between Chicago and Los Angeles as Route 60. It wasn't a transcontinental highway, strictly speaking: It only spanned two-thirds of the United States from east to west, and in fact ran more north and south for a considerable distance. So why did it merit an exception to the rule that only transcontinental roads be given numbers ending in zero?

The answer to that question lies with three powerful members of decision-making board. B.H. Piepmeier, Frank Sheets and Cyrus Avery each served on a five-man panel tasked with assigning numbers to the routes the board had chosen. And three of them represented states through which the north-south section of the proposed Route 60 passed. Piepmeier came from Missouri, Avery spoke for Oklahoma, and Sheets — who wielded particular clout as president of AASHO — was from Illinois, where Route 60's eastern end was anchored.

Avery wielded plenty of influence, as well. He had been an early champion of the Ozark Trails, Coin Harvey's regional network of auto trails formed in 1915 that ran from St. Louis in the east to El Paso in the southwest. The main highway centered on Tulsa, where Avery owned a farm and where the Ozark Trails Association elected him vice president in 1919. His work in that capacity led him to become involved in the American Association of State Highway Officials, where he eventually became a key player. When the time came to choose routes and numbers for the proposed new federal highway system, Avery was appointed to the 24-member board.

Cyrus Avery

Once there, he immediately started thinking about the city he called home. Although it was at the heart of the Ozark Trails, Tulsa wasn't on any of the major transcontinental or north-south highways. While it was true that a section of the Jefferson Highway ran through Oklahoma, it traversed the eastern edge of the state, skirting both Tulsa and the state capital, Oklahoma City. Meanwhile, the east-west Santa Fe Trail passed to the north through Kansas, while the Old Spanish Trail and Jefferson Davis Highway were far to the south in Texas.

Avery used his position on the board to change the dynamic. He placed Tulsa at the center of an entirely new proposed highway from Chicago to Los Angeles, on a diagonal section where it morphed from a north-south highway into an east-west route. The highway board, with its reliance on economic and population data, wasn't supposed to indulge in this sort of improvisation. But Avery — with the support of Sheets and Piepmeier — had the clout to make it happen.

They dubbed their creation U.S. Highway 60.

Their decision, however, didn't go unnoticed.

# AMERICA'S FIRST HIGHWAYS

Even the head of the Oklahoma Good Roads Committee recognized the artifice Avery had used. The road through Tulsa, he wrote, had "never been recognized as a tourist route and was created at the insistence of Mr. Avery, who wanted an east and west route through his home city of Tulsa and Oklahoma City, the state capital."

Folks from Virginia and Kentucky were immediately up in arms. They had presumed that Route 60 would be a transcontinental route that ran from Newport News, Va., on the Atlantic Coast, to Los Angeles. The section from Virginia to Springfield, Mo., would have followed the remainder of Avery's proposed route from there to Los Angeles as a single highway. Instead, under the "group of five" proposal, it stopped at Springfield and was given the less-impressive route number 62.

As a result, neither Avery's proposed Route 60 nor the truncated Virginia-to-Missouri Route 62 met the definition of a transcontinental highway. Making matters worse, and more offensive to Kentucky's governor, it left that state as the only one in the Mississippi Valley without an east-west "zero" highway. The governor first vowed to simply ignore the new federal highway numbers, then pressed the matter further at a Chicago meeting of the board's executive committee in January 1926.

He pulled no punches, accusing Chicago-based interests of rigging the process in their favor.

It was suggested that the Chicago-to-Springfield section of the bifurcated highway be designated "60-North," but Avery and his supporters nixed that idea because it made the highway seem like a second-class road. Still, Avery didn't want to appear inflexible, so he said it didn't much matter much to him whether his route were numbered as 60 or 62, as long as it was the same the entire way.

In February, however, Piepmeier wrote Avery, urging him to stick to his guns. He pointed out that a road from Chicago to Los Angeles would carry more traffic than just about any other route in the system — a claim that turned out to be quite correct. "We cannot afford to lose Route 60," he wrote. "I think if we three (Piepmeier, Sheets and Avery) stand pat we will mark No. 60 through Chicago." Piepmeier included in his letter a copy of a freshly printed map from the Missouri Highway Department showing their road as U.S. Highway 60.

A total of 600,000 such maps had already been printed, and workers had even started placing U.S. 60 signs along the northern section of the highway.

It was becoming clear, however, that the arguments being posed by Kentucky and

Virginia weren't just going to go away. W.C. Markham, the AASHO executive secretary, remarked in a letter to Avery that the selection of the routes themselves had been "more or less contentions," but that it was "nothing in comparison to the contention that is going on between the States in reference to the numbering system."

As March came to a close, members of Congress were starting to make noise about intervening; if they did, some worried, all of the committee's work might come undone. Thomas MacDonald, head of the Bureau of Public Roads, said as much in a letter to Avery in which he parroted his earlier words back to him: "I do not feel it makes one bit of difference to the States along the route from Chicago to Los Angeles whether it is Route No. 60 or 62 or any other number so long as the number is carried continuously." To drive home the point, he reminded Avery that he himself had said so: "That," he said, "has been conceded."

The screws were beginning to tighten.

Making one last attempt to salvage 60 for his highway, Avery turned a previous argument on its head by suggesting that the Virginia-Missouri route be designated "60-South." "North" and "South" designations had been used to paper over other disputes that had arisen: Two sections of the Victory Highway had been transformed into U.S. 40 North and U.S. 40 South, while the Old and New Santa Fe Trails were designated as U.S. 50 north and south.

But Piepmeier was unwilling to accept that solution regarding Highway 60.

The issue remained unresolved in April, after all the other quarrels over numbering had been settled. On the final day of that month, Piepmeier, Avery and John Page, the chief engineer for the state of Oklahoma, met in Springfield, Mo., to consider their options. During that meeting, Page noticed a number that had yet to be claimed. Avery and Piepmeier agreed that it just might work, and sent a telegram to federal officials saying they'd be willing to accept that designation.

They had to wait until July 23 for a formal response from the Bureau of Public Roads. When it came, in the form of a letter from the bureau's division of design, it read as follows:

"Kentucky has just assented to an arrangement which will require the assignment of number 60 to the route from Springfield, Missouri, across Kentucky and Virginia to Newport News, with the understanding that the route from Chicago to Los Angeles will be given the number 66."

# AMERICA'S FIRST HIGHWAYS

Which rhymes with "kicks," conveniently enough.

What about those Route 60 signs that had already started going up along the highway? Avery admitted: "We will have to junk them."

Avery became known as the "Father of Route 66." And Route 66, of course, became known as the nation's most iconic road, a symbol of the era that followed the auto trails — an era still recalled fondly, even as memories of its predecessors, such as the National Old Trails Highway, fade slowly from our collective memory. There was even a television program in the 1960s set on (and titled) Route 66.

There's plenty of demand for Route 66 nostalgia, as museums in Clinton, above, and Elk City, Okla., left, testify.
*Author photos*

**Above:** A Route 66 shield is stenciled into the highway in the California desert. *Author photo*

**Right:** Martin Milner and George Maharis starred in Route 66, a television show that ran from 1960 to 1964 on CBS.

## After the Trails

A road sign off Interstate 81 in western Virginia points to U.S. Highway 11 (foreground right), which is still called the Lee Highway here. *Author photo*

# The End is the Beginning

It's easy to view the age of auto trails as a short, fleeting period of about a dozen years starting with the dedication of the Lincoln Highway and ending with the adoption of numbered routes. But to do so would be to miss the bigger picture. Many of the roads that made up the auto trail network were there before the trails came along. The trail associations just improved and connected what was already there.

The same can be said for the federal highway system, which, in turn, improved on the trails. Roads like the Lincoln and Pacific highways served as vital links between the era of unimproved, disconnected roads and the age of the modern highway. The roads didn't disappear; they just got renamed and shuffled around, and even that didn't solve all the perceived problems with the trail system.

Some of the numbered roads, like the trails before them, shared the same segment of highway over long stretches: The same road was U.S. 99, 70 and 60 through much of Southern California, just as a single road in Arizona had once been marked as the Bankhead Highway, Dixie Overland Highway and Old Spanish Trail through Arizona. More clarity would have to wait for the age of the interstate, when 99, 70 and 60 would be consolidated to form I-10.

Our nation's roads have always been evolving, and they continue to do so. In 1996, the last California stoplight was removed on Highway 99, in Livingston; that was some three decades after the federal government decommissioned the road and turned it over to the state. Also in California, U.S. 101 bypassed Willits in 2016. And signs along U.S. 220 in Virginia read "Future Interstate 73 corridor," speaking of changes still to come.

Edwin Meredith

The auto trails didn't exist in isolation. They were a key part of that evolution. People like Henry Joy, Edwin Meredith and, especially, Carl Fisher picked up the torch for good roads when no one else would. They poured millions of their own money into creating the building blocks for a national highway system while the federal government stayed on the sidelines. They were pathfinders, not just in a literal sense, but in the examples they set, as well. They did, or at least attempted, what no on else at the time was willing to do.

Some of the roads already existed before they came along. But they were poorly maintained and isolated from one another by long stretches of open space. Perhaps there were a few wheel ruts here and there, but beyond that, roads existed like spokes on a wheel leading from farmland into town, where the train awaited to take passengers who wished to travel beyond their home counties.

Auto trail groups started with those rutted wagon paths, Native American traces, and a few 19th century turnpikes. Businesses and homes already lined these roads. Trail organizers cobbled them together, at least as much as they could, and improved them.

# AMERICA'S FIRST HIGHWAYS

**Above:** Martha Washington College in Abingdon, Va., was built in 1832, nearly 90 years before the Lee Highway ran past its front door.

**Left:** The Frederick Wolfe House in Gettysburg (1753) preceded the Lincoln Highway by more than a century and a half.

*Author photos*

**Above:** Mount Pleasant Methodist Church was founded in 1871 in Marion, Va., and moved to this site in 1914. The black congregation met beside what became the Lee Highway in 1920, named for the Confederate general. The church endured, but the highway became U.S. 11 in 1926.

**Right:** Mission San Juan Bautista was founded in 1797, and El Camino Real was built to connect this and other California Catholic missions. The road served as the basis for an auto trail and, later, U.S. Highway 101. *Author photos*

# AMERICA'S FIRST HIGHWAYS

**Above:** The Tavern in Abingdon, Va., is the oldest bar in Virginia and one of the nation's 10 oldest, having been built in 1779. It was still open and serving food in 2020 beside the road that became the Lee Highway and, afterward, U.S. 11.

**Left:** The Old Stone Tavern, also on U.S. 11, was built in 1815 in Atkins, Va.

*Author photos*

The John Krepps Tavern was built in 1820 on what was then the National Pike or Cumberland Road, west of Brownsville, Pa. It's seen here in 1933. *Library of Congress*

When the auto trails came along, some of their names contained echoes of the primitive past: the Old Spanish Trail, El Camino Real, the Ozark Trails, the National Old Trails Road.

Other names sounded more modern: They were "highways," not trails. It was a dichotomy that reflected the nature of the times: These were years of transition, when the nation was finding its way gradually from dirt and gravel byways to asphalt autobahns.

When the federal highway system came along in 1926, it chopped up many of the auto trails into bits and pieces, dividing the old names among several different numbers. Some of those names became lost to history: No one calls Highway 99 the Pacific Highway anymore, in part because there's a Pacific *Coast* Highway that hugs the ocean off California and is famed for its views of the waves on one side and majestic cliffs on the other.

A street sign in southern Dalton, Ga., preserves the Dixie Highway name. *Author photo*

The Pike's Peak Ocean to Ocean Highway is, similarly, a distant memory: It was split into so many different segments, often far from major population centers, that few recall it today. The Jefferson Davis Highway is fading amid concerns over honoring men who fought for secessionists who sought to preserve slavery. And you'll probably find few people today who know the Dixie Overland Highway ever existed, let alone how it differed from the Dixie Highway.

Indeed, the name "Dixie" has come under fire, as well. It's been used as a generic term for the South and dates back to the creation of the Mason-Dixon Line drawn between Maryland and Pennsylvania in 1767. A song titled *Dixie* written in 1859 became so popular that Abraham Lincoln once called it "one of the best tunes I have ever heard." But it was also performed by minstrels in blackface and became the anthem of the Confederacy, so in that light, it's offensive.

Miami-Dade County recently voted to rename its portion of the road for Harriet Tubman. And in 2015, Riviera Beach in Palm Beach County renamed its section in honor of Barack Obama, thus adding a modern president's name to the list of auto trails named for some of his predecessors: Lincoln, Jefferson, Jackson, et. al., who served as inspirations to road-builders a century ago.

But the Dixie Highway and a few other auto trails remain alive in the public consciousness, if only on the fringes.

The band Journey clearly remembered the Dixie Highway, even penning a song by that name. In his introduction to the tune on their 1981 live album *Captured*, singer Steve Perry announced the band was going to do "a brand-new song about a highway that runs from Detroit all the way down to Florida: the Dixie Highway."

Country music Hall of Famer Alan Jackson grew up not far from the highway, waiting tables in high school at a barbecue place called Spayberry's in Newnan, Ga. The eatery's still there on State Route 34, and it dates back to 1926, the heyday of the Dixie Highway.

Even though he was born more than three decades later, the Dixie Highway made enough of an impression on Jackson that he wrote a song about it. Its lyrics are full of evocative imagery, with references to Georgia pines, red clay, willow trees, clotheslines and lightning bugs. Not only that: The song *Dixie Highway* appears on an album titled *Thirty Miles West*, because the highway was just that far from his hometown.

"There's this highway that's been in existence for forever now — it's called the Dixie Highway and it runs from north of Michigan all the way down to South Florida, and I wrote a song about it that's on the album," he said. "I grew up on Highway 34 outside of Newnan, Georgia, and that's where we came up with Thirty Miles West. I think we were about thirty miles west of the official part of the Dixie Highway that runs through Georgia."

Others ranging from Roger McGuinn of the Byrds to Carole King have written songs paying tribute to the road. And "Dixie Highway" remained on signs and businesses into the 21st century. So did the Lincoln Highway, Lee Highway and El Camino Real.

A Lincoln Highway sign is incorporated into a bridge spanning Mud Creek in Tama County, Iowa
*Joe Elliott, Historic American Engineering Record*

# AMERICA'S FIRST HIGHWAYS

Those nearly 400 bells still mark El Camino Real in California, and the Lincoln Highway is still marked by painted pole signs bearing its distinctive insignia. The Lincoln Highway Association disbanded in September of 1928. But at the same time, a group of Boy Scouts put up 3,000 concrete posts along the old route featuring a bronze bust of the 16th president and bearing the words, "This highway dedicated to Abraham Lincoln."

The old auto trail was no more, but its legacy endured along the path it had once taken.

**Left:** El Camino Real. *Orange County Archives, Creative Commons CCBY2.0*

**Left:** The Lincoln Theatre in Cheyenne, Wyo., opened in March 1927. This photo was taken in 2011. *Wikimedia Commons*

The Lincoln Lanes Bowling Center in Chambersburg, Pa., and the Lincoln Theatre in Massillon, Ohio, both reference the Lincoln Highway name. The theater opened all the way back in 1915 and was taken over by Warner Bros. in 1931.

*Author photos*

The Lincoln Highway is memorialized in mural form on the front of Lincoln Lanes, which sits along the old road in Chambersburg.

*Author photos*

**Above:** The Lincoln Highway Motor Court in Bedford County, Pa.

**Left:** This cast-iron marker at the west end of the Calhoun Street Bridge in Morrisville, Pa., has been there for more than a century, across the Delaware River from Trenton, N.J.

*Historic American Engineering Record photos*

# AMERICA'S FIRST HIGHWAYS

Murals on buildings along the Lincoln Highway. *Author photos*

A sign for Lee-Hi Lanes in Virginia offers a reminder that U.S. Route 11 in the region started out as the Lee Highway. *Author photo*

In addition to the Lincoln Highway's concrete posts, murals went up on barns and buildings, reminding passing motorists of the old road and its history. Segments in various places still carry names like Lincoln Way and Lincoln Street, and businesses by the side of the road still include "Lincoln" in their names.

The same can be said along the Lee Highway, despite its association with a general who fought for the right to keep human beings in chains. More than two decades after the federal highway system took over the old auto trails, a drive-in theater called the Lee-Hi went up along a section of the Lee Highway between Roanoke and Salem, Va. The drive-in is gone now, but there's still a bowling alley near the spot with the same name.

And perhaps just as importantly, the roads became home to more and more businesses as time went on. Even as numbers replaced their names, they remained the vital arteries that bound a nation together. Theaters, bowling alleys, skating rinks and miniature golf courses sprouted up beside them, alongside gas stations, motels, liquor stores and strip malls. In a very real sense, the auto trails didn't disappear; on the contrary, they came of age.

And they retain their importance even today. Some have been bypassed by modern interstates, but many remain *the* way to get from here to there. Their legacy endures, and our debt to their builders is one we'll have a hard time ever repaying.

The 11-70 Motor Court was built along a section of road shared by the Lee and Dixie Highways, later U.S. 11 and 70 south of Knoxville, Tenn. The road is now known as the Kingston Pike.

*Author photo*

**From top:** The Rainbow Autel chose a less-popular alternative to "motel" by conflating "auto" (instead of "motor") with "hotel" along U.S. 11 in Abingdon, Va.; the Robert E. Lee motel nearby was one of the first three places you could buy Kentucky Fried Chicken; the Moonlight Theatre opened in 1949 and is one of the few drive-ins on the National Register of Historic Places. *Author photos*

# AMERICA'S FIRST HIGHWAYS

**Top:** The building that houses Barter Theatre on U.S. 11 in Abingdon, Va., was built as a church in 1833 and is the second-oldest theater in the United States. The Barter opened in 1933 and charged 30 cents admission, or the equivalent in bartered goods. **Above:** The Shady Bend gas station, grocery and diner in Grand Island, Neb., was built in 1931 on U.S. 30. Until a few years earlier, it had been the Lincoln Highway, which built a seedling mile nearby. *Author photos*

The Airplane Filling Station in Powell, Tenn., was built in 1931 on U.S. 25W, previously part of the Dixie Highway and now known as the Clinton Highway. Constructed by Elmer and Henry Nickle, it stopped dispensing fuel in the 1960s and has served as a bait and tackle shop, used-car lot, produce stand, and as of this publication, a barber shop. It's on the National Register of Historic Places. *Author photos*

# AMERICA'S FIRST HIGHWAYS

Sir Goony's Family Fun Center operates on a section of road once shared by the Dixie and Lee Highways south of Knoxville, Tenn., and known for many years as the Dixie Lee Highway. It's part of a chain that, at one time, included more than 30 locations across the country. The course features figures including a rocket ship, Humpty Dumpty, a snake, a princess in a castle tower, elephants, a kangaroo and a pirate ship. The first Goony Golf was built in 1960. *Author photos*

The same building in 1921, top, and 2019, above, in Gettysburg, Pa., on the Lincoln Highway. It opened as the Meade School in 1897 and was transformed into a luxury hotel in 2013. *Top photo University of Michigan Library (Special Collections Research Center, Transportation History Collection); author photo above*

The Lincoln Highway in Pennsylvania today. *Author photo*

# Timeline

**1625** — Street in Pemaquid, Maine, earliest known U.S. paved road

**1795** — Philadelphia-Lancaster Turnpike, first engineered U.S. road

**1823** — First macadam road in U.S. built, Boonsborough, Md.

**1830** — 73-mile section of Cumberland Road/National Pike paved with macadam

**1877** — Pennsylvania Avenue in Washington, D.C., first section of paved asphalt in U.S.

**1880** — League of American Wheelmen formed

**1891** — *Gospel of Good Roads* published

**1893** — First rural brick road built, Ohio
Office of Road Inquiry founded

**1896** — Rural Free Delivery service established

**1897** — Oldsmobile founded by Ransom E. Olds

**1900** — 8,000 motor vehicles registered in U.S.

**1902** — Nine auto clubs combine to form American Automobile Association

    Charles and Lucy Glidden become first to circle the world in an automobile

**1903** — Horatio Nelson Jackson and Sewall Crocker first to drive across the U.S.

**1904** — Henry Ford sets land speed record

    AAA tour to St. Louis World's Fair

    Prest-O-Lite headlight company founded as Concentrated Acetylene Co.

**1905** — First Glidden Tour

    AAA publishes first street map

    Office of Road Inquiry becomes Office of Public Roads

**1906** — First Bituminous macadam road built, Rhode Island

    Stanley Rocket steam-powered car sets land speed record of 127 mph

    Hepburn Act authorizes Interstate Commerce Commission to set rail rates

    Bell guideposts placed along El Camino Real in California

**1908** — First Ford Model T produced

    U.S. entry wins New York-to-Paris Race

    General Motors founded

**1909** — Indianapolis Motor Speedway opens

    Glidden Tour takes participants west of the Mississippi River

**1910** — 468,500 motor vehicles registered in U.S.

**1911** — First Indy 500

    Meridian Highway dedicated

    Sam Hill sets up $100,000 road to test different surfaces in Oregon

    Jackson Highway conceived

    Des Moines-Kansas City-St. Joseph Interstate Trail Association formed

    Glidden Tour to South, New York to Jacksonville

**1912** — National Old Trails Road dedicated

    Los Angeles vs. San Diego race to Phoenix

    Pike's Peak Ocean to Ocean Highway formed

    Carl Fisher conceives of Lincoln Highway

    Cadillac introduces electric starter to replace hand crank

# AMERICA'S FIRST HIGHWAYS

        Yellowstone Trail Association formed
**1913** — Lincoln Highway Association formed
        Final Glidden Tour
        Pacific Highway dedicated
        Ozark Trails Association formed
        Gulf Oil opens first drive-through service station in Pittsburgh
        Number of state motor vehicle registrations passes 1 million for first time
**1914** — American Association of State Highway Officials (AASHO) founded
        Dixie Overland Highway Association formed
        First Lincoln Highway "seedling mile" built in Malta, Ill.
        AAA places 4,000 road signs on National Old Trails Highway
**1915** — Dixie Highway dedicated
        Old Plank Road built over Algodones Dunes east of San Diego
        Office of Public Roads becomes Bureau of Public Roads (BPR)
        Jefferson Highway Association formed
        Ridge Route opens over Tehachapi Mountains in California
**1916** — Federal Road Aid Act of 1916 passed
        Jefferson Highway route finalized
        Old Plank Road rebuilt with new design
        AAA opens Yellowstone National Park to automobile traffic
**1917** — Wisconsin establishes system of numbered roads
        First center lines added on roads in Michigan, Oregon and California
**1918** — Proposed 2-cent federal gas tax, opposed by AAA, fails
**1919** — Eisenhower participates in Army cross-country convoy
        Lee Highway Association formed
        Oregon adopts first gasoline tax, a penny a gallon
**1920** — National Park to Park Highway dedicated
**1921** — Federal Road Aid Act of 1921 passed
        Number of motor vehicle registrations in U.S. tops 10 million
**1922** — "Ideal section" of Lincoln Highway built in Indiana

**1923** — Mississippi Valley Association of State Highway Depts. adopts uniform signs
**1924** — AASHO recommends selection of federal transcontinental and interstate routes
**1925** — Agriculture secretary creates Joint Board on Interstate Highways
**1926** — Federal highway system of numbered roads established
Old Plank Road abandoned

The Midland Trail between Mojave and Willow Trail, Calif. *University of Michigan Library (Special Collections Research Center, Transportation History Collection)*

# Index of Trails

A partial list of auto trails and notable roads in this volume. Page numbers for photos and illustrations are *italicized*.

**Atlantic Highway** — 195, *233*

**Atlantic-Pacific Highway** — 171, 176

**Bankhead Highway** — 176, 195, 248, 256

**Blue J Route** — 182, 186-189

**Boone's Lick Road** — 100-101

**Cincinnati-to-Lookout Mountain Airline Highway** — 144, 148

**Cumberland Road (National Pike)** — 23, *24*, *25*, 88, 255, *260*, 275

**Dixie Highway** — 25, 93, 101, 135-156, *154 (map)*, 158, 171, 173, 178, 195, 239, 244, 249, 261-262, 277

**Dixie Overland Highway** — 93, 195, 248, 256, 261, 277

**El Camino Real** — 8, 88, 182, 195, *213*, 248, *258*, 260, 262-263, *263*, 276

**Great Valley Road** (Virginia) — 18, 174

**Great White Way** (Iowa) — 8

**Jackson Highway** — 173, 180-182, *183 (map)* 195, 276

**Jefferson Davis Highway** — 172, 177-179, *179 (map)*, 193, 250, 261

**King of Trails** — 182, 189, 195

**Lee Highway** — 148, 170-177, *171, 172, 174, 175, 176 (map)*, 179, 181, 195, *255*, 262, 268, *268, 269*, 277

**Lincoln Highway** — 8, 12, 25, *25*, 99-133, *99, 107, 111, 112, 113, 115, 119, 120, 121, 123, 126-129, 131-133*, 143, 154, 159, 162, *162, 163*, 164, 165, 169-170, 177-178, 182-183, 192, 194-195, 201, *212, 213*, 218, 228, 231, *232*, 235, *235, 242*, 249, 255, *257*, 262, *262-267*, 268, *271, 274, 275*, 276-277, 281, 283

**Louisville and Nashville Turnpike** — 17, 149

**Meridian Highway** — 8, 182, 195, 248, 276

**Midland Trail** — 115, *117*, 195, 279

**Mississippi River Scenic Highway** — 182, 189, 195

**National Bee Line Highway** — 181-182

**National Old Trials Road** — 8, *88*, 100, 107, 116, 195, 260, 276

**National Park to Park Highway** — 195, 216-217, 221, *225 (map)*, 277

**New Santa Fe Trail** — 171, 195, 252

**Old Santa Fe Trail** — 171, 252

**Old Plank Road** — 91-94, *91, 92, 93, 94*, 114, 277

**Old Spanish Trail** — 171, 176, 182, 195, *245*, 248, 250, 256, 260

**Oregon Trail (Emigrant Trail)** — 100-101, 114, *114 (map)*

**Ozark Trails** — 8, 195, 204-210, *208 (map), 210*, 250, 260, 277

**Pacific Highway** — *7*, 8, 26-27, *27, 28*, 193, 214, 219, 246, 253, 258, 275

**Pershing Way** — 189, 191, 195

**Pikes Peak Ocean to Ocean Highway** — 8, 93, 191-196, *192, 193 (map)*, 236, 276

**Route 66** — 8, 23, 25, 101, 151, *151*, 204, 210, *210*, 249-253, *253*,

**Theodore Roosevelt International Highway** — 195

**Victory Highway** — 116-118, *116*, 169-170, 195, 237, 252

**Yellowstone Trail** — 8, 195-203, *203 (map)*, 234

The party of F.W. Hough crosses the Mojave Desert in 1924. *NOAA Photo Library*

# Sources

"1901 Ford 'Sweepstakes' Race Car," thehenryford.org.
"1909 Glidden Tour – Indianapolis Star," firstsuperspeedway.com.
"1910 Chalmers Detroit Model 30," conceptcarz.com.
"2,636-mile Glidden Tour ends, eight cars have perfect scores," Munster (Ind.) Times, p. 3, July 31, 1909.
"A Short History of U.S. Freight Railroads," aar.org, July 2019.
AAA Highways Green Book, 1922.
"A.A.A. Urges Need of Military Roads," Automobile Topics, p. 399, June 2, 1917.
Abbott, Karen. "Paris or Bust: The Great New York-to-Paris Auto Race of 1908," smithsonianmag.com, March 7, 2012.
Address of Hugh Shepard to Good Roads convention, May 1928, iowadot.gov.
"Airline route to be reality in short time," Chattanooga Daily Times, p. 5, April 1, 1922.
"Alex Winton's Fast Mile," Detroit Free Press, p. 1, Oct. 11, 1901.
"An Old Friend Goes," San Francisco Examiner, p. 38, Jan. 30, 1929.
Andrews, Evan. "Pedal Your Way Through the Bicycle's Bumpy History," history.com, Aug. 22, 2018.
Andrews, Stefan. "The historic New York to Paris Race in 1908," thevintagenews.com, Jan. 1, 2017.
Andrews, Evan. "Why is the South known as 'Dixie'?" history.com, June 8, 2017.
"Another race Phoenixward," Arizona Republic, p. 9, Oct. 4, 1912.

Ascher, Charlie. "From a single Hupmobile to a fleet of 1,552 buses, Greyhound turns 100," hemmings.com, Aug. 14, 2014.
"Assessing and Managing the Ecological Impacts of Paved Roads," nap.edu, 2005.
"Auto at Golden Gate," New York Tribune, p. 8, March 25, 1908.
"Auto Tourist Camps," Western Magazine, p. 74, September 1924.
"Automobile Journal," p. 24, Pawtucket, R.I., Feb. 10, 1917.
"Automobiles in New York-St. Louis run arrive here," Buffalo Evening News, p. 1, July 30, 1904.
"Automobiles ran too fast," Buffalo Sunday Morning News, p. 9, Oct. 12. 1902.
"Automobiling," Minneapolis Journal, p. 16, Nov. 18, 1902.
"Autos Reach Aberdeen on Second Day of Run," Minneapolis Sunday Tribune, p. 1, Oct. 2, 1910.
"Autos to abandon route by Alaska," San Francisco Examiner, p. 21, April, 12, 1908.
Beck, Darrell. "The Old Plank Road Across The Imperial Sand Dunes," ramonajournal.com, Feb. 6, 2020.
Bedell, Mary Crehore. "Modern Gypsies," Brentano's, New York, 1924.
Belasco, Warren James. "Americans on the Road," MIT Press, 1979.
"Bender, Melissa M. and Szlezak, Klara Stephanie. "Contested Commemoration in U.S. History," Routledge, New York, 2020.
"Boone's Lick Road History," booneslickroad.org.
"Borderland Route maps will feature Hig auto highway," Bisbee (Ariz.) Daily Review, p. 5, Aug. 4, 1915.
Bowman, Nick. "Why Seattle's cobblestone streets are here to stay," mynorthwest.com, June 25, 2019.
Boyer, Warren E. "The Park-to-Park Highway," Western Highways Builder, Braff, Carolyn Stanford.
"Brick and Stone Pavements to be Added To Historic Register," tacomanorthslope.org.
Brown, Gary. "Campaign seek HOF enshrinement for Ralph E. Hay, an NFL founder," the-daily-record.com, Sept. 8, 2014.
Buettner, Michael G. "In search of ... the Yellowstone Trail in Ohio," lincolnhighwayoh.com, December 2005.
Bulger, Bozeman C. "On a Circular Track with Barney Oldfield," The Age-Herald, April 1, 1906.
"Carl Fisher's Record Setting Premier," firstsuperspeedway.com.
"Carl Fisher's World Beater," theoldmotor.com, Oct. 25, 2011.
"Carl Fisher Wins Match Race – 1904," firstsuperspeedway.com.
"Chalmers Automobile Registry," Vo. 13, Issue 1, January 2008.
Chaney, Raymond C. Jr. "Racetrack to Highway: San Diego's Early Automobile Days," sandiegohistory.org, April 1971.
"Chevrolet, 1911-1996," gmheritagecenter.com.
Claypool, Ethelbert M. "Platte County Plows Mud," The Modern Highway, p. 3, April 1919.
"Cleveland, the City of Brick Streets," Seattle Star, p. 8, June 9, 1906.
"Col. 'Coin' Harvey Blazes Ozark Trail," Afton American, p. 1, May 15, 1913.
Cole, Drusilla. "1000 Patterns," Chronicle Books, San Francisco, 2003.
"Contributions and Crossroads: Timeline" ftwa.dot.gov.
Crawford, Richard. "Civic pride on the line in Phoenix road race," sandiegouniontribune.com, March 11, 2010.
"Cullom offers a highway bill," Rock Island Argus, p. 1, Aug. 11, 1911.
"Daredevil Driver Fred Marriott Sets Land Speed Record," racingnelliebly.com.
"Death demands toll in record speedway races," Indianapolis Star, p. 1, Aug. 20, 1909.
Deshais, Nicholas. "Beneath the asphalt: Spokane's historic brick streets endure the decades," spokesman.com, Aug. 3, 2017.
"'Dixie Highway' by Alan Jackson, songfacts.com.
Donnelly, Jim. "Louis Chevrolet: A Racer, Not Just a Brand of Automobile," Hemmings Muscle Machines, 2006.
"Dr. S.M. Johnson Tells Story of Building of Lee Highway," Kingsport (Tenn.) Times, p. 26, Oct. 1, 1924.
Duin, Steve. "The story behind the Confederate flags on I-5, just north of Portland," oregonlive.com, June 9, 2017.
"Durant-Dort Carriage Company Office" nomination to National Register of Historic Places, npgallery.nps.gov.
Durbin, Jeffrey L. "Section B: The Dixie Highway in Georgia," sca-roadside.org.
Rexford, Peter V. "Earlier Line," The (Portland) Oregonian, p. 3M, Dec. 4, 1954.
"Editorial Gleanings: Numbered Highways," Canonsburg (Pa.) Daily Notes, p. 4, July 8, 1930.

# AMERICA'S FIRST HIGHWAYS

"Famous Mules are Coming to Gaffney," Gaffney (S.C.) Ledger, p. 1, Nov. 1, 1919.

Fimrite, Peter. "Long before the interstates, there was a Winton," sfgate.com, June 16, 2003.

Fisher, Jerry M. "The Pacesetter: The Complete Story," Friesen Press, Victoria, BC, 1998.

Flink, James J. "The Automobile Age," MIT Press, Cambridge, Mass., 1990.

"Florida's Post-World War I Boom and Bust," polk-fl.net.

"Free Auto Camps," history.nebraska.gov.

"George Schuster," hemmings.com, November 2015.

"Glidden Tour cars ditched in Virginia," The New York Times, p. 9, Oct. 18, 1911.

"Glidden Tour press car is demolished," Richmond Times-Dispatch, p. 9, Oct. 17, 1911.

"Glidden Tour Postponed," Brooklyn Standard Union, p. 12, Sept. 26, 1912.

"Glidden Tour Route Has Been Mapped Out," Brooklyn Times Union, p. 4, Aug. 29, 1912.

"Good Roads Apostle Here," Los Angeles Evening Express, p. 13, April 2, 1913.

Gosselin, Rick. "State Your Case: Ralph Hay," mavensports.io, July 26, 2016.

"Governors in Full Control," Chattanooga Daily Times, p. 1, April 4, 1915.

Greenwell, Caitlin. "A Rich History for Lost River Cave," bgkyliving.com, 2019.

Guroff, Margaret. "American Drivers Have Bicyclists to Thank for a Smooth Ride to Work," smithsonianmag.com, Sept. 12, 2016.

Hanks, Douglas. "Dixie Highway name condemned by Miami-Dade commissioners," miamiherald.com, Feb. 5, 2020.

Hanlon, Mike. "The fastest cars in history: 1894 to 1914," newsatlas.com, Jan. 3, 2017.

"Harding likes Florida and Florida 'Crackers,' He Tells Metropolis Reporter," Miami News, p. 1, Jan. 31, 1921.

Harris, Nelson. "Streets of Roanoke: Lee Highway," theroanoker.com.

"Henry Ford and racing 1901 to 1913," myautoworld.com.

"High Praise for our Tourist Camp," Muskogee Democrat, p. 5, Aug. 5, 1921.

"Hill, Samuel (1957-1931)," historylink.org.

"Hines, Good-Roads Pioneer, Dies Unexpectedly in Home," Detroit Free Press, p. 1, June 5, 1938.

"History Of Asphalt Roads In The U.S.," dykespaving.com.

"History of the AAA Glidden® Tours," exchange.aaa.com.

"History of the Stop Sign in America," signalfan.freeservers.com.

"History of WisDOT," wisconsindot.gov.

"Indy 'Brickyard' is completed," history.com.

Ingram, Tammy. "Dixie Highway," University of North Carolina Press, Chapel Hill, N.C., 2014.

"Itinerant Booster Of Roads Dead," Cushing (Okla.) Daily Citizen, p. 8, Aug. 19, 1927.

Jakle, John F. and Sculle, Keith A. "The Gas Station in America," Johns Hopkins University Press, Baltimore, 1994.

"January 12, 1904 – Ford sets new land speed record," automotivehistory.org, Jan. 12, 1917.

Jessup, Elon. "The Motor Camping Book," G.P. Putnam's Sons, New York and London, 1921.

"John Anderson, My Jo, John," Tampa Times, p, 3, Aug. 23, 1913.

Jones, Meghan. "Stop Signs Used to Be Yellow – More Recently Than You Think," rd.com.

Katz, Brigit. "Parts of Florida Highway … Will Be Renamed in Honor of Harriet Tubman," smithsonian.com, Feb. 25, 2020.

Kelly, Susan Croce. "Father of Route 66: The Story of Cy Avery," University of Oklahoma Press, Norman, Okla., 1988.

Kelly, Susan Croce. "Route 66: The Highway and its People," University of Oklahoma Press, Norman, Okla., 1988.

Kernan, Michael. "Wow! A Mile a Minute!" smithsonianmag.com, May 1998.

Klein, Christopher. "The Epic Road Trip That Inspired the Interstate Highway System," history.com, Oct. 28, 2018.

Klein, Christopher. "The First Great American Road Trip," history.com, June 29, 2012.

Lelande, Harry J. The Grizzly Bear, September 1911.

"Let the Enemy Build Our Roads," Motor Age, p. 14, April 25, 1918.

Lewis, David Lanier. "The Public Image of Henry Ford," Wayne State University Press, Detroit, 1976.

Lin, James. "A Brief History of the Lincoln Highway," lincolnhighwayassoc.org.

Loberg, Alice. "Yellowstone Trail: 'granddaddy' of the interstate highway," Stevens Point Daily Journal, p. 13, Oct. 24, 1979.
Longfellow, Rickie. "The National Road," fhwa.dot.gov.
Lord, Allyn. "Historic Monte Ne," Arcadia Publishing, 2006.
"Louis Chevrolet," indyracingmuseum.org.
"Mad dog routs tourist camp," Spokane Spokesman-Review, p. 6, Aug. 14, 1921.
"Massachusetts Highway Association," Good Roads, p. 23, Jan. 12, 1918.
McCaughan, Sean. "The Lincoln Hotel," miami.curbed.com, Nov. 6, 2012.
McDonough, Doug. "Obelisks once marked Ozark Trail," myplainview.com, April 23, 2010.
McIver, Stuart. "Speedway on the Sands," sun-sentinel.com, Feb. 16, 1992.
Mitchell, D. "Indianapolis Motor Speedway's first races in 1909 were marked by death and danger," usatoday.com, Aug. 9, 2019.
"Motor Travel," Vol. 11, 1919.
Murphey, John and Kris. "Miss Alma Makes a Bee Line: The Story of One Woman and Two Auto Trails," sca-roadside,.org.
"Muskogee's Auto Tourist Camp," 3riversmuseum.blogspot.com, Aug. 6, 2013.
"Nashville Left Off Proposed Route," Nashville Banner, p. 13, April 8, 1915.
Neal, Robert J. "Liberty Engine: A Technical & Operational History," Specialty Press, North Branch, Minn., 2009.
"Neosho Heights and Maywood Will Get Sidewalks," Miami (Okla.) Daily Record, p. 1, April 29, 1919.
"New York to Paris Race," nyheritage.org.
"Noted Deputy Gives Up Post," The (Portland) Oregonian, p. 22, June 29, 1947.
"Now for the Glidden Tour," Salina (Kan.) Daily Union, p. 4, June 7, 1910.
"Ocean to Ocean in an Auto," New York Sun, p. 5, July 27, 1903.
"Old Plank Road: Imperial Sand Dunes," desertusa.com.
"Oppose Parmley's Road Bill," Aberdeen Democrat, p. 6, Feb. 15, 1907.
Orliff, Martin. T. "Getting Out of the Mud," University of Alabama Press, Tuscaloosa, 2017.
"One of the biggest and finest ever given in South," Chattanooga News, p. 4, May 21, 1915.
Orliff, Martin T. "Alma Rittenberry," encyclopediaofalabama.org.
"Ozark Trail Pillar at Central and Main Removed as Menace," Miami (Okla.) Record-Herald, p. 1, May 16, 1919.
"Ozark Trail Winds Through Rich Southwest," Grove (Okla.) Sun, p. 1, May 30, 1913.
"Ozark Trails Association Projects New Tulsa-Kansas City Route," Tulsa Democrat, p. 13, Sept. 15, 1918.
Palermo, Nick. "On fire: Automotive Lighting History," knowhow.napaonline.com, Jan. 27, 2015.
"Parks for Aberdeen," Pierre Weekly Free Press, p. 2, Sept. 8, 1910.
Pascale, Jordan. "Jefferson Davis Highway Will Be Renamed By October," dcist.com, May 15, 2019.
"Pathfinders and Map Makers – Part One," randomconnections.com, Oct. 28, 2015.
"Pathfinder arrives," Reno Gazette-Journal, p. 7, Oct. 28, 1912.
Peek, Jeff. "Marmon: The rise, fall, and rarity of a forgotten American automaker," haggerty.com, Dec. 15, 2017.
"Perfect Scores Suffer Heavily," South Bend Tribune, p. 10, July 22, 1909.
"Perryville," Kentucky Advocate, p. 3, June 13, 1921.
Petroski, Henry. "The Lines on the Road: Infrastructure in Perspective," watermark.silverchair.com.
"Pikes Peak Ocean to Ocean Highway," ppoo.org.
"Poles along all main roads of state numbered," Harrisburg (Pa.) Evening News, p. 13, Aug. 25, 1924.
Potter, Isaac B. "The Gospel of Good Roads: A Letter to the American Farmer," New York, 1891.
"Prest-O-Lite History," firstsuperspeedway.com.
"Primary Road Guide for Iowa," Denison (Iowa) Review, pt. 2, p.5, Sept. 15, 1920.
"Protest Ruling on Trail Names," Richmond Times Dispatch, p. 2, June 8, 1927.
"Pyramid is a Traffic Guide," Chanute Daily Tribune, p. 1, May 16, 1919.
"Railroad Land Grants," loc.gov.
Reid, Carlton. "Roads Were Not Built for Cars," Island Press, Washington, D.C., 2015.

# AMERICA'S FIRST HIGHWAYS

"Reliability Run," Brooklyn Daily Eagle, p. 3, Aug. 2, 1902.

"Reliability Run," Boston Globe, p. 5, Oct. 9, 1902.

"Reliability run is at an end," Buffalo Evening News, p. 8, Oct. 17, 1902.

"Return in time to the Lincoln Hotel, Miami Beach, Late January, 1921," wolfsonianfiulibrary.wordpress.com.

Rong, Blake Z. "The First Speed Limit Law Was Passed On This Day In 1901," roadandtrack.com, May 21, 2016.

"RV History: The Tin Can Tourists," tincantourists.com.

Schreiber, R. "Why Henry Leland, founder of Cadillac and Lincoln, is practically unknown in Detroit," hagerty.com, Oct. 6, 2019.

"S.M. Butler is killed," Chattanooga Daily Times, p. 1, Oct. 26, 1911.

"Sam Hill paved the way for state roads," kitsapsun.com, March 9, 1988.

Sears, Stephen W. "Ocean To Ocean In An Automobile Car," americanheritage.com, June/July 1980.

Shupert-Arick, Jan. "Cabin Camp Project," indianalincolnhighway.org.

Smith, Bert C. "Twelve cars for big race," Los Angeles Times, p. 29, Oct. 11, 1912.

Society for Commercial Archaeology. "Tour Guide: Drivin' the Dixie," sca-roadside.org, 1998.

Spears, R.S. "On the Yellowstone Trail," Outing, Vol. 68, 1916.

"Speeding 'Henry' Hits O.T. Marker at Central and Main; Car Stopped," Miami (Okla.) Record-Herald, p. 3, Feb. 28, 1919.

"State Motor Vehicle Registrations, by Years, 1900-1995," fhwa.dot.gov.

Street, Jullan. "Abroad at Home," The Century Co., New York, 1914.

Stutz Bearcat, autoswalk.com.

"Summary of Auto Races on Saturday," Indianapolis Star, p. 1, Aug. 21, 1909.

"Swamp Turned Into Swanky Lincoln Road By Carl Fisher," Miami News, p. 4B, March 21, 1937.

"Ten Delegates Left Last Night," Fort Scott Daily Tribune-Monitor, p. 7, Nov. 16, 1915.

"The 1905 Glidden Tour," vmcca.org.

"The Automobile Record Broken," Great Falls (Mont.) Tribune, p. 4, Oct. 11, 1901.

"The Glidden Tour Years," pierce-arrow.org.

"The Highway Magazine," p. 10, August 1924.

"Ten Men Jumped from Windows," Detroit Free Press, p. 1, March 10, 1901.

"Tennessee Mini Golf," roadarch.com.

"The Complete Official Road Guide to the Lincoln Highway," Lincoln Highway Association, Detroit, Mich., 1916.

"The Curved Dash Oldsmobile: Putting America on Wheels," studebakermuseum.org, Jan. 28, 2019.

"The Five Natural Asphalt Lake Areas In The World," worldatlas.com.

"The Founder of Oldsmobile: Ransom E. Olds," michiganhistory.leadr.msu.edu.

"The Ghosts of the Old Golden Belt Route," seelincolncounty.com.

"The Perfect Time to Ride," American Bicyclist, bikeleague.org, November-December 2007.

"The Roadway Centerline," Sikeston, Mo., Daily Standard, p. 2, July 5, 1969.

"The Stanley Steamer, Why The Fascination?" stanleymotorcarriage.com.

"The Yellowstone Trail," City of Ipswich, South Dakota, Ipswich-sd.com.

"Thirteen Highways to New Orleans," The Modern Highway, p. 20, May 1919.

Thompson, William h. "Transportation in Iowa: A Historical Summary," Iowa Department of Transportation, 1989.

"Thousand Saw Tank Clime Ozark Trail Pillar," Miami Daily Record-Herald, p. 1, April 20, 1919.

"Three lives pay price for closing auto races," Indianapolis Star, p. 17, Aug. 22, 1909.

Tobin, Gary Allan. "The Bicycle Boom of the 1890's," assets.theatlantic.com.

Trexler, Keith A. "The Tioga Road; a History 1883-1961," yosemite.ca.us, 1961, 1980.

Tuhy, John E. "Sam Hill: The Prince of Castle Nowhere," Timber Press, Portland, Ore., 1983.

"Union Pacific explains refusal," Rochester Democrat and Chronicle, p. 12, March 23, 1908.

U.S. Congress. "The Old Oregon Trail: Hearings ... on H.J. Res. 232, H.J. Res, 328, and S. 2053," January-February 1925.

U.S. Congress. "Unfair Competition from the Public Sector in the Tourism Industry and Tourism-related Areas," 1993.

"U.S. government takes over control of nation's railroads," history.com,

Van de Water, Frederic Franklyn. "The Family Flivvers to Frisco," D. Appleton and Company, New York, 1927.

Van Pelt, Lori. "Eisenhower's 1919 Road Trip and the Interstate Highway System," wyohistory.org, Jan. 4, 2018.

Wapling, Greg. "Ford 999," gregwapling.com.

Warnick, Ron. "Ozark Trail obelisk near Stroud cleaned of graffiti," route66news.com, April 28, 2019.

"Washington Bricks: Denny Clay Company, Taylor," washingtonbricks.com.

Weingoff, Richard F. "Celebrating a Century of Cooperation," fhwa.dot.gov.

Weingoff, Richard F. "Creation of a Landmark: The Federal Aid Road Act of 1916," fhwa.dot.gov.

Weingoff, Richard F. "From Names to Numbers: The Origins of the U.S. Numbered Highway System," fhwa.dot.gov.

Weingoff, Richard F. "Jefferson Davis Memorial Highway," fhwa.dot.gov.

Weingoff, Richard F. "The Pikes Peak Ocean To Ocean Highway," fhwa.dot.gov.

Weingoff, Richard F. "U.S. Route 80: The Dixie Overland Highway," fhwa.dot.gov.

"Where did the band get its name?" speedwagon.com.

Whitaker, Sigur E. "The Indianapolis Automobile Industry: A History, 1893-1939," McFarland & Co., Jefferson, N.C., 2018.

Williams, David B. "Good Old Cobblestones," geologywriter.com, March 11, 2009.

Wilner, Barry. "The humble Hupmobile lends support in start of NFL," apnews.com, April 11, 2019.

"Winton Remembered in New Book," wintonhistory.com.

"Wisconsin Highways: Historical Overview," wisconsinhighways.org.

"Work for Good Roads," Junction City (Kan.) Republican, p. 1, May 18, 1882.

"World's Record for Mile Drive," Spokane Chronicle, p. 5, May 20, 1905.

*Photo by Samaire Provost*

# About the author

Stephen H. Provost is an author and historian who has written several books about life in 20th century America. During more than three decades in journalism, he has worked as a managing editor, copy desk chief, columnist and reporter at five newspapers. Now a full-time author, he has written on such diverse topics as American highways, dragons, mutant superheroes, mythic archetypes, language, department stores and his hometown. He currently lives in Martinsville. And he loves cats. Read his blogs and keep up with his activities at stephenhprovost.com.

# Did you enjoy this book?

Recommend it to a friend. And please consider rating it and/or leaving a brief review online at Amazon, Barnes & Noble and Goodreads.

STEPHEN H. PROVOST

# Also by the author

*Works of Fiction*

*The Talismans of Time (Academy of the Lost Labyrinth, Book 1)*
*Pathfinder of Destiny (Academy of the Lost Labyrinth, Book 2)*
*Astral Academy*
*Memortality (The Memortality Saga, Book 1)*
*Paralucidity (The Memortality Saga, Book 2)*
*The Only Dragon*
*Identity Break*
*Feathercap*
*Nightmare's Eve*

*Works of Nonfiction*

*Yesterday's Highways*
*Highway 99: The History of California's Main Street*
*Highway 101: The History of El Camino Real (Spring 2020)*
*The Great American Shopping Experience (Fall 2020)*
*Martinsville Memories*
*Fresno Growing Up*
*A Whole Different League*
*The Legend of Molly Bolin*
*Please Stop Saying That!*
*Undefeated*
*Media Meltdown*
*The Osiris Testament (The Phoenix Chronicles, Book 1)*
*The Way of the Phoenix (The Phoenix Chronicles, Book 2)*
*The Gospel of the Phoenix (The Phoenix Chronicles, Book 3)*
*Forged in Ancient Fires (The Phoenix Principle, Book 1)*
*Messiah in the Making (The Phoenix Principle, Book 2)*

# Praise for other works

"If you have any interest in highways, old diners and motels and such, or 20th century US history, this book is for you. It is without a doubt one of the best highway books ever published."
— Dan R. Young, founder OLD HIGHWAY 101 group, on **Yesterday's Highways**

"The complex idea of mixing morality and mortality is a fresh twist on the human condition. … **Memortality** is one of those books that will incite more questions than it answers. And for fandom, that's a good thing."
— Ricky L. Brown, Amazing Stories

"Punchy and fast paced, **Memortality** reads like a graphic novel. … (Provost's) style makes the trippy landscapes and mind-bending plot points more believable and adds a thrilling edge to this vivid crossover fantasy."
— Foreword Reviews

"The genres in this volume span horror, fantasy, and science-fiction, and each is handled deftly. … **Nightmare's Eve** should be on your reading list. The stories are at the intersection of nightmare and lucid dreaming, up ahead a signpost … next stop, your reading pile. Keep the nightlight on."
— R.B. Payne, Cemetery Dance

"**Memortality** by Stephen Provost is a highly original, thrilling novel unlike anything else out there."
— David McAfee, bestselling author of 33 A.D., 61 A.D., and 79 A.D.

"Profusely illustrated throughout, **Highway 99** is unreservedly recommended as an essential and core addition to every community and academic library's California History collections."
— California Bookwatch

"An essential primer for anyone seeking an entrée into the genre. Provost serves up a smorgasbord of highlights gleaned from his personal memories of and research into the various nooks and crannies of what 'used-to-be' in professional team sports."

— Tim Hanlon, Good Seats Still Available, on **A Whole Different League**

"As informed and informative as it is entertaining and absorbing, **Fresno Growing Up** is very highly recommended for personal, community, and academic library 20th Century American History collections."

— John Burroughs, Reviewer's Bookwatch

"Provost sticks mostly to the classics: vampires, ghosts, aliens, and even dragons. But trekking familiar terrain allows the author to subvert readers' expectations. ... Provost's poetry skillfully displays the same somber themes as the stories. ... Worthy tales that prove external forces are no more terrifying than what's inside people's heads."

— Kirkus Reviews on **Nightmare's Eve**

"… an engaging narrative that pulls the reader into the story and onto the road. … I highly recommend **Highway 99: The History of California's Main Street**, whether you're a roadside archaeology nut or just someone who enjoys a ripping story peppered with vintage photographs."

— Barbara Gossett,
Society for Commercial Archaeology Journal

*Martinsville*

Made in the USA
Monee, IL
12 November 2021